THE
SmartMoney
STOCK
PICKER'S
BIBLE

THE
SmartMoney
STOCK
PICKER'S
BIBLE

NELLIE S. HUANG

PETER FINCH

JOHN WILEY & SONS, INC.

Published by John Wiley & Sons, Inc., New York.
Published simultaneously in Canada.

Library of Congress Cataloging-in-Publication Data:

Huang, Nellie S.
    The SmartMoney stock picker's bible / Nellie S. Huang & Peter Finch.
      p.   cm.
    Includes index.
    ISBN 0-471-15204-8 (cloth : alk. paper)
    1. Stocks. 2. Securities. I. Finch, Peter, 1960– II. SmartMoney. III. Title.
HG4661 .H83 2002
332.63'22—dc21   2001046914

Printed in the United States of America.

10 9 8 7 6 5 4 3

CONTENTS

FOREWORD

When I was in graduate school studying economics in the early 1980s, I remember reading financial publications for the sheer enjoyment of the narratives and the human spectacle of success and failure. The best writers seemed to be taking a page from Erasmus's *In Praise of Folly* as they warned us about Wall Street promoters, go-go stock brokers, IPO pitchmen, dubious leveraged buyout deal makers, creative accountants, life insurance salespeople, and all the supposed get-rich-quick schemes that their fertile imaginations kept dreaming up.

Nothing wrong with that, of course. The articles and columns of people like Alan Abelson of *Barron's* are classics of journalistic prose—still fun to read today. But taken together, the implicit message you'd get from reading the most respected financial journalists came down to this: Beware of Wall Street and the stock market. Those shysters aren't your friends. No one said it explicitly, but the message I glimpsed between the lines was simple: Only the foolhardy stray from guaranteed Treasury bonds and solid, dependable blue-chip stocks. Little in the financial press of that time made me—a Wall Street outsider and not a natural gambler—want to be an active investor at all.

It took me several years to figure out why my friends (also struggling graduate students, for the most part) and I got so little personal use from financial coverage. But with the benefit of hindsight, it now seems pretty clear.

Sophisticated publishers 20 years ago assumed their readers were already people of substance—retirees with substantial nest eggs, successful middle-aged professionals, trust fund babies, business practitioners, and established investors. These were people whose biggest worry was losing what they already had. Naturally, the most useful articles and columns for that kind of reader were stories that helped them preserve their wealth rather than help them multiply it.

That accounts for the very conservative investing bias of the more venerable financial publications. They were just serving a much smaller, narrowly focused audience. By turning a skeptical light on all the con artists, on all the well-intentioned but misguided gurus, on the corporate executives whose latest business plan didn't quite add up, or just anything new, different, and unproven, the press worked in the service of the typical reader by helping him or her (mostly him) avoid losing what he had.

But what about the reader who wasn't there yet? What about the reader whose main problem was building wealth rather than preserving it? That was less of a concern. Back in the early 1980s the average person wasn't interested in personal finance. It was not a popular subject. And for the few dedicated investment junkies, a healthy investment newsletter business catered to them. Then the demographics started to change.

When pensions and guaranteed employee retirement benefits began to melt away in the 1980s, building wealth became a concern for everyone—not just the ambitious and the well-to-do. Today, most of us recognize that the nest eggs we will need to retire comfortably will have to be substantially larger than those required by our parents and grandparents. Baby boomers in particular woke up to the potential disaster waiting 20 or 30 years into the future if they didn't get better returns on the assets they already had.

By the late 1980s several publications had tapped into the rising popularity of mutual funds as a way for the typical family to safely build wealth. *SmartMoney*, an offshoot of the *Wall Street Journal*, took personal finance a step further with its first issue in early 1992. It was the first magazine that devoted as much effort to informing readers about building successful stock portfolios as it did to covering the mutual fund industry.

I remember reading the first issue and being stunned by the boldness of its new approach to personal finance. (I was so excited I started thinking about quitting my job and going to work for the fledgling publication.)

Why the bold, new positive emphasis on stocks? A couple of reasons stand out. First and foremost: Over the past three-quarters of a century, no other investment asset available to the average investor—bonds, cash, life insurance, real estate—has come close to providing the same wealth-building potential.

The statistical superiority of stocks over fixed-income securities like bonds and money-market securities has been documented over and over by respected researchers like Jeremy Siegel of the Wharton School and Roger Ibbotson of Ibbotson Associates. With the coming of the Internet, anyone with access to a historical stock database and good spreadsheet software can replicate their findings—something we've done at *SmartMoney* on several occasions.

Mutual funds had initially promised a painless way to tap into the potential of the stock market, but many longtime observers feel that the mutual fund industry has failed to live up to that promise. Not only have fees remained high at many fund companies, but new fees have cropped up where they didn't exist before. Performance hasn't lived up to expectations, either. As the number of funds multiplied into the thousands, managerial talent was spread thinner and thinner. The result: Most stock mutual funds can't keep up with their benchmark indexes—some of the very market indexes that researchers used to establish the superiority of stock market investing in the first place.

The perceived failure of most mutual funds as well as the falling cost of stock trading for individuals had the natural result of convincing more and more Americans to strike out on their own. Main Street discovered Wall Street, and it became common for the rest of us to start putting together our own stock portfolios to supplement or replace our mutual fund investments.

That shift has been reflected in *SmartMoney's* outlook since the magazine's inception. The stock market should be a place where we can start to build a better future for ourselves and our families. You can be a passive investor in mutual funds, or you can be more active and aggressive by choosing your own stocks. Most of us will want to do some of both, and we'll only do as much as we feel comfortable with.

And what of that notion of Wall Street as a dangerous place for the uninitiated? That is still something to be concerned about. The promoters, the pitchmen, and all the other con-artists are still out there. Their efforts have multiplied with a flood of new baby boomer savings available.

You'll face other risks as well. While the stock market as a whole is never in danger of going bankrupt, that's not true of the companies whose shares you might buy. Studying the historical market averages leaves out a lot of the detail of what can happen to the individual stocks that make up the averages. You can never realize the benefits of stocks' long-term wealth-building superiority if your shares of stock don't make it to the long term.

That's where the experience of a magazine like *SmartMoney* comes in. We're just as skeptical about financial products as the older generation of financial journalists. But we don't want to let that skepticism get in the way of offering readers some positive advice amid the warnings. We don't want to worry you so much that you miss out on the benefits of owning equities.

There are many risks in stock investing and countless ways to squander that potential if you don't fully understand the risks. That certainly proved true for many investors who bought into the so-called "new paradigm" of telecommunications stocks in 1999. The past few years have been a rude awakening for many.

The message in our coverage is that you need a disciplined program that balances those risks, playing them one against the other so that your overall prosperity is not put in danger—even in difficult times like the past two years, with the largest Nasdaq decline ever, followed by the terrorist attacks of September 11. This book will sum it all up for you. Our advice has worked for readers for a decade. We've made over 500 stock suggestions in our features over the years. The average appreciation for the group beats the average gains on matching S&P 500 index investments.

One thing we've learned is that there is no one way to build wealth safely with stocks. There are several different ways you can go about breaking down the risks associated with stock equity. The stock market is too complex and constantly evolving for any one set of hard-and-fast rules about investing to work for each investor every time. *SmartMoney* has always promoted multiple viewpoints when it comes to investment strategy.

However, our research and a decade of experience in some of the most volatile and eventful markets ever suggest that you can draw some broad conclusions about basic principles. These are principles and attitudes you will find common to many, if not most, of the successful stock strategies out there.

Nellie S. Huang and Peter Finch are in a good position to highlight those for you. They have been with *SmartMoney* since its early days and have been an integral part of the team covering the stock market for the magazine. In this book they bring together some of the most important lessons for active investors that we've learned over the years. While they include lots of useful advice on bonds and mutual funds, the emphasis here, like the emphasis in our magazine, is on understanding the stock market and getting the most out of it.

JERSEY GILBERT
Financial Editor
SmartMoney

ACKNOWLEDGMENTS

Every issue of *SmartMoney* magazine has always been a collaborative effort. This book is no different.

We would like to thank the reporters, writers, and editors of *Smart-Money* magazine (past and present) for their enthusiastic and innovative contributions over the years. Their work was instrumental in creating and refining the *SmartMoney* investing philosophy, and it was no less important in the creation of this book. In particular, we'd like to single out editor-at-large James B. Stewart, author of the incredible "The 10 Stocks for the '90s" feature in *SmartMoney*'s premiere issue, and Jersey Gilbert, the magazine's exceptionally talented financial editor. Thanks, too, go to Mike Oneal of SmartMoney.com and the award-winning team of writers and programmers at SmartMoney University, a terrific online tool for learning the investing basics. Finally, we would like to acknowledge Steven Swartz and Stuart Emmrich, former president and editor of *SmartMoney*, respectively. In the magazine's early years, they encouraged and occasionally browbeat many of us *SmartMoney* staff members into approaching the market in new and creative ways, always with the goal of making investing more accessible. This book was written in that spirit.

NELLIE S. HUANG
PETER FINCH

INTRODUCTION

THE CASE FOR STOCKS

The market, we realize, hasn't exactly been a winning advertisement for investing in stocks lately. Even supposedly safe companies such as Procter & Gamble and General Electric have taken investors on a roller-coaster ride, careening from new lows to new highs to new lows all over again. The market's massive sell-off in the days after September 11's terrorist attacks may have been frightening, but it was not a new phenomenon.

The important thing to remember, however, is this: Despite their short-term ups and downs, stocks do make great long-term investments. Over the past 74 years, while the stock market has grown by an average of 11 percent a year, a typical savings account accumulated just 2 percent on average every year—a difference of nine percentage points a year! That's a huge difference. And the longer the time horizon, the bigger difference those nine percentage points will make, thanks to the beauty of compounding. After 10 years, $10,000 invested in stocks is worth $16,204 more than the same amount invested in a savings account; after 25 years, the difference between the two has grown to more than $120,000.

It's simple. Over time, nothing does better than stocks. True, bonds will do a bit better than that savings account we just mentioned. But over the long term they probably won't improve the return you'll earn on stocks. For a retirement article we published in May 2000, we studied every possible time span going back to the 1920s, testing several different mixes of U.S.

stocks, bonds, and cash in a hypothetical tax-deferred account. While we found many 10-, 12-, and 14-year periods in which adding bonds or cash to your holdings resulted in higher gains than a diversified stock portfolio produced (and they were mostly periods that started in the Depression), we could find no period longer than 18 years where adding some bond assets improved the outcome.

This is a message *SmartMoney* has been spreading for the past 10 years. And, we're glad to say, our readers have benefited from it.

Our premiere issue in April 1992, when the United States was still recovering from a recession and the debilitating savings and loan debacle, featured an article called "The 10 Stocks for the '90s." Readers who followed our suggestions and bought those 10 stocks have since witnessed gains of better than *530 percent.* (The big winner in that portfolio was semiconductor-equipment company Applied Materials, up an amazing 3,458 percent since we wrote about it.)

Happily, our successes didn't end there. In 1994, a generally miserable year for stocks, our annual "Best Investments" portfolio climbed an average of 31 percent, in contrast to the 1 percent loss of the Standard & Poor's 500-stock index (S&P 500). More recently, when the rocky market started to roil our readers' portfolios, we responded with an article that highlighted seven stocks with healthy dividends—"The New Income Stocks" for our March 2001 issue. That portfolio, which included Ford Motor Company, railway company CSX Corporation, and energy play Occidental Petroleum, climbed a healthy average 18 percent in the first eight months of 2001, a nice contrast to the 9 percent decline in the S&P 500.

How do we do it? How do we go about researching our stocks and why do we make the choices we do? That's what you're going to learn over the following pages. We'll introduce you to a disciplined, proven stock-picking strategy that has worked for *SmartMoney*—and can work for you, too.

Yes, it will take a certain amount of commitment (after all, nothing good ever comes easily). To invest successfully you need to diligently research the companies you're thinking about buying. That means reading annual reports and keeping up with the daily news on the stocks you're considering. And even after you've invested in a company, you need to make a commitment to at least scanning the newspaper every day—to see if there's any important news about one of the stocks that you own—and reading those annual reports when they arrive in the mail.

It would be easier, certainly, to put all of your long-term money into stock mutual funds. And some funds *are* real highfliers, generating returns that are vastly bigger than what you'd expect from most individual stocks. In 1999, the Janus Venture fund racked up a spectacular 141 percent return, 120 percentage points ahead of the surging S&P 500-stock index. In 2000, Vanguard Health Care soared 60 percent as the S&P slid by 9 percent.

But here's the problem: Though many funds may outrun the broader market in any given year, only a few manage to do it consistently over time. As of mid-2001, the average fund boasted a 10-year average return of 15.7 percent. Not bad, except that it trails the S&P 500 index by 1.6 percent. Over 10 years, that margin could cost you $6,580 on a $10,000 investment.

It's not that we think mutual funds are a bad idea. On the contrary, at *SmartMoney* we believe in diversification. Mutual funds, bonds, and cash should each be a part of every individual's portfolio. But individual stocks offer the prospect of superior returns. The very safety of mutual funds' diversification drags their returns toward a distressingly predictable norm. And the truth is, we're not content to do only as well as everybody else.

We're not going to sit here and claim our stock-picking system is foolproof. Frankly, we've picked our share of duds over the years. It happens to the best professional managers and it will happen to you, too. You can't anticipate everything about the companies you invest in. And your stocks will almost certainly undergo rocky periods when they underperform market averages. Sometimes that will happen for no other reason than a broad market sell-off. Other times, a stock can implode for a very good reason, albeit one that's unforeseeable.

Who could have guessed in late 1994, for instance, that Intel's brand-new Pentium chip wouldn't be able to do floating-point division, a complex math function? In a matter of three weeks, the stock—one of our "Best Investments" for the year—slipped 10 percent. More recently, nearly everyone—including us—was shocked at the brisk way that Cisco Systems' revenue dropped in the first quarter of 2001. As of mid-2001, the stock was 77 percent off its peak.

So, yes, it often takes a strong stomach to be a stock picker. But it's our view that if you spend a little time on it, you'll have far more winners than losers. If you keep a cool head, you'll see some of these implosions as great buying opportunities. And you'll probably even have fun doing it.

1

STOCK AND BOND BASICS: STARTING AT THE BEGINNING

There are numerous people out there who would like you to believe that investing is complex. Many of them—brokers, financial advisers, "life planners," and the like—have a vested interested in this; the scarier and more forbidding they can make it seem, the more likely you are to hire them for their advice.

It's our view that investing is only as complicated or difficult as you allow it to be. So let's dive right in. We think you'll be surprised at how simple it really is.

Stock

Stock is ownership. It's as basic as that. Buy a share of Microsoft and you acquire a tiny sliver of the software giant. This is ownership in the most literal sense: You get a piece of every desk, contract, and trademark in the place. Better yet, you own a slice of every dollar of profit that comes through the door. The more shares you buy, the bigger your stake becomes.

The stock market itself is basically a daily referendum on the value of the companies trading there. Surely you've seen pictures of guys standing around screaming at each other on a stock exchange floor. Their job is to take in the day's news and distill it down to a single question: Will it help the companies I own make money in the future, or will it prevent them from doing so?

Look at the chart in Figure 1.1. It tracks the price movement of Microsoft stock from 1996 through mid-2001. You can see how it had a tremendous run-up in the late 1990s. Traders felt Microsoft could do no wrong. But then its antitrust case—which came to a head in 2000 when Judge Thomas Penfield Jackson ordered that the company be split in two—helped to send the company's stock spiraling downward. Clearly, traders were no longer so sanguine about its prospects. (Since then, as the decision was overturned, investors came to see the split-up as less likely and bid the stock back up a bit—only to send it back down as the economy sputtered in 2001.)

Whether it's Microsoft or any other stock, the supreme measure by which companies are valued is their earnings (a.k.a. profits). Wall Street is obsessed with them. Companies report their profits four times a year, and investors pore over these numbers—expressed as earnings per share—trying to gauge a company's present health and future potential.

The stock market rewards both fast earnings growth and stable earnings

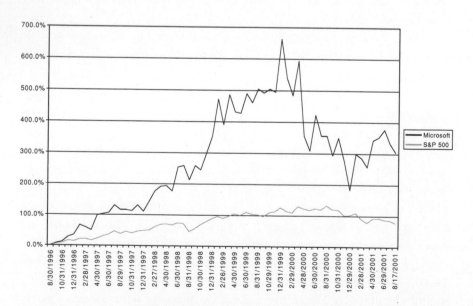

FIGURE 1.1   Microsoft vs. S&P 500

growth. But what about a company with a great idea but no immediate prospects for profitability? As Internet investors learned, Wall Street won't tolerate that situation for long. In 2000, the stock prices of many dot-coms went into a free fall as the market reevaluated the worth of these companies. Unfortunately, that left many investors with huge losses.

The market also has little patience for companies with declining earnings or unexplained losses. Bottom line? Companies that surprise Wall Street with bad quarterly reports almost always get punished.

Unlike a bond, which promises a payout at the end of a specified period plus interest along the way, the only assured return from a stock is created if it appreciates on the open market. (While many companies pay shareholders dividends out of their earnings, they are under no obligation to do so.) The worst-case scenario is that a company goes bankrupt and the value of your investment evaporates altogether. Happily, that's rare. More often, a company will run into short-term problems that depress the price of its stock for what seems an agonizingly long period of time.

Big Stocks

Market capitalization—or market value—is a term you'll come across a lot, so we'll define it right here. It's the number of shares a company has outstanding in the market, multiplied by the share price. If a company has 5 million shares outstanding and each one trades for $5, its "market cap" would be $25 million.

As the name suggests, large-capitalization stocks are the biggest players in the market (see Table 1.1). How big? A market value of $5 billion is generally considered the low end of large-cap stocks, while a behemoth like Microsoft weighs in at more than $300 billion. Then there's General Electric, the biggest of them all, which toward the end of 2000 temporarily had a market capitalization greater than $500 billion. Taken together, stocks with market values over $5 billion account for 82 percent of the market's total $16.1 trillion in value.

These companies play an especially significant role in driving the economy. That's why everybody pays so much attention to them. The two most-watched indexes—the Dow Jones Industrial Average and the Standard & Poor's 500-stock index—are both composed of large-cap stocks. The Dow tracks 30 of the biggest stocks on the New York Stock

TABLE 1.1   THE 10 BIGGEST STOCKS IN AMERICA

Company Name	Market Value as of mid-2001
1. General Electric	$432.1 billion
2. Microsoft	353.2
3. ExxonMobil	288.1
4. Pfizer	260.2
5. Citigroup	252.7
6. Wal-Mart Stores	249.9
7. AOL Time Warner	201.3
8. Intel	200.5
9. American International Group (AIG)	194.2
10. IBM	184.9

Source: Morningstar.com. Reprinted with permission.

Exchange. The S&P tracks 500 companies with an average market value of $21.8 billion.

The bigger you are, the harder it is to grow quickly, so large caps don't tend to expand as fast as your average technology upstart. But what they lack in flash, they make up in heft. The classic blue chip has steady revenue, a consistent stream of earnings, and a dividend. It also has critical mass, which means it can withstand ill economic winds better than its smaller cousins.

The 1990s ushered in a new breed of large caps that grow much faster than most blue chips. We're talking about mature technology wonders like Microsoft, Intel, and Cisco Systems. They're a little more volatile—okay, sometimes a *lot* more volatile—than a blue chip like Wal-Mart. But when it comes to catching a piece of future economic growth, they're hard to beat.

One caveat: Some small companies achieve large-capitalization status because of unbounded investor enthusiasm. In 1999, for example, some Internet companies like Priceline.com soared to large-cap status, even though they were unprofitable and lacked a proven track record. In April 1999, Priceline.com was valued at more than $23 billion—but that didn't last long. Near the end of 2000 its market capitalization had shrunk down to a mere $316 million. Lesson learned? Some companies might look like large caps, when they're really just bloated small or mid-caps. Clearly, there's nothing steady about companies like these.

Because of their size and stability, large-cap stocks are not generally speculative in nature and appeal to a more cautious investor. That's not to say they can't run into serious trouble, but they tend to grow along predictable trend lines and, since they are well known to Wall Street analysts, their problems often come with ample warning. Big companies (with the notable exception of many technology blue chips) also tend to pay regular dividends, which act as ballast by attracting income-oriented, long-term investors. Don't be fooled: Large caps can experience jarring price swings. But there's no doubt they are less volatile than small, hot-growth stocks.

Lower risk comes with a price, however. Except during periods of rampant uncertainty, large-cap stocks tend to produce lower returns than small caps (11.2 percent annually versus 12.8 percent).

Small Stocks

Small-capitalization stocks are known as the market's speed demons. That's not entirely accurate, since there are plenty of small, stodgy banks and rust-belt manufacturers in the group. And there are periods when small caps suffer because investors have no stomach for high volatility. But companies with a market value below $1 billion can also grow more quickly than bigger companies. Indeed, the good ones can post explosive earnings that drive double-digit returns for investors.

There are several indexes that track small-cap stocks. Probably the most widely referenced is Frank Russell Co.'s Russell 2000, which tracks 2,000 companies with an average capitalization of $530 million. Companies in Standard & Poor's small-cap index, the S&P 600, average about $625 million in market value. Most people, however, consider any company below $1 billion a small cap.

Small-cap companies tend to have correspondingly small revenues. And that means many of them have either just started up or are poised to expand their markets, either geographically or with new products. Dianon Systems is a good example. The Stratford, Connecticut–based operator of medical testing labs had a market value of right around $300 million as 2000 turned into 2001. Yet, because it was so small, it was able to grow much faster than a health-care giant like Johnson & Johnson, which had a market value of more than $130 billion.

Johnson & Johnson makes everything from Band-Aids to replacement hips. And over the five years from 1996 to 2000, its stock gained 131 percent, based on annual earnings growth of 15 percent. Not bad for a large cap. But over the same period, Dianon gained more than 1,000 percent as its earnings soared, on average, 444 percent per year. (See Figure 1.2.)

Of course, Dianon was also more volatile than Johnson & Johnson. And the smaller company ought to be much more vulnerable than the mighty Johnson & Johnson during an economic downturn. But Dianon's incredible performance over the past few years would have been a great sweetener to any diversified portfolio.

There are other risks as well. When the economy is uncertain, as it was, for example, in 1997 when the Asian crisis sent global stock markets reeling, investors looking for safety and stability will often abandon small caps for blue chips. Also, because small companies have fewer shares outstanding, their price movements are necessarily more erratic. When good news hits, investors clamoring to get in will drive the price up quickly. When bad news hits, the opposite is true, and it can sometimes be difficult to get out. Because fewer Wall Street analysts cover these stocks, there's also less reliable in-

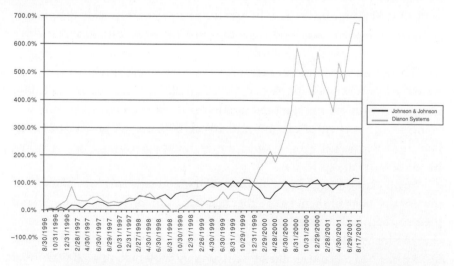

FIGURE 1.2   Johnson & Johnson versus Dianon Systems

formation on them. That means bad news can strike out of the blue, decimating stock prices overnight.

For all of that, however, most investors—especially young ones who have the time to make up any losses—want exposure to small caps. As we saw with Dianon, the upside potential is simply too great to pass up.

Foreign Stocks

At a time when the world economy has become increasingly interconnected, investors can hardly afford to ignore foreign stocks. There's too much opportunity out there and too many ways to tap it. And since the economies of the world's different regions tend to boom and bust in cycles that often offset each other, international stocks can provide excellent diversification for a portfolio heavy on U.S. equities.

Like stocks on the U.S. exchanges, foreign stocks vary in size and do not move as a single group. So you can't really say how a "Japanese stock" behaves, or how an "Italian stock" will perform. It's also true that foreign companies are subject to different rules of accounting and far less government scrutiny than U.S. investors are used to. It all adds up to this: Investing abroad is more complicated than buying stocks in the United States.

That's why most U.S. investors get international exposure either by investing in large, well-established overseas companies like Finland's Nokia or by putting their money in professionally managed mutual funds that have the expertise and resources to assemble winning portfolios from a host of different foreign stocks.

Buying an international mutual fund is no different from buying a domestic one. As for individual stocks, you can either buy the stocks through a broker directly on foreign markets or purchase what are known as American depositary receipts (ADRs) on U.S. exchanges. These shares are surrogates for foreign shares, but have dollar values and move according to the performance of their foreign issuers.

International markets are nothing if not volatile. They are highly susceptible to changes in foreign exchange rates, as well as shifts in regional and global economies. As the global economy slowed in 2000, for instance, stocks in most areas of the world slowed, too. But international markets are rarely that monolithic. Usually one region is up while another is down.

A dramatic example of that sort of divergence came in 1998 during the meltdown among the Asian economies. Economic turmoil in a region that was once the financial world's darling taught a lot of investors about the treachery of betting your money abroad. Japan's Nikkei index lost almost 40 percent between June 1997 and October 1998, as trading partners throughout the Pacific Rim imploded due to financial mismanagement and corruption. The ripple effects were felt worldwide as companies with exposure to those markets lost revenues.

At the same time, however, European markets blossomed as the Continent came closer to true economic union and a rash of U.S.-style corporate restructurings began to pay dividends. One region collapsed; another made up for it. That's why it makes sense to diversify your foreign investments, or let a professional money manager do it for you.

Tech Stocks

We live in an age when technology can change our lives seemingly overnight, and that ability creates rich new markets and explosive earnings growth for countless companies.

Of course, as investors learned in 2000 and 2001, there's a dark side to all that opportunity. Fearful of an economic slowdown, investors abandoned growth stocks and looked for safety in less volatile sectors like pharmaceuticals. Profitless Internet stocks like Amazon.com felt the worst impact. But even big, established technology companies like Cisco Systems and Sun Microsystems took a drubbing.

New markets are by nature filled with danger, and that means actual earnings—or the prospect of future earnings—can fluctuate wildly. News of a personal computer (PC) sales slowdown at Christmas can cause investors to flee any number of related stocks—from PC maker Gateway to Novellus Systems, which makes the equipment that fabricates the chips that power the PCs that Gateway sells. Investors will return to the good companies once the dust has cleared. But unless you have patience and staying power, such crises can easily wipe you out.

As the tech roller-coaster ride of the past few years has demonstrated, technology stocks as a group tend to be more volatile than the broader market. Still, a selection of high-tech blue chips should be in everyone's long-term portfolio, since the volatility they do exhibit is easily offset by their superior growth over time. We'll talk about where to find them—and a lot more—in the pages ahead.

But before we get to that, let's have a few words about another candidate for your investment portfolio.

Bonds

Think of a bond as an IOU. Buy one and you are in effect lending money to the issuer—whether it's the U.S. Treasury or U.S. Airways Inc. The issuer promises to pay you interest until the bond is due, at which point you'll get your principal back.

Bonds, with their steady stream of income, can add much-needed ballast to an otherwise volatile long-term portfolio. Here are the main types of bonds you should consider buying. We'll help you decide how much exposure to bonds you want in Chapter 3, when we discuss your ideal asset allocation.

Buying Directly from the Treasury

If you are just starting out, you can simply buy five-year Treasury securities, or—if you have a large amount of assets allocated for bonds—you can put together a so-called ladder of Treasurys. We'll show you how in a moment. Either way, your best bet for buying bonds and notes is the government's commission-free Treasury Direct program, which allows you to bypass brokers and their fees. An application to open an account may be obtained online by visiting the Treasury Direct web site (www.treasurydirect.gov) or by contacting your nearest Federal Reserve Bank. You can also call the U.S. Bureau of Public Debt at 800-722-2678.

Two-, three-, five-, and ten-year notes are available for a $1,000 minimum investment. You can set up an account online. If for some reason you need to sell the Treasurys in this account before they mature, you will have to have them transferred to a broker, who will charge at least $50 per transaction. In addition, Treasury Direct accounts of $100,000 or more face an annual $25 maintenance fee.

Agency Bonds

Also extremely safe and liquid, but offering a slightly higher yield, are government-agency bonds issued by the likes of the Tennessee Valley Authority, Farm Credit Financial Assistance Corporation, Federal National Mortgage Association (FNMA), and Government National Mortgage Association (GNMA). (These debentures should not be confused with the mortgage-backed bonds that are also issued by FNMA and GNMA; mortgage-backed securities are extremely sensitive to fluctuations in interest rates and should be avoided.)

It's hard, however, to gain any edge with these agency bonds over Treasurys. That's because they're generally available only through brokers and thus incur commission costs that cut into their yields. How much? The standard retail brokerage fee comes out to 0.5 percent, or in the lingo of the bond world, 50 basis points. Even if you have $100,000 to invest and negotiate a lower commission, perhaps 20 basis points, the advantage over Treasurys will probably come to only around $50 a year.

There might be an exception if you have a very large portfolio and can sink perhaps $1 million into agency bonds; you might then be able to get the institutional commission rate of just 10 basis points. Or, at a more modest level, you might be able to hook up with a financial adviser who specializes in making bulk government-agency bond purchases directly from banks, lumping clients' investments together in order to build million-dollar packages of agency debentures.

Muni Bonds

Investors with substantial income should also consider combining tax-free municipal bonds with their Treasurys. While the stated yields of munis are lower than those of Treasurys, the effective return for investors in high tax brackets is almost always better. As with Treasurys, individual muni bonds can also be laddered to limit your interest-rate exposure. But because they tend to trade in fairly large lots (usually $5,000 to $25,000) and because investors should spread their money among a variety of different locales as a precaution against default risk, building a muni portfolio requires a commitment of $100,000 at a bare minimum.

If you don't have enough now to build a muni ladder, the next best option is to look to a series of municipal-bond mutual funds. The best are Vanguard's Limited-Term Tax-Exempt and Intermediate-Term Tax-Exempt funds (which both have a minimum initial investment of $3,000). They maintain a low 0.18 percent expense ratio and are run with minimal maturity fluctuation and risk-taking.

What About Corporates?

While investors have traditionally been steered to corporate bonds because they offer higher interest income than government bonds, we are dubious about endorsing them. In part, it's a question of costs eating into those higher yields. First there are the taxes: Income from corporates is fully taxed at all levels. If your state and local rates (which are not applicable to government bonds) are a mere 6 percent, that would cut the effective return of an 8 percent yield to 7.5 percent. Next come the transaction costs: both brokerage commissions and the cut taken by the bond dealers (known as the spread). All told, they can easily eat up 1 percent or more of your investment.

Perhaps most important, though, is that the best bonds are usually callable by the issuer, meaning the corporation can, at its discretion, pay off its obligation at a stated price and stop paying interest. That becomes a heads-you-win, tails-I-lose proposition for investors. If interest rates decline and the value of the bonds goes up, the corporation may call them, disrupting your expected income stream and cutting off a potential capital gain. Alternatively, if interest rates rise you are stuck holding a less valuable security that is yielding below-market rates.

Up the Ladder

Diversification is as important in bond investing as it is in stock investing. It's best to spread your risk over a series of different maturities, while maintaining an average maturity of your liking in your portfolio. The best way to do that is to set up a ladder of Treasurys—in essence, a series of notes with a range of maturities. (Treasury notes have maturities of 1 to 10 years, while bonds have maturities of more than 10 years.)

Here's how it works: You buy equal amounts of Treasurys due to mature in one year, three years, five years, seven years, and nine years. That portfolio would have an average maturity of five years (one+three+five+seven+nine, divided by five, equals five). The next year, when the first batch comes due, you would reset the ladder by putting the money into new 10-year notes. Your portfolio would then have an average maturity of six years.

Two years later, when the next round of notes matures, you would buy more 10-year notes, continuing to buy new 10-years whenever a note matures. That would always keep the average maturity in the five- to six-year range.

One advantage to this scheme is that you don't need to worry about fluctuations in interest rates—especially if the ladder you construct has notes coming due each year. If rates do rise soon after you bought this year's bonds, you can take comfort in the fact that soon you will have money coming available to take advantage of the change by purchasing your new 10-years at lower prices. Similarly, if rates decline after you buy, you've managed to lock in the higher rates for that portion of your portfolio. The bottom line is, you won't get stuck one way or the other.

Treasurys for your ladder may be purchased straight from the U.S. government through the Treasury Direct program (mentioned earlier), with few fees and low minimum investments.

A ladder may also be constructed of municipal bonds, but that would typically require a bare minimum of $100,000 in capital to gather a diversified group of issues. Trading in a muni, which you can do through most brokerage firms, also creates higher transaction costs, but if your tax rate is high enough—probably anywhere above 28 percent—the tax savings may make the costs worthwhile.

Bond Funds versus Your Own Portfolio

Bonds are complex—there's no doubt about it—especially if you're a novice investor with little experience in the markets. That's why a lot of people opt for bond funds when they seek to diversify their investments with some fixed-income exposure. Our view is that if you're willing to put in the effort, you're better off buying individual bonds instead of bond funds. But in the real world, the convenience of a fund is sometimes worth the drawbacks.

Here's what you have to consider:

Like a stock mutual fund, a bond fund is managed by a professional investor who buys a portfolio of securities and makes all the decisions. Most funds buy bonds of a specific type, maturity, and risk profile—15-year corporates, for instance, or tax-free municipals—and pay out a coupon (interest rate) to investors, often monthly, rather than annually or semiannually like a regular bond.

The chief advantage of a bond fund is that it's convenient. It's also true that when it comes to buying corporate and municipal bonds, a professional manager backed by a strong research organization can make better decisions than the average individual investor. Consequently, if you want to dabble in junk bonds or shelter your income with triple-tax-free New York City 30-year bonds, you may be better off going the easy route and picking a good fund.

The main disadvantage of a bond fund is that it's not a bond. It has neither a fixed yield nor a contractual obligation to give investors back their principal at some later maturity date—the two key characteristics of individual bonds. Then there are the fees and expenses that can cut into returns. Finally, because fund managers constantly trade their positions, the risk-return profile of a bond-fund investment is continually changing: Unlike an actual bond, whose risk level declines the longer it is held by an investor, a fund can increase or decrease its risk exposure at the whim of the manager.

The other thing about building your own portfolio of bonds is that you can tailor it to meet your circumstances, meaning the bonds will mature precisely when you need them. A bond fund cannot deliver that sort of precision.

Our advice is this: If you lack the time or interest to manage a bond portfolio on your own, or if you want a mixed portfolio of corporates or municipals, buy a bond fund. But if you want a tailored portfolio of Treasurys to mature when your child goes to college, and you want to avoid the fees and added risk associated with bond funds, go ahead and take the plunge yourself.

2

THE SMARTMONEY WAY

"The Best Investments for the Year." "Five Ways to Beat This Market." "The One Investment Guide You Need Now."

To judge from the headlines on *SmartMoney*'s covers, you might get the impression we are all about market timing—that is, jumping in and out of stocks at precisely the right moment to get the maximum profits. Actually, nothing could be further from the truth. The magazine advocates—and always has advocated—buying stocks and holding onto them for the long run. It's our view that an individual investor should own most of his or her stocks for a minimum of three to five years . . . and often much longer.

The advantages of this long-term approach were summarized by our editor at large, James B. Stewart, in the very first issue of *SmartMoney*:

- *Taxes are deferred.* Long-term stock investing strikes us as the easiest yet most underanalyzed approach to minimizing taxes. Think of your portfolio as an IRA that can be liquidated at any time without penalty.

- *Brokerage commissions are minimal.* Spreading brokerage costs over a 10-year period can significantly boost total returns.

- *Decision making is minimized.* Stock performance doesn't have to be monitored daily. Market timing—a hopeless task even for most professionals—isn't a factor. Most investors simply don't have the time to be worrying constantly about their stock portfolio.

So why, you might wonder, do we routinely offer up those headlines like "The One Investment Guide You Need Now" and "Six Stocks Ready to Rally"? For the same reason we are writing this book: Most of us do not invest one lump sum per year and then forget it. There are going to be times *throughout* the year when we find ourselves with new cash—whether it's a bonus or a tax refund or the profit we made from cashing out of another stock—and we want to put it to use as intelligently and effectively as we can. The point is, we want to buy stocks that are most attractively priced right now, even if we intend to hold onto them for 10 years or more. That's how you get the kind of "pop" in your portfolio that produces market-beating results.

What we're looking for is opportunity. We don't necessarily want stocks that are cheap (because there's often a good reason for that), but we do want them to be trading at a discount to their normal levels. This can happen during times of market distress, say, or when an industry is going through an inevitable down cycle, or even when a company that's been beaten down is about to embark on a turnaround.

The Value of "Value"

Fundamentally, what we're talking about is closer to value investing than just about any other style.

In case you're not familiar with the term, let us explain. The investing world is divided into two broad groups: growth and value. Growth investors seek companies that are growing earnings and sales at annual rates that beat the market, and they are will to pay a hefty price for growth—generally speaking. Cisco in the late 1990s was a classic growth stock. Its earnings and revenue were growing 30 to 40 percent a year, easily double what you'd find at the average company. But that came at a price. Cisco stock had a price-to-earnings ratio of 50 or 60, again easily double what you'd pay for most stocks. (A price-to-earnings ratio, or P/E, is the price of the stock divided by its earnings per share. For more on this and other important valuation measures, see "Our Favorite Ratios" on page 74.)

Value investors, on the other hand, wouldn't touch Cisco stock if you paid them—well, maybe they would have in 2001, after its stock fell to $13 a share from $70, but certainly not the year before. Value investors want bargains, or stocks that trade at a discount, and that discount can be measured in a variety of ways against the market or its peer group. We're not talking about a low price, necessarily. A $10 stock might seem very expensive to a value investor if the company has no assets and no earnings.

We would never suggest you turn your back entirely on growth. After all, investors are never going to get excited about a company (and bid its stock price up) if they hold out zero hope for any earnings growth. This is why the *SmartMoney* style of investing is in effect a hybrid: To us, the ideal stock will have a low P/E ratio and a rapid rate of earnings growth. It's an investing style some call growth at a reasonable price (GARP).

But we can't stress enough the importance of that value underpinning, for study after study shows that value trumps growth over time. If you had invested $10,000 in large-company value stocks in 1974, you'd have $639,200 today, according to a well-respected research outfit called the Leuthold Group. But pity the poor investor who put the same amount in big-name growth stocks: A $10,000 investment in 1974 would be worth just $405,500 today, a shortfall of nearly 37 percent.

Value wins out among small and midsize companies, too. Another influential study, conducted by, among others, Josef Lakonishok, a professor of finance at the University of Illinois at Urbana-Champaign, examined all the companies listed on the New York and American stock exchanges between 1968 and 1990. Deep-value stocks beat their growth-stock counterparts by an average of 10 percent per year over most five-year periods.

But performance isn't the only reason we like value investing. It requires a certain amount of discipline to buy cheap stocks, and that can save even the most inexperienced investors from the biggest pitfall: impulse investing. All too often, investors let panic take over when the market starts to tank—they sell when they should buy—and they let greed tell them to buy when the market is climbing, which is just when they should sell.

Knowing When to Say "Sell"

The best way to invest, clearly, is to buy good companies and hold onto them. But you can't hold them *forever*. Companies change, industries change, your circumstances change. At some point, you're going to need to bail out of some of your stocks.

The question is, when?

It is one of the toughest decisions any investor will ever make, and unfortunately there are no clear-cut rules about when you ought to sell. But here are some guidelines we've devised over the years:

A stock's price/earnings ratio exceeds its earnings growth rate. The so-called forward P/E ratio is simply the current price of a company's stock divided by analysts' estimates for its earnings in the next year. If this figure tops the expected earnings growth rate (as a percentage) for the next three to five years by a wide margin—say, 20 percent or more—consider bailing out. The one exception is when the company is in a commodity-based business, such as energy, mining, or food processing. In these cases the growth rate matters little, since the market is focused on the outlook for industry prices.

The company's profit margins are trending down. A company's sales and earnings may be on the rise, yet it may still be in trouble. Check its profit margin (net income after taxes divided by sales). A better measure of a company's health is its operating margin (operating income divided by sales). If it has eroded over three consecutive quarters—you can track this on the quarterly income statements—dig into the company's 10-K filing to find out why.

Most analysts are revising their estimates downward. Analysts tend to be an optimistic lot, so whenever they begin lowering their three-to-five-year earnings estimates, watch out.

The dividend is too high. A dividend cut on a stock yielding at least 2.5 percent will surely send the share price lower. To assess a company's ability to meet its current payout, calculate its payout ratio (dividends per share divided by earnings per share). Anything over 60 percent is unusual, except for utilities, which shouldn't be above 80 percent.

A strong, well-known company has announced a competing product. Your company may be among the industry leaders in its niche, but if a familiar company with deep pockets announces it's targeting that same niche, your stock may lag until it proves it can defend its territory. If a costly price war seems to be in the works, don't be among the casualties. Sell.

Now, let's assume your stock has really gotten crunched, with a decline of greater than 40 percent since you bought in. That's really a tough one to sell, because you're going to take a bath on it. But will it ever come back? Is the worst over—or are the problems just beginning?

Ask yourself:

Is the stock's sector in fundamental decline? If yes, sell.

Is the same management team in place? If yes, sell. If there's been a change in the past year or so—and the new CEO has proven turnaround experience—consider hanging on.

Have pretax earnings fallen more than the stock price? Over the long haul, stock prices follow earnings. If the earnings decline is greater in percentage terms than the stock's decline, it's probably just a matter of time before the price drops even further. Sell.

Finally, here are some words of advice from Peter Lynch, the legendary former manager of Fidelity's Magellan fund and now vice chairman of the company's investment arm.

"Ask yourself, '**What inning is it in this company's life?**' If it's a growth company, the game might last 10 to 30 more years. But eventually, growth companies have to come up with a new story. When you're everywhere, where is there to go?

"I watched Avon Products fall 90 percent in the early '70s. You could have sat in your broker's office all the time, but you wouldn't have [known what was wrong just] by watching the stock. What you needed to know was there were too many Avon ladies—at one point maybe one out of every 10 women in America. Who were they going to sell to? Once the story starts to deteriorate, get out. I know one person whose system was that when the company stopped hiring, he sold.

"Cyclicals such as paper or steelmakers are different. When a cyclical stock goes from good to terrific, what's left? It's not going to stay terrific for long. . . . **When the balance sheet starts to slip, I'm out.**"

Most would-be growth moguls wind up selling off their winners too early and hanging onto their losers too long. According to a study of discount brokerage customers conducted by University of California at Davis finance professor Terry Odean, the stocks investors sold from 1987 to 1993 went on to outperform the stocks they held by more than three percentage points a year. "People tend to get excited about growth stocks. They build up expectations, and they end up getting quite disappointed," Lakonishok says.

The Proof Is in the Profits

We wish, of course, we could claim our investment strategy was 100 percent accurate. But buying stocks this way—buying them *any* way, for that matter—is risky. From time to time you'll unwittingly pick up a stock that truly is cheap and will stay that way forever. Maybe its industry is hopelessly doomed and never does turn around. Or maybe the "new, improved" management is worse than the group that preceded it. Whatever. The important thing is, with a diverse collection of holdings often all it takes is one or two really great performers to lift a portfolio to astronomical heights.

In 1996, as part of an article called "Ten Stocks under $20," we alerted readers to Vitesse Semiconductor, then a little-known chip company. Investors had been spurning any stock associated with semiconductors, and the stock had fallen 16 percent from its 52-week high. (Aha—value!) What most of Wall Street didn't understand was that Vitesse doesn't use silicon to make its chips. It uses digital gallium arsenide, and the result is a chip that's four to five times faster than the average silicon version. Vitesse owned a 60 percent share of a market that was poised to boom. Boy, were we right: Three months after we wrote up the stock, it had climbed more than 100 percent, and it spent the next 18 months hitting new 52-week highs. It's up more than 650 percent since then.

Naturally the whole "Ten Stocks under $20" portfolio hasn't done that well, on average. But it's still up a remarkable 80 percent, with Vitesse's spectacular performance smoothing over some of the, *ahem*, less than stellar performers in that portfolio. (Auspex Systems and Previo, which was previously known as Stac, were down 60 and 92 percent, respectively.)

It happens time and time again. On the following pages you'll see charts representing a handful of representative *SmartMoney* portfolios from the past few years (Figures 2.1 to 2.7). In each case they are ahead of the S&P 500, with a few stocks truly leading the way and one or two holding back the average.

No, diversity is not a guarantee of great results. We published our "Ten Stocks under $25" portfolio in May 1998, for instance, on the eve of an 18-month decline in the Russell 2000, an index of small stocks. Through mid-2001, the companies we profiled in that article were down by an average of 30 percent. (To our credit, we did note that these small companies "may experience 30 or 40 percent price swings from time to time, especially if they are in heavily traded sectors like technology or health care.")

By and large, however, our portfolios have performed exceptionally well. The average stock picked in *SmartMoney*'s feature articles has increased in price about 1 percent faster per year than the Standard & Poor's 500 index. That may not sound like much, but compounded over time it leads to much larger returns.

At its core, our system for finding good, undervalued stocks has two steps. It starts with a computer screen, a kind of process of elimination that winnows down the universe of 7,000+ stocks into a smaller group of potential invest-

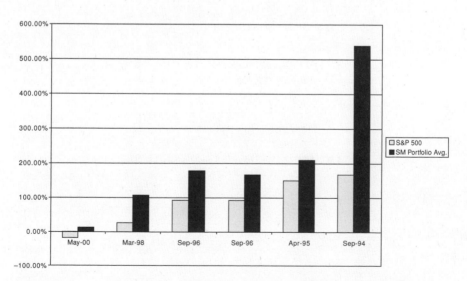

FIGURE 2.1   Selected *SmartMoney* Portfolios versus S&P 500 (through July 20, 2001)

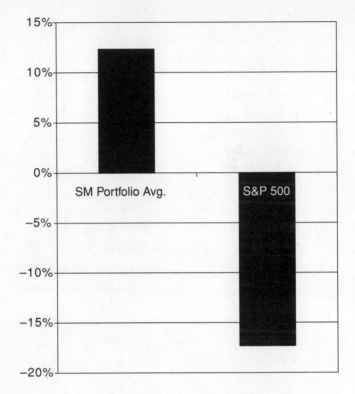

Selected returns from this portfolio:

Abbott Laboratories	56%
Avon Products	48
Hershey Foods	36

Honeywell International	−21

FIGURE 2.2 "Living Large"—May 2000

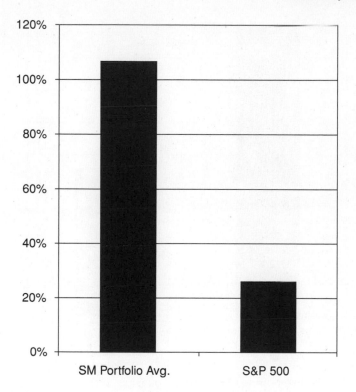

Sample returns from this portfolio:

Adobe Systems	315%
Dell Computer	141
ASM Lithography	71
Autodesk	−6

FIGURE 2.3   "Silicon Values"—March 1998

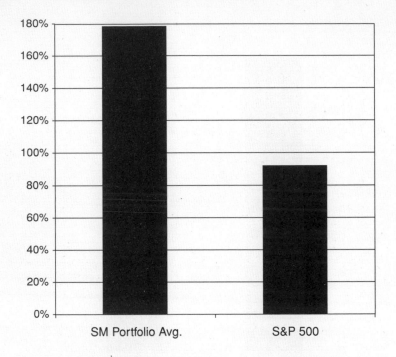

Sample returns from this portfolio:

TJX Companies	395%
Microsoft	367
Sun Microsystems	357

CompUSA	–54

FIGURE 2.4   "Bargain Stocks to Buy Now"—September 1996

ments. Is the stock a bargain compared to its peers and the market? To figure this out, we do what many other investors do: We use ratios like price-to-earnings (the share price divided by earnings over a 12-month period) or price-to-sales (market capitalization divided by revenue) to place a relative value on a company share.

Then we analyze the company's fundamental nitty-gritty: Is the company run by a reliable and trustworthy management team? Why is it trading at a discount? Is there a catalyst for growth, something that will juice the earnings of the company and thus drive up the stock?

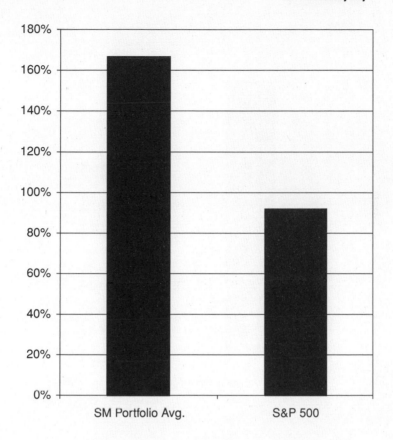

Selected returns from this portfolio:

Analog Devices	503%
Cisco Systems	228
Microchip Technologies	168
U.S. Robotics	−59

FIGURE 2.5   "Sifting Through the Debris"—September 1996

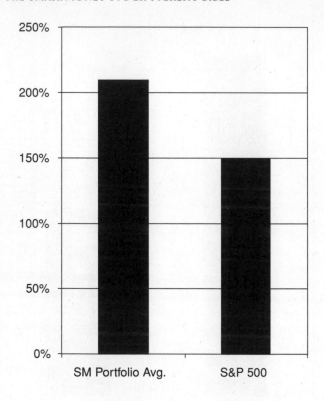

Selected returns from this portfolio:

AES Corporation	716%
Gentex	433
American Power Conversion	29
--	
Sports & Recreation	−100

FIGURE 2.6 "A League of Their Own"—April 1995

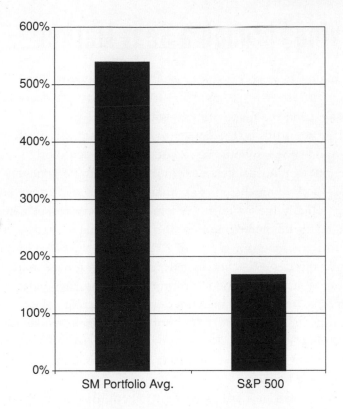

Selected returns from this portfolio:

Concord EPS   2,721%
Patterson Denta   488
Fair, Isaac & Co.   315

Wall Street Deli   −95

FIGURE 2.7   "The New Growth Stocks"—September 1994

Living Through a Bear Market

No matter how you define a bear market—down 10 percent, as some say, or down 20 percent—it's not pretty. It's scary and depressing and seemingly fraught with danger.

But the truth is, the consequences are not as cataclysmic as the handwringers would have you believe. According to research firm Ibbotson Associates, bear markets tend to be relatively short-lived—and when the market finally does recover, the resulting surge quickly makes up for whatever losses were sustained. According to Ibbotson's figures, the average bear market lasts 10 months and results in a loss of 28 percent in the value of the S&P 500. In the past 55 years, investors caught in a bear market have had to wait, on average, 18 months from market's bottom to recover their money and then are poised for big, *big* gains. The average total return in the first 12 months after a bear market ends is a whopping 36 percent. That's sufficient to make back all of your losses—and then some—if you're patient enough to stay in the market and hold on.

Yes, it can be hard to be that patient. But there are ways to confront and cope with the painful feelings associated with falling stock prices. *SmartMoney*'s editor at large, James B. Stewart, recently shared his thoughts on the subject with our readers. Here are some of the bear-market survival techniques that have worked for him:

Recognize your emotions about the market, but don't act on them. There's no point in trying to pretend you feel good when you don't. But your feelings should never dictate an investment strategy. If you have a sensible investment plan in place, stick resolutely to it. If you don't, the time to forge one is probably not when you're in the depths of despair. But vow to make one when you're feeling better.

Understand that to act rationally at times of intense emotion is difficult. It is one thing to recognize that you should be buying stocks at times of severe market weakness. It is another to act. You will think of every possible excuse to avoid it. Be disciplined. The greatest investment returns are realized by those with sound judgment and the fortitude to go against the herd.

All bear markets eventually end. Even the Great Depression, the worst economic contraction in 500 years, came to an end. At their lowest, stocks lost 90 percent of their value. They never lost all of it. The average bear market in the S&P 500 from 1926 till now lasted 11 months.

Avoid getting fixated on the market value of your assets. Market prices are simply a snapshot of investor sentiment at a particular moment. Unless you have to sell just then—and hopefully you do not—those prices are interesting but largely irrelevant. You still own exactly the same assets that you did at the market peak, assuming you haven't sold.

Don't become trapped by hindsight. It's easy now to fantasize about having sold at the market's peak. Media stories trumpeting the good fortune of people who did don't help. But you weren't clairvoyant then, and you aren't now. And even if you had sold, what would you have done with the proceeds? Would you have bought on the dips, putting your cash back into the market? If so, you'd be only slightly better off. The point is that no one has discovered an infallible strategy for market timing, so you shouldn't feel bad about missing a market peak.

If you have cash, concentrate on buying stocks at bargain prices. For anyone who's a net buyer rather than a seller of stocks, which should be just about anyone under 60, a bear market is a godsend. It's as if the department store of the nation's economy launched a huge sale.

If you don't have any available cash, it's okay just to ignore the market until it turns around. If you don't want to look at CNBC or your stock portfolio because it's too painful to do so, don't. If you have other interests in life, concentrate on them and forget about the market. If you don't have any other interests in life, now might be a good time to cultivate some.

Remember, there's no reason to feel paralyzed. This may be as good a time as any to examine your asset allocation. Given the huge decline in tech stocks as a group, for example, you might wish to sell a sector that has become overweighted in your portfolio, such as pharmaceuticals, and buy more tech. As long as you buy as much as you sell, you're remaining neutral on the market. But unless you are a pure momentum investor, don't bet on further declines. Do not sell into the depths of a bear market.

Whatever happens, don't despair. Over the long term, stocks have historically produced the highest returns of any category of investment.

In the chapters that follow, we'll show you how we typically run our screens and then tell you how to gather research on a company (how to get your hands on information, what to read, and how to understand it). Finally, we'll explain how to pull it all together and assess whether the stock will make a good investment.

But before you get to that, we suggest you take 15 minutes and fill out our SmartMoney One asset allocation worksheet, which appears in the following chapter. It's a quick, easy way to get a handle on the *types* of stocks you should be buying now, so that you end up with a fully rounded and well-diversified portfolio.

3

YOUR IDEAL
ASSET ALLOCATION

E ven with the market's meltdown in 2000 and 2001, the past few years
have been spectacular for big, blue-chip stocks. If you'd bought and
held nothing but the brand-name stocks of the Standard & Poor's
500-stock index since the first issue of *SmartMoney* was published back
in 1992, you'd have earned 21 percent a year on average, for a total gain of
197 percent.

But the truth is, in the real world it's not always a bull market for those
big stocks. Unless you're saving for a retirement that's 20 years or more away,
you can't just put 100 percent of your money in the S&P 500 and expect it
will all be there when you need it. What you need is a diverse portfolio—a
mix of big and little stocks, some international companies, even some bonds
and some cash. Because if you allocate your assets correctly, your portfolio
will be safer at the top of a bull market and more rewarding in a bear market
than if you tried to time your way in and out.

Think about it: If you spread your assets widely enough, some of them
will be doing well at any given time. So over time, you shouldn't be forced to
cash out at the bottom of a bear market in any one of your investments if
you need to tap some of your savings. You'll have losses in part of your portfolio occasionally, but they'll be only on paper—to be much reduced or even
eliminated over the years.

Or at least that's the way it works if you do it correctly. But we'd venture that very few people know exactly how their assets are divvied up at any given point. Even fewer, we'd guess, have any idea of how to get it right.

Which brings us to the SmartMoney One asset allocation worksheet in Figure 3.1. (We call it that because we consider it the one asset allocation program you'll ever need.) Though it may look a little daunting, don't sweat it. You should be able to complete our worksheet in 15 minutes or less—and when you're done you will have a very good idea of how to spread your assets among large, small, and international stocks (as well as bonds and cash).

Before we move on to the worksheet, a couple of important points:

- The allocation we're designing here is for your *wealth building* portfolio. By that we mean the money that you've set aside for your long-term savings, including your retirement accounts. However, money that you have already earmarked for shorter-term goals, such as a vacation or a down payment on a new house, should not be included. Those kinds of savings demand a more conservative approach than we're advocating here.

- This is a *guide* to asset allocation; the mix you derive after running through the calculations is not meant to be carved in stone. The more you learn about the range of investments within each asset category—and the way they interact with other investments—the better you'll be able to fine-tune your own portfolio over the years.

SmartMoney Allocation Principles

The basics of the SmartMoney One program are as follows: You assign yourself a score based on your age. Then you make adjustments to your score depending on your answers to eight different questions about your financial situation. Certain answers will increase your stock or bond allocations. Other answers will lead to neutral or negative adjustments, reducing your exposure to market volatility.

Age

We start with age because it is arguably the most important factor influencing asset allocation. The longer you have to save and invest, the less you need to cut back your exposure to equities. When you have decades of investing

The SmartMoney One Worksheet

Your age is the most important, but by no means the only, factor in choosing a reasonable allocation among investments. Your portfolio's size, your tax exposure, your spending needs and your tolerance for volatility should all play a role. Therefore the worksheet has two parts. Part A (below) will let you account for what makes your financial situation different from other people your age. Scores from that table will be used in Part B (next page) to adjust the allocation mix according to your needs.

Keep in mind that the suggested allocations are guidelines only. In that spirit, feel free to round the final percentages off to the nearest whole number and drop any asset with an allocation under 4 percent. Amounts that small add little to your overall performance or your overall risk reduction.

PART A To fill out the SmartMoney One asset-allocation worksheet, you will first need to answer the following questions about your financial situation and your investment outlook. We suggest you highlight or circle the entire row (under columns A through D) of the response that best fits. Then, when the worksheet requires you to make adjustments to your allocations based on this table (lines 2, 4, 11, and 18), it will be easier to find the required score from the appropriate column. Note: You will not know the correct response to the last question (Interest-Rate Exposure) until you fill in line 7 of Part B.

	A	B	C	D
Portfolio Size				
What is the value of your investment portfolio?				
Less than $50,000	3	0	0	0
Between $50,000 and $250,000	−1	15	4	4
Greater than $250,000	−3	20	6	10
Yearly Savings				
How much do you save a year?				
Less than $2,000	2	N/A	0	0
Between $2,000 and $10,000	−1	N/A	2	2
Over $10,000	−2	N/A	8	6
Spending Needs				
What portion of your investments do you plan				
to spend (for education, home, etc.)				
over the next 10 years?				
0 to 30 percent	−3	N/A	15	10
31 to 60 percent	2	N/A	5	4
61 to 100 percent	7	N/A	0	0
Investment Income				
How much income do you need to generate				
from your investments?				
Less than 1 percent	N/A	10	10	N/A
Between 1 and 4 percent	N/A	15	4	N/A
More than 4 percent	N/A	25	0	N/A
Federal Tax Bracket				
What is your marginal federal tax rate?				
15 percent	0	N/A	0	N/A
28 percent	−1	N/A	2	N/A
31 percent or greater	−4	N/A	6	N/A
Volatility Tolerance				
How much volatility can you live with?				
As little as possible	2	5	0	0
A moderate amount	−1	10	5	3
A lot	−5	15	14	6
Economic Outlook				
What is your reading on the U.S. economy				
over the next 12 months?				
Weak	2	20	0	10
Average	−5	10	6	0
Strong	−8	0	10	−10

FIGURE 3.1 The SmartMoney One Worksheet

	A	B	C	D
Interest-Rate Exposure				

To make sure you are not overly exposed to interest-rate risk, you will adjust your small-cap and foreign allocations for the size of your bond holdings. When you get to line 7 of Part B, note if the bond allocation is . . .

	A	B	C	D
Less than 15 percent	N/A	N/A	0	0
Between 15 and 35 percent	N/A	N/A	6	10
Greater than 35 percent	N/A	N/A	10	20

PART B

1. **Enter your age.** _____
   (If you are younger than 25, enter 25; if you are older than 80, enter 80. If you are filling out the worksheet as a couple, average your ages.)

2. **FIXED INCOME:** Choose the score in column A from Part A.
   a. **Portfolio Size** _____
   b. **Yearly Savings** _____
   c. **Spending Needs** _____
   d. **Federal Tax Bracket** _____
   e. **Volatility Tolerance** _____
   f. **Economic Outlook** _____

3. Add lines 1 and 2a through 2f. (If result is greater than 100, enter 100.) _____

4. **BONDS:** Choose the score in column B from Part A.
   a. **Portfolio Size** _____
   b. **Investment Income** _____
   c. **Volatility Tolerance** _____
   d. **Economic Outlook** _____

5. Add lines 4a through 4d. _____

6. Divide line 5 by 100. _____

7. Multiply line 3 by line 6.
   This is your Bond allocation. _____%

8. Subtract line 7 from line 3.
   This is your Cash allocation. _____%

9. **STOCKS:** Subtract line 3 from 100. _____

10. Subtract your age from 70. (If answer is less than zero, enter zero.) _____

11. **SMALL CAPS:** Choose the score in column C from Part A.
    a. **Portfolio Size** _____
    b. **Yearly Savings** _____
    c. **Spending Needs** _____
    d. **Investment Income** _____
    e. **Federal Tax Bracket** _____
    f. **Volatility Tolerance** _____
    g. **Economic Outlook** _____
    h. **Interest-Rate Exposure** _____

12. Add lines 10 and 11a through 11h. _____

13. Divide line 12 by 200. _____

14. Multiply line 9 by line 13. *This is your Small-Cap allocation.* _____%

15. **FOREIGN STOCKS:** Enter 40. Then, if you are younger than 60, skip to line 18. Otherwise continue with the next two lines. _____

16. Subtract 60 from your age. _____

17. Subtract line 16 from line 15. Use this result on line 19. _____

18. Choose the score in column D from Part A.
    a. **Portfolio Size** _____
    b. **Yearly Savings** _____
    c. **Spending Needs** _____
    d. **Volatility Tolerance** _____
    e. **Economic Outlook** _____
    f. **Interest-Rate Exposure** _____

19. Add either the amount in line 15 or line 17 to the sum of lines 18a through 18f. (If the result is negative, enter zero.) _____

20. Divide line 19 by 200. _____

21. Multiply line 9 by line 20. *This is your Foreign Stock allocation.* _____%

22. Add line 14 and line 21. _____

23. Subtract line 22 from line 9. *This is your Large-Cap allocation.* _____%

24. **YOUR INVESTMENT MIX:** Enter the total value of your portfolio. $_____

25. **ALLOCATION AMOUNTS:**
    a. Multiply line 24 by percent on line 8.
       Cash $_____
    b. Multiply line 24 by percent on line 7.
       Bonds $_____
    c. Multiply line 24 by percent on line 23.
       Large-cap U.S. stocks $_____
    d. Multiply line 24 by percent on line 14.
       Small-cap U.S. stocks $_____
    e. Multiply line 24 by percent on line 21.
       Foreign stocks $_____

FIGURE 3.1   *(Continued)*

returns to look forward to, market volatility is reduced to minimal importance. It's the eventual outcome that's most important, not how you get there.

As you age, aggressive equity strategies remain important for wealth building. But wealth preservation is also important. This is particularly true as you set aside big chunks of your savings for college tuition or retirement. The less time you have to let your investments run freely, the more of an impact stock market fluctuations will have on your final results. This program will methodically shrink your stock allocation as you get older.

Portfolio Size

While age is a primary consideration, it can't be the only one. Your own financial circumstances play a huge role in how you allocate your assets. First, we'll consider the amount you have invested. The general rule is a simple one: The less you have, the more you need to exercise caution.

If you have savings that even approach $50,000, you're ahead of most of your fellow Americans. Unfortunately, even a little misstep at this point can make a big difference in your portfolio, because you still do not have much extra cushion to break your fall. There's another concern: The less money you have, the harder it is to completely diversify your holdings.

For the person with less than $50,000, scoring in this section of the worksheet will ensure that more of your money goes toward the safest asset: cash. Among the other assets, bonds and large caps will be favored for their lower volatility.

With $50,000 to $250,000, you ought to feel reasonably comfortable. You have enough assets to diversify over a wide variety of investments. However hard it was to build up your nest egg, your good fortune means you can afford to risk some of these assets.

At the same time, we're not going to ignore the need to preserve capital; a big loss can still drag down your lifestyle even if the days when it would wipe out your savings are behind you. If you have more than $250,000, that's sufficient to get all the diversity you need and take on as much risk as is appropriate for your age. Our point system takes all of this into account.

Yearly Savings

It's a lot easier to accept extra risk if you have a steady flow of new savings each year. That's because new money gives you a chance to make up for losses if part of your portfolio takes a hit. It's also a lot easier—and cheaper—to adjust your allocations. You can simply apply the new money where needed to restore balances, rather than selling part of your holdings and using the proceeds to buy more of other holdings—a process that often involves commissions, fees, or tax liability. The SmartMoney One program hikes your equity position if you maintain a steady stream of new savings.

Spending Needs

Most people plan to enjoy their wealth as they age. Thus, our asset allocations tend to be more aggressive for young investors and more conservative for those who are older. But your spending plans can reverse that pattern. Let's say you must dip into your nest egg in your 30s or 40s because you need the money to buy a house or even pay for a big vacation. If you need it within 10 years, there is no guarantee that the market will recover from any setback it experiences.

So the more you plan to spend in the foreseeable future, the more you need to shift into large caps from small caps and foreign stocks—and, generally, the more you need to move out of equities.

Investment Income

Not everyone has the luxury of reinvesting his or her income to boost total return. Some of us need to supplement our other earnings with income from our investments. This is especially true for retirees, and our age adjustments take that into account. This program, however, will boost the bond portion of your allocation further if you need more than 4 percent in annual income from your holdings. It will also put more money in large caps—the ones most likely to have substantial dividends.

Federal Tax Bracket

In general, the higher your tax bracket, the more you want to avoid distributions such as dividends and bond coupons while your investments grow.

Otherwise, taxes will bleed your total return. So, regardless of your age, we decrease your bond allocations and large-cap allocations in favor of small caps when your tax rates are high. Most small-cap appreciation gets assessed at the low 18 or 20 percent capital gains rates, because you don't get much in the way of dividends from these stocks.

There is, however, one important caveat to that rule. If most of your wealth is in tax-advantaged retirement accounts such as 401(k)s and individual retirement accounts (IRAs), your current tax bracket is of little concern. Gains on assets in the account are not taxed until the money is withdrawn when you're retired. If most of your investments are in such accounts, we suggest you choose the 15 percent response to complete this question. If your investments are evenly split between taxable and nontaxable accounts, choose the 28 percent response.

Volatility Tolerance

In the most rational of worlds, concern over volatility would be confined to those of us with short investment horizons. But this question recognizes that there is a substantial emotional component to any successful investment program. We know lots of perfectly sane, intelligent people who simply cannot stomach even a small decline in their stocks, let alone the occasional free fall.

Only you can measure your true tolerance of price fluctuations, and you have to be honest. Some people like to think they are risk tolerant, even like to boast of it, and yet are actually risk averse. If you have never owned a stock that has plunged—if you didn't experience the October 1987 crash, not to mention the bear market of 1973 to 1974—you don't know what losing money on paper feels like. Until you do, you shouldn't assume that you have a strong appetite for risk.

Here are some questions to ask yourself: Have you ever panicked and sold a stock that was going down? Do you tend to buy stocks only after your friends and acquaintances have already bought in? Do you look at stock tables only on days when the market is up? Are you uncomfortable admitting to friends that your stocks have experienced declines? Do you agonize over interest-rate swings? Do you worry about the value of your home, even though you have no intention of selling? If the answer to any of these questions is yes, you may not be able to live with volatility as easily as you think. Stick to either the medium or low answer. Those responses will put less of your assets in stocks and bonds and more of them in supersafe cash.

Economic Outlook

How do you think things are going for the U.S. economy? Are you optimistic or pessimistic? We don't mean the next quarter or two. Trying to make that kind of prediction will destabilize most portfolios very quickly. Think instead in terms of where we are in the business cycle: Are we toward the beginning, the middle, or the end of the current expansion? Generally speaking, the more optimistic you are, the more heavily you should be weighted in U.S. stocks, because the stock market rises with corporate earnings and national income. If you're a pessimist, you don't need the extra risk of stocks. But you might want to increase your bond allocation.

That's because when the economy slows, interest rates usually fall. And bond prices rise. Pessimism should also lead you to increase your overseas equity portion, because the timing of recessions in different global regions seldom coincides.

So what's the bottom line for our recommendations? If your outlook for the economy is strong or average—roughly equivalent to the beginning and middle of economic expansion—then the scoring will indicate a stronger mix of cash and small stocks. The stepped-up mix of cash in good economic times may surprise you, especially if you are younger than 45 or so and fixed income makes up only a small part of your investment. Even though bonds typically have higher yields than Treasury bills or money market funds, they offer almost no protection against rising prices or rising interest rates. Since strong economies are much more likely to spur price and interest rate hikes, sacrificing a little yield gives you better protection against loss of capital.

Interest-Rate Exposure

This can be answered only after you've worked through question No. 7 on Part B of the worksheet. Here, what we're trying to do is make sure that if you end up requiring a lot of bonds in your mix, you don't load up with large-cap stocks. That's because bonds, which pay a stated interest (coupon), and large-cap stocks, which tend to pay dividends, have similar reactions to changes in interest rates. (As interest rates go up, the coupon payments and dividend payouts seem less attractive.) Therefore, even though small caps and foreign stocks are more volatile than the other assets in this model, in combination with bonds they can help reduce your interest-rate risk.

THE RIGHT MUTUAL
FUNDS FOR YOU

This is a book about picking stocks. So why a chapter on funds? That's easy: diversification.

Yes, picking stocks is fun and you can significantly boost your returns if you invest in great companies. But the truth is, the more stocks you own, the less your portfolio suffers if one of them tanks. The trick is to build and maintain a well-diversified portfolio—not an easy thing to do for the average investor. To do it right, you might have to keep an eye on 20 to 60 different stocks at once. Some people thrive on that sort of thing; others lack the time, interest, or experience to give a complex portfolio the attention it demands.

Enter mutual funds—pools of stocks or bonds that are managed by professional investors. By combining your investment money in a number of individual stocks as well as funds, you'll get the best of both worlds. The only problem is, there are nearly as many mutual funds out there as there are common stocks—more than 8,800 at last count. They seem to multiply like rabbits, drinking from the wide stream of baby-boomer retirement savings. All together, they comprise a staggering $7 trillion in assets. And then there's the most chilling statistic of all: More than 75 percent of them routinely fail to beat the benchmark S&P 500 index when it comes to annual returns.

In this chapter we'll tell you what you need to know to take control of your mutual fund investing. You'll need to learn some basics first: Why mutual funds make sense. How they work. What to look out for in terms of fees and expenses. And how to sort through the different types of funds. The fund bazaar can be daunting, but finding your way around isn't as hard as it looks.

Different Flavors of Funds

Funds come in all shapes and sizes, from Fidelity's $84 billion Magellan fund—the largest in the United States—to the $1 million Rainbow fund. Most of them work this way: A sponsor company like Fidelity or Vanguard rounds up money and pays a portfolio manager to buy groups of securities according to a specific investing strategy. The company then sells shares in the fund to the general public at a price reflecting the value of the pooled securities. Buy a share of the fund, and you own a small percentage of the total portfolio, meaning you participate in any of the fund's investment gains or losses. Depending on the fund, you can own a piece of 20 to 500 different stocks.

The fund industry has gone on a rampage of market segmentation in recent years with ever more exotic offerings to attract new fee-paying customers. Now there are funds geared to just about any investment objective—from funds that buy only Internet-related stocks to those that invest only in Latin American utilities. In fact, Morningstar, the Chicago-based fund database firm, tracks 29 distinct kinds of equity funds—and that includes the newly hatched breed of exchange-traded funds (see Sidebar 4.1, "Even Cheaper Than Index Funds").

For investors, this diversity provides the opportunity to tailor a portfolio of funds to meet particular objectives. Take a 55-year-old man eyeing retirement in a few years. Seeking some growth but not much risk, he may put part of his money into a steady, large-company equity fund, while protecting the bulk of his nest egg in a money-market fund with lower—but virtually guaranteed—returns. A 30-year-old woman, on the other hand, has years to make up for any short-term investment losses. So she may want to put most of her money in a more aggressive, small-company equity fund that promises more risk, but higher returns.

Unfortunately, the outcrop of high-flying funds has encouraged some investors to move in and out of funds like stock traders, trying to time the market. What gets lost in the shuffle is a simple, time-honored principle: Investors do best if they pick a set of promising stocks or funds and leave their money in them for the long term.

If all this sounds hopelessly confusing, it doesn't have to be. Most people's investment objectives can be satisfied without getting fancy. The truth is, there are only a few broad categories of funds that really matter to most people. And if you are investing through your retirement plan at work, you'll probably be limited to those groups, anyway.

In Table 4.1 you'll find the essential fund categories to know about and

TABLE 4.1   ESSENTIAL FUND CATEGORIES

Type of Fund	10-Year Return through Mid-2001	Standard Deviation	Expense Ratio
Blend	11.86	16.75	1.30
Bond	6.69	4.65	1.09
Financial	19.77	21.91	1.66
Foreign	7.12	16.11	1.68
Growth	12.46	23.98	1.53
Index	11.94	14.18	0.79
Large-cap	12.63	16.96	1.35
Microcap	13.91	16.70	1.91
Mid-cap	13.91	16.70	1.91
Money market	4.70	1.42	0.59
Small-cap	13.47	21.80	1.53
Technology	20.69	39.01	1.68
Utilities	11.30	13.00	1.40
Value	13.41	14.90	1.42
World	8.85	17.10	1.79

Source: Morningstar.com. Reprinted with permission.

how they stack up next to each other in terms of average return, risk, and expense ratios.

One more thing before we move on: Every fund has to publish a document called a prospectus that states clearly its strategy, or investment style. Managers have been known to drift from this strategy—something you have to watch out for—but the good ones toe the line.

Index Funds

Many investors find that index funds are by far the easiest, most effective way to go. They charge the lowest fees, they are tax efficient because there's very little turnover in the portfolio, and you don't have to worry about what the fund manager is doing. If your goal is long-term growth without having to pay much attention, these workhorse funds are the best solution.

How do they operate? Technically, index funds do have fund managers, but the managers don't do a whole lot. They simply buy all the stocks or bonds in a chosen index with the goal of matching that group's performance.

What's an index? It's a grouping of stocks chosen to represent a certain market segment. The S&P 500 index, for instance, is comprised of large stocks. The Nasdaq Composite index is heavy on technology companies. By purchasing any index, a fund tries to mimic the returns of that particular segment.

Sounds boring, but it works. Consider the Vanguard 500 Index fund. In the middle of 2000, it was the biggest fund in the world, with $110 billion in assets—largely because investors flocked to its exceptional 21.75 percent five-year annual return. By merely mimicking the S&P 500, it beat 93 percent of the active fund managers out there over the same period.

A really good fund manager should be able to beat the index. But index funds have two other advantages: low expenses and tax efficiency. Since the fund manager doesn't have to look actively for stocks, these funds are relatively cheap to run. And low turnover limits tax liability. The Vanguard 500 Index fund has an incredibly low annual fee of 0.18 percent of your investment. A typical, actively managed large-cap fund can charge more than six times as much.

Even Cheaper Than Index Funds

Spiders. Webs. Diamonds. Qubes.

Though they sound vaguely like names for comic-book characters, these are actually names for exchange-traded funds (ETFs), one of the hottest new products to come out of Wall Street in a long time. As their name suggests, these funds trade just like common stocks. And they are extremely popular: A mere 12 months after Qubes, which tracks the Nasdaq 100 index, went on sale in early 1999, the ETF had amassed $9.7 billion in assets. By mid-2001, the fund had $22.8 billion in assets—three times as much as the biggest tech fund (that's T. Rowe Price Science & Technology, at $6.8 billion).

Investors can now choose from nearly 100 different ETFs, including SPDRs (short for Standard & Poor's Depositary Receipts), called "Spiders," which track the Standard & Poor's 500; WEBS (world equity benchmark shares), which track international indexes; and Diamonds, which track the 30 stocks in the Dow Jones Industrial Average. Then there's Barclays Global Investors' line of iShares—there are iShares for 68 different indexes, from the Nasdaq Biotechnology index and the Russell 3000 Growth index to the Morgan Stanley Capital International (MSCI) Malaysia index.

Many investors are day trading ETFs, just like stocks. (The average holding period for Qubes is just 5.3 days.) It's easy to see why. After all, you can buy and sell ETFs throughout the day and place limit orders and stop orders, short them, even buy them on margin—none of which you can do with mutual funds, which you trade once a day, after the market closes.

Michael T. Porter, a former managing director at Salomon Smith Barney, calls ETFs "a product that suits the times," in that they have "all the good features of other index funds formats, but with more flexibility." As a result, investors can be much more nimble, acting immediately on market-moving information that occurs throughout the day. In the event of bad news, "You can't do much about it with a traditional mutual fund, but you can quickly short any of these index funds, act on the news, and partially protect your portfolio."

Of course, just because you can do all that doesn't mean you should. Even the people who issue exchange-traded funds say it's better to buy and hold them. "The benefits for iShares are their low cost and tax efficiencies, which will accrue most to the people who hold them for the long term," says Lee Kranefuss, CEO of Individual Investor Business at Barclays Global Investors. And they're more cost-effective, largely because of their lower operating costs. (For one thing, they don't require all the necessary mutual fund infrastructure and the shareholder accounting.)

So should you buy shares in an ETF?

There are basically three ways to use ETFs in your portfolio: as substitutes for conventional index funds, as replacements for actively managed country funds, or as a way to play small slices of an industry. ETFs boast lower expenses than most index funds. Vanguard 500 Index, for instance, will cost you 0.18 percent of your assets per year; Barclays iShares S&P 500, which tracks the same index, comes in at 0.09 percent. On a $100,000 investment over 20 years, assuming a 10 percent annual increase, you would save more than $11,000 with the Barclays ETF.

Say you want to invest in an emerging market, such as Korea or Malaysia, but you don't want to pay the hefty loads and fees that come with most foreign-stock funds, or you can't buy equities in that country on your own. ETFs could be the answer. (Barclays' low-cost MSCI Taiwan iShares may be your best option to home in on that country's booming tech market.) And because they are index portfolios, the stocks within the ETFs rarely change—so you always know which stocks you own, unlike the situation with managed mutual funds, which are required to report holdings only twice a year.

If you want to bet on a small part of an industry that sector funds don't typically cover exclusively, such as Internet e-commerce (at this point, though, we'd wonder why) or consumer staples, but you'd prefer broader exposure to the group over buying just one or two stocks, an ETF is probably your only option. To cite one example: Merrill Lynch offers ETFs called HOLDRs (for holding company depositary receipts—there are a total of 17) in five different Internet sectors, including broadband, business-to-business (B2B), and Internet infrastructure as well as biotechnology. Each portfolio holds a basket of about 20 of the sector's largest stocks.

Like index funds, ETFs avoid capital gains liabilities due to their very low turnover. But unlike conventional funds, they won't generate the potentially large capital gains liabilities that managers can rack up to meet shareholder redemptions, thanks to the unique way they trade.

Mutual fund database firm Morningstar tracks ETF portfolios just as it does mutual funds (www.morningstar.com). Nearly all ETFs trade on the American Stock Exchange, and their closing prices are listed daily in newspapers. You can get intraday quotes on web sites like www.smartmoney.com and http://finance.yahoo.com. Some ETF families, like Barclays' iShares, have web sites with basic information on yearly returns and stock composition (www.ishares.com). Finally, the American Stock Exchange web site also has basic data on many ETFs—which it calls "index shares"—including up-to-date prices, annual returns, and a breakdown of stocks within each portfolio (www.amex.com).

SIDEBAR 4.1

Stock Funds

Stock funds are often grouped by the size of the companies they invest in—big, small, or tiny. By size we mean a company's value on the stock market: the number of shares it has outstanding multiplied by the share price. This is known as market capitalization, or cap size. Big companies, as we've noted, tend to be less risky than small fry. But smaller companies can often offer more growth potential. The best idea is to have a mix of funds that give you exposure to large-cap, midsize, and small companies, as well as some international holdings.

LARGE-CAP FUNDS

Large-capitalization funds generally invest in companies with market values of greater than $8 billion. Some, like the Vanguard 500 Index fund, merely mimic the index and invest in all 500 companies. Others, like Fidelity's huge Magellan fund, try to beat the index by picking a mix of large caps that will outperform the broader market.

As you can see from Figure 4.1, large-cap funds are less volatile than funds that invest in smaller companies. Usually that means you can expect smaller returns. But until recently, large caps had outperformed all others. The last few years of the 1990s dished up an odd combination of economic stability in the United States, but turmoil in Asia, Latin America, and Russia. That made the stock market extremely volatile and convinced many investors to run for the relative stability of large, established companies like General Electric and Oracle. But lately, large caps have suffered devastating returns. Even so, it's worth noting that despite the market correction, large-cap funds have managed to post returns that stay in step with more risky funds. Maybe that's why for most investors a large-cap fund is their core

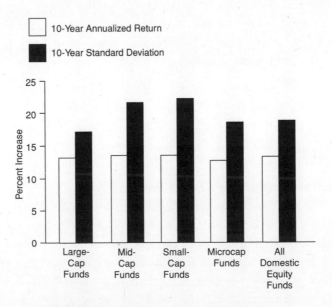

FIGURE 4.1   Risk versus Return in Funds
Source: Morningstar.com. Reprinted with permission.

long-term holding. A good one is a reliable—but far from stodgy—place to park your savings.

MID-CAP FUNDS

As the name implies, these funds fall in the middle. They aim to invest in companies with market values in the $1 billion to $8 billion range—not large caps, but not quite small caps, either. The stocks in the lower end of the range are likely to exhibit the growth characteristics of smaller companies and therefore add some volatility to these funds. They make the most sense as a way to diversify your holdings.

SMALL-CAP FUNDS

A small-cap fund, like T. Rowe Price Small-Cap Stock, will focus on companies with a market value below $1 billion. The volatility of the fund often depends on the aggressiveness of the manager. Aggressive small-cap managers will buy hot growth and technology companies, taking high risks in hopes of high rewards. More conservative "value" managers will look for companies that have been beaten down temporarily by the stock market. Value funds aren't as risky as the hot growth funds, but they can still be volatile.

Because of their volatility, buying small-cap funds requires that you have enough time to make up for short-term losses. There are times when the market turns away from small-cap companies altogether for extended periods, as we witnessed in 1997 and 1998. Since then, however, small-cap managers have had more reasons to smile, as small-cap growth funds excelled in 1999 and small-cap value funds proved strong in 2000 and 2001.

As history has recently indicated, after periods of slow growth, small companies eventually will regain favor. And during times like these they are likely to grow more quickly than their larger cousins—which can provide a good kicker for aggressive investors who need to build as much wealth as possible while they're young.

MICROCAP FUNDS

We're talking truly small companies here—outfits with market values below $250 million. These funds tend to look for either start-ups, takeover candidates, or companies about to exploit new markets. With stocks this small, the volatility is always extremely high, but the growth potential is exceptional. Fremont U.S. Microcap, for instance, sported a three-year average annual growth rate of 31.3 percent at the beginning of October 2000, but it had just come off a 12-week stretch in which it lost 8.7 percent.

If you have the time and inclination to pay attention to a fund like this, you might be willing to put some money in. But beware: Microcap funds can rear up and bite you. In 1997 and 1999, for example, the 24 funds in Morningstar's database with a median market cap of $250 million or below posted stellar returns of 26.4 and 21.9 percent, respectively. But in the year in between, 1998, the 24 funds lost 14.1 percent, trailing the S&P 500 by 42.7 percentage points.

Strategy

There is yet another distinction in the way funds are categorized—investment strategy. Every manager is different, but there are three broad archetypes when it comes to investment strategy: growth, value, and blend. (See Figure 4.2.) We've already explained what makes a growth investor different from a value investor. When it comes to funds, it all boils down to whether the manager is willing to chase popular (a.k.a. expensive) stocks, hoping to cash in on their momentum, or seeks to discover cheap stocks, betting that eventually the market will discover them, too.

GROWTH FUNDS

As their name implies, growth funds tend to look for the fastest-growing companies on the market. Growth managers are willing to take more risk and pay a premium for their stocks in an effort to build a portfolio of companies with above-average earnings momentum or price appreciation.

For example, Cisco Systems and EMC Corporation are generally considered "expensive" stocks, because their prices have been bid high relative to their profits. But because they enjoy vibrant markets and have rapid earnings growth, managers like Scott Schoelzel of the Janus Twenty fund have no qualms about paying big prices. Schoelzel knows that investors crave these supercharged growth stocks and will keep piling into them as long as the growth keeps up. But if the growth slows, watch

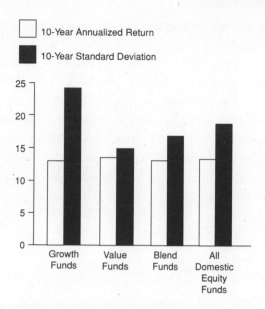

FIGURE 4.2   Growth versus Value: Where the Risk Is
Source: Morningstar.com. Reprinted with permission.

out—the more momentum a stock has, the harder it is likely to fall when the news turns bad.

That's why growth funds are the most volatile of the three investment styles. It's also why expenses and turnover (which leads to tax liability) are also higher. For these reasons, only aggressive investors or those with enough time to make up for short-term market losses should buy these funds.

VALUE FUNDS

These funds like to invest in companies that the market has overlooked. Managers like Marty Whitman of the Third Avenue Value fund search for stocks that have become "undervalued"—priced low relative to their earnings potential.

Sometimes a stock has run into a short-term problem that will eventually be fixed and forgotten. Or maybe the company is too small or obscure to attract much notice. In any event, the manager makes a judgment that there's more potential there than the market has recognized, and bets that the price will rise as others come around to the same conclusion.

Whitman, for instance, bought passive-component manufacturer AVX Corp. in late 1998 before it was discovered by most people on Wall Street. The stock rose 198.3 percent in 1999 and still traded at 28 times the previous 12-month earnings—a steal when you consider that peer Analog Devices registered similar performance while trading at 85 times earnings.

The big risk with value funds is that the undiscovered gems they try to spot sometimes remain undiscovered. That can depress results for extended periods of time. Volatility, however, is quite low, and if you choose a good fund, the risk of lousy returns should be minimal. Also, because these fund managers tend to buy stocks and hold them until they turn around, expenses and turnover are low. Add it up, and value funds are most suitable for more conservative, tax-averse investors.

Blend Funds

These portfolios can go across the board. They might, for instance, invest in both high-growth Internet stocks and cheaply priced automotive companies. As such, they are difficult to classify in terms of risk. The Vanguard 500 Index fund invests in every company in the S&P 500 and could therefore qualify as a blend. But because it's also a large-cap fund, it tends to be steady. The Legg Mason Special Investment fund is more aggressive, with heavy weightings in technology and financials. In order to determine whether a particular blend fund is right for your needs, you'll probably have to look at the fund's holdings and make a call.

International Funds

International stock funds allow you exposure to overseas markets at varying levels of risk. Some are fairly tame. Others can make your hair stand on end. Consider the experience of the summer of 1998, when the Asian economies fell like dominoes and decimated stocks in the region. Funds like Pioneer Emerging Markets and Ivy Developing Markets, with heavy exposure to Asia, got hammered. Even when foreign economies are doing reasonably well, currency fluctuations can have a negative effect on stock prices.

Of course, economic and currency risk can also swing very strongly in a positive direction. So, as always, diversification is the key to managing risk. Funds investing overseas fall into four basic categories: world, foreign, country-specific, and emerging-markets. The wider the reach of the fund, the less risky it is likely to be, as you can see from Figure 4.3.

WORLD FUNDS

World funds are the most diverse of the four categories. But don't be fooled by their cosmopolitan-sounding name. They're able to invest in any region of the world, including the United States, so they may not actually offer as much diversification as a good foreign fund. A prime example: Dresdner RCM Global Small Cap fund, which in mid-2001 had 57 percent invested in the United States and Canada, 24 percent in Europe, 9 percent in Japan, 1.3 percent in the Pacific Rim, and the rest in smaller regions. Over the past 10 years world funds have tended to be among the safer international-stock investments, but that's because they typically lean on better-known U.S. stocks.

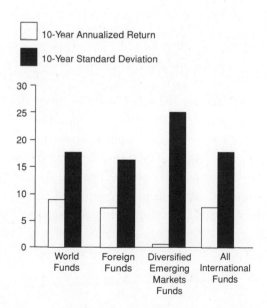

FIGURE 4.3 International Funds: The Wider the Reach, the Lower the Risk
Source: Morningstar.com. Reprinted with permission.

FOREIGN FUNDS

These funds invest most of their assets outside the United States. Depending on the countries selected for investment, foreign funds can range from relatively safe to more risky. Fidelity Diversified International, for instance, has its assets spread over 38 different countries, many of which are in Europe. In mid-2001, Oakmark International Small Cap, on the other hand, had significant exposure (40 percent of the portfolio) to some of the most traditionally volatile regions in the world: Japan, Hong Kong, South Korea, and Singapore. It's wise to try to choose a fund with the best balance, or make sure the manager has done a good job of moving in and out of regions profitably.

COUNTRY-SPECIFIC FUNDS

These funds invest in one country or region of the world. That kind of concentration makes them particularly volatile. If you pick the right country—Japan in 1999, for example—the returns can be substantial. The average Japan fund, according to Morningstar, returned a whopping 120 percent that year. But pick the wrong one, and watch out. In 1997, for example, the average Korean fund dropped 66 percent. Only the most sophisticated investors should venture into this territory.

EMERGING-MARKETS FUNDS

Emerging-markets funds are the most volatile. They invest in undeveloped regions of the world, which have enormous growth potential but also pose significant risks—political upheaval, corruption, and currency collapse, to name just a few. Don't go near these funds with anything but money you are willing to lose. If you need proof: Over the past 10 years, the average emerging-markets fund has returned just 0.7 percent, not even beating inflation. Still, that doesn't mean that these funds don't pack a punch once in a while: In 1993 and 1999 these types of funds posted better than 70 percent returns.

Sector Funds

Sector funds do what their name implies: They invest in stocks in a particular segment—or sector—of the market. A fund like Firsthand Technology

Leaders, for instance, buys only tech companies for its portfolio. Fidelity has a whole stable of sector funds such as Fidelity Select Insurance and Fidelity Select Wireless. The idea is to allow investors to place bets on specific industries or sectors whenever they think that industry might heat up.

While such a strategy might appear to throw diversification to the wind, it doesn't entirely. It's true that investing in a sector fund definitely focuses your exposure on a certain industry. But it can give you diversification within that industry that would be hard to achieve on your own. How? By spreading your investment across a broad representation of stocks. Fidelity Select Financial Services fund holds 124 different stocks; the Evergreen Health Care fund includes 117; and T. Rowe Price's Media & Communications fund has 66. Individual investors can't achieve that kind of diversity within a single sector without sacrificing overall diversity in their portfolios.

Of course, such concentrated portfolios can produce tremendous gains or losses, depending on whether your chosen sector is in or out of favor. In 1999, Firsthand Technology Leaders soared 152.6 percent because software and semiconductor companies were hot. Real estate fund Franklin Real Estate lost 5.6 percent in the same year because the category sputtered.

Because of this specialization, any sector fund carries more risk than a generalized fund. But some sectors are clearly more volatile than others. For example, Vanguard Utilities Income, which invests in staid electrical companies, has about one-third the volatility of PBHG Technology & Communications, which invests in supercharged software makers.

Charges and Fees

If there is a single drawback to investing in mutual funds, it's the corrosive effect that fees and taxes have on returns. If you aren't careful, management expenses and capital gains taxes can shave hundreds—if not thousands—of dollars from your returns over the years.

Check into SmartMoney.com's "Fund Fee Analyzer" (an interactive tool on the site's SmartMoney University) to see for yourself how much a high load or expense ratio can eat into returns. The address is www.smart-money.com/fundfeeanalyzer.

Say you invest $10,000 in a fund that charges 4.7 percent every time you put money in (a front-end load) and a 1.5 percent expense ratio per year (to pay management fees). (Both charges are about average for the fund industry.) After one year, assuming a steady 10 percent return, the fund will have made you $999 in profit, but after fees (about $660), your profit dwindles to $339. That means fees swallowed 66 percent of your profits in one year. After five years, that percentage diminishes—to 29 percent—but after 20 years, you'll have paid a whopping $18,522 in fees, which will diminish your overall profit of $57,144 to just $38,622.

The good news is that it's still possible to find excellent funds with relatively low costs. You just have to know what to look for.

Loads: Front-End and Back-End

A load is simply a sales charge—like the commission you pay when you buy or sell shares in a stock—that's tacked onto the price of a mutual fund to compensate the broker or financial adviser who sells it to you. Loads work in two ways: You pay them either up front when you buy your shares or when you sell them, depending on the fund. Of the 8,881 equity funds in existence in mid-2001, 4,613 (52 percent) charged a load; 4,268, or 48 percent, did not.

A front-end load is charged when you buy your shares. It typically ranges between 1 percent and 5.75 percent of your initial investment, and some funds charge you again for reinvesting your dividends in new shares of the fund. A back-end load is a fee the fund charges when you sell—or redeem—your shares. These deferred fees are essentially a tactic to keep you invested in the fund for the long term. A typical scenario would work this way: In the first year of ownership, you'd pay a charge in the range of 4 percent to 5.75 percent if you sold out of the fund. After that, the percentage declines each year until it disappears altogether after about six to eight years.

The obvious problem with a load is that it immediately trims your investment return. That might be acceptable if you believe the fund will post such superior returns that the load will pay for itself over time. But since there are plenty of quality no-load funds out there, why pay a fee if you don't have to? We never say "never" when it comes to paying fees, but at *SmartMoney* we tend to recommend no-load funds.

Expense Ratios

Even a no-load fund requires its shareholders to pay for the costs of doing business. These include everything from the advisory fee paid the fund manager to administrative costs like printing and postage. These costs are expressed as an "expense ratio," which is an annual percentage of the fund's average net assets under management. Published fund returns are usually calculated net of annual expenses, but you should definitely pay attention to them. When you get your statement at the end of the year, you can count on the costs being skimmed off the top.

There's a temptation to associate high expenses with good fund management. Some people figure it's like anything else: You get what you pay for. The fact is, however, that low-expense funds are more likely to outperform high-expense funds over the long haul. Recently, the average expense ratio for domestic equity funds was about 1.4 percent. For fixed-income funds it was about 1.1 percent. Foreign funds have higher expense ratios, averaging around 1.7 percent. There is no reason to buy funds with expense ratios higher than that.

12b-1 Fees

Included in the expense ratio, but often talked about separately, are 12b-1 fees. They go to pay the fund's marketing and distribution expenses. These fees are charged in addition to a front- or back-end load, and you'll find that many no-load funds charge them, too. Note that once a 12b-1 fee rises above 0.25 percent, the fund is no longer considered a no-load. Our advice? If a 12b-1 fee puts a fund's expense ratio above the average for that class of fund, think twice before buying.

Share Classes

Ever wonder what all those As, Bs, and Cs are that you often see after the names of some funds? These letters indicate the different share classes a fund offers. Although these classes are not standardized, they primarily apply to load funds and determine the various ways that investors can pay the sales charge. For example, A shares traditionally indicate a front-end load, while

B shares most often indicate a back-end load. Other share classes include C shares, which usually incorporate a small back-end load and a higher 12b-1 fee.

Taxes

When a fund manager sells a stock for a gain, the law says it becomes a taxable event. That transaction may be offset by any losses the manager incurs when selling a losing stock. But if the sum of all the transactions during the year adds up to an overall gain, somebody has to pay the tax bill. We'll give you one guess who that ends up being.

These gains are paid out in the form of taxable distributions. It's disconcerting to end the year with a fat one you weren't expecting. It's even more costly when the gain falls into the short-term category—a big problem with fund managers who trade often. Short-term gains are taxed as regular income instead of at the lower, 20 percent tax levied on long-term capital gains. Distributions usually occur once or twice per year and can be taxed as long-term or short-term gains, depending on how long the fund manager held the securities. So, before you buy shares in a mutual fund, make sure it is not right before a distribution. A call to the fund family's 800 number will clear that up. Otherwise, you'll get hit with a tax bill for money you didn't even earn.

A high turnover ratio can be a sign of a high capital gains distribution further down the line. And clearly, one way to avoid this potential problem is to be wary of managers who trade a lot. A fund with a turnover ratio of 500 percent indicates that the average holding in the fund lasted less than three months. And all that trading could produce a capital gains liability for you. That is, unless the manager is able to offset his or her gains with losses.

Fund Picking Made Easy

You could save yourself a whole lot of trouble and just about guarantee success by simply choosing an index fund and holding onto it for the long haul. They're cheap. They're tax-efficient. And, as we've noted, they routinely beat the vast majority of actively managed funds.

We think index funds make good core holdings, for sure. But the fact is, you *can* do better than the market. Twenty-two percent of all domestic equity funds have outpaced the S&P 500 over the past 20 years, which amounts to over 1,000 portfolios. Unless you truly don't know what you're doing—you're chasing last year's hot fund, for instance—we think it is possible to pick one, even a few, market-beating winners.

At *SmartMoney*, we run screens to find good funds nearly every month. Sometimes our approach, as with our stock stories, hinges on some market event. In April 2001, for instance, as investors grappled with an uncertain market, we highlighted seven funds in a story we called "Tough Funds for Tough Times." (Those portfolios as a group climbed an average of 2.7 percent, compared to a 9.4 percent drop in the S&P 500-stock index, in the first six months. One did far better than others—Wasatch Core Growth fund climbed 22 percent—but every fund outpaced the S&P 500, mostly returning in the 2 percent to 3 percent range.) And every so often, we'll highlight the best of the newest crop of funds. Our most recent group of "Best New Funds" (from June 1999) have a combined average three-year return of 20.8 percent, which beats the S&P 500 return over the same period by 16.9 percentage points.

As you can see, you can find good funds. You just have to know how to look for them. That's what the next sections are all about. We've devised a five-point strategy that addresses the basic elements that make a good fund. All should play a role in the way you screen for funds.

1. Nail down your goals.
2. Check long-term performance.
3. Assess risk and volatility.
4. Minimize fees and taxes.
5. Know your managers.

Goals

Before you start sleuthing around for a good fund, you have to know what the money is for: Are you saving for retirement? Holding some money aside for a down payment on a house? Looking to sink your bonus into a speculative play on China? Your answers could lead you in several different directions, and that could narrow the field of appropriate funds significantly.

If you're not sure what your goals are, at the very least you should set up an asset allocation program and then consider matching your fund picks to your suggested allocations (large-cap stocks, small-cap value, etc.). Most studies show that a properly allocated portfolio is crucial to maximizing your returns.

Part of this decision will hinge on how much risk you're willing to take. The more time you have until you need your money, the more aggressive you can be. But you also have to consider how comfortable you are with volatility. If your fund dips 5 percent or 10 percent in any given month, is it going to keep you up at night? Then you won't want an especially volatile fund, like an emerging-markets fund that specializes in Latin America or Southeast Asia. A tech sector fund probably shouldn't be on your list, either.

Performance

You may have heard the phrase before: "Past performance is no indicator of future results." It's written in tiny print at the bottom of every mutual fund advertisement—right below the part where the ad brags about the fund's past performance. It's true that investors should never assume that the past will repeat itself. But those who ignore a mutual fund's historical record do so at their own peril. It's the best measure we have of a fund manager's competence.

Interestingly, past performance is probably a better predictor for the stinkers than it is for the highfliers. A 2000 study of ongoing performance by Fordham University found that while Morningstar's four- and five-star funds (the best performers) didn't necessarily remain atop the charts, its one- and two-star funds did continue to flounder. The lesson is pretty obvious: Avoid the perennial losers.

How do you evaluate performance beyond that? First, examine multiple time periods. Many investors get burned by heeding the siren song of last year's hot fund. Take the American Heritage Fund, which finished 1997 first in its group with a 75 percent gain, then plunged 61 percent the following year, ending up at the bottom of the barrel. Had you been wowed by the 1997 gain, but checked the fund's five-year record (a 1.1 percent annualized return), you would have seen its erratic history. That's a red flag that management isn't fully in control.

What if you have a more ordinary fund with, say, 7 percent, 15 percent, or 20 percent annual returns? How do you tell how consistently good that fund really is?

The best way is to compare its numbers to a relative benchmark index (compare a large-cap fund to the large-cap S&P 500; a small-cap growth fund with the Russell 2000) as well as other funds with similar objectives. Check out the Morningstar snapshot for Legg Mason Value Prime Trust in Figure 4.4. In the left side, you'll find the fund's performance for four time periods—the year-to-date return, as well as the past three calendar years. Below those figures are the average returns for the category, in this case, large-cap value funds. As you can see, this is a high-powered fund.

Risk and Volatility

If your fund choice is going to make you sick with worry, what's the point? That's why it pays to make sure you're comfortable with a fund's risk profile and its propensity for short-term volatility.

Risk is generally a function of investing style. Growth funds—run by managers who chase popular but risky companies with huge earnings growth—tend to suffer wider short-term price swings and more turnover. Value funds—in which the managers look for undiscovered bargain stocks,

FIGURE 4.4   A Morningstar Quicktake Report
Source: Morningstar.com. Reprinted with permission.

hoping that their prices will pick up over time—are less volatile on the downside, but you sometimes pay for that with less dramatic upside. The lesson (true for stock investing as well): The lower the risk, the lower the potential return; the higher the risk, the higher the potential return.

One easy way to assess the risk of each fund is Morningstar's star rating system. These ratings, while not perfect, aim to quantify the risk-return trade-off of each fund. The ratings, which range from one to five stars (five being the best), take into account both a fund's performance and risk for the life of the fund. Basically, Morningstar subtracts the fund's risk score from its performance score. A five-star rating means a fund has scored in the top 10 percent of its broad investment class. Funds with four stars fall into the next 22.5 percent of their broad class, and so on down the line.

You can find the rating for any fund at Morningstar.com or in Smart-Money.com's "Fund Snapshots."

If you want to dig deeper into a fund's risk profile, you can track its beta. This is a measure of a fund's volatility relative to its benchmark—typically the S&P 500 for equity funds. The beta of the benchmark is always 1.00; so it follows that if an equity fund has a beta of 1.00, it has experienced roughly the same up and down movements as the S&P 500. An equity fund with a beta of 1.25, on the other hand, is expected to do 25 percent better than the S&P 500 in an up market and 25 percent worse in a down market. This information, and more, is available at SmartMoney.com.

Fees and Taxes

You can never predict what a fund will earn next year. But you can almost always predict what its expenses will be. So, why not control what you can? That's the reasoning behind *SmartMoney*'s preference for no-load funds with low annual expenses.

Try not to buy funds with expense ratios greater than the sector average. For large-cap funds, that was 1.35 percent in mid-2001. For small-cap funds, it was 1.53 percent. For foreign funds, it was 1.68 percent. And for bond funds, it was 1.09 percent.

When viewing similar load and no-load funds with equal returns, choose the no-load. Remember, the returns of the load funds are not adjusted for the sales charges shareholders pay. (If you're interested, you can find adjusted returns in the fund's prospectus.)

That said, don't be so rigid as to always rule out load funds. Some funds have actually made up for their loads with strong returns and low volatility. Take Smith Barney Aggressive Growth. It has returned an impressive 28 percent annualized gain in the past five years, and that includes an adjustment for the fund's 5 percent load. The fund ranks in the top 1 percent of all large-cap growth funds.

Furthermore, many of the best sector funds, like Fidelity Select Brokerage and Investment Management and Fidelity Select Utilities Growth, come with 3 percent loads. The Select Brokerage and Investment Management fund boasted a 27 percent five-year annualized record; the Select Utilities Growth fund, a 17 percent five-year return. Generally, the longer you plan to stay in a fund, the less an up-front load matters.

If you do buy a load fund, long-term investors should select the class A shares that charge a high up-front load but have little or no annual 12b-1 fees (used for marketing and distribution). Short-timers should stick with share classes that have low loads, like the B or C shares, but higher 12b-1s.

Then there are taxes. They can sneak up and bite you, too, if you're not careful. Unless you hold your fund in an IRA or tax-advantaged retirement account, a fund's taxable distributions reduce your after-tax gain.

The best way to avoid big distributions is to find funds with low turnover. That means the manager isn't churning the portfolio all year, generating capital gains in an attempt to make returns look good. Our basic guideline is this: Investors should avoid funds with turnover above 80 percent. (A turnover of 100 percent means the manager replaced holdings representing the entire value of the fund during the latest 12-month period.) The rule doesn't apply so easily to bond funds, whose securities mature and must be replaced.

Tax-conscious investors should also avoid funds with high dividend yields. That's because dividends are taxed at income-tax rates as high as 39.6 percent rather than the lower capital gains rate (for holdings of 12 months and longer). And, if you're really opposed to taxes, you should consider index funds, which are generally the most tax-efficient type of funds. Their holdings should only change when the composition of their benchmark index does or when the fund needs to pass out redemptions to shareholders.

While we're on the topic of expenses, make sure to see whether the minimum initial investment of this fund is within your means. For most funds, you'll need $500 to $1,000 to open any type of account—regular, IRA, or automatic investment plan (AIP)—while subsequent payments range from $100 down to $50. But you'd be surprised at how many successful funds call for a minimum investment of $5,000 or $10,000. Of course, sometimes you can buy shares for less through a no-fee network through Charles Schwab or Fidelity.

Your Manager

The great intangible in all fund investing is the fund manager. The kinds of numbers SmartMoney.com includes on its snapshots can tell you a lot, but data does not breed familiarity. If all the numbers add up, the last step is to research who it is you are about to entrust your money to. And given that fund managers tend to come and go like flies through an open window, that is often the hardest part.

You can find the manager's name and tenure on the fund company's web site (and it will typically include a short biography). Or click onto Morningstar.com or SmartMoney.com. Obviously, the longer a manager has been around generating good returns, the better. Keep in mind, though, that only a handful of managers—Bill Miller of Legg Mason Value is one of them—have been around for longer than 10 years. The average tenure of fund managers is just 4.5 years.

If it turns out a fund manager is new—he or she has been running the fund for less than two years—track down his or her previous record (often the manager transferred from another fund at the same fund company). If the manager's history is cloudy, consider holding off before you buy shares in the fund. You should also keep in mind that a change in fund management can often lead to high portfolio turnover (and high taxes) as the new manager shapes the fund to his or her own liking.

Getting Information

Where can you get fund information? First, hit the fund company's web site for reports, prospectuses, and (sometimes) updated commentary from fund managers. If you're looking for up-to-the-minute information on a fund, you're going to find it here. Or simply pick up the phone and call the fund company directly—the toll-free number is listed under "Purchase Info" on all SmartMoney.com "Fund Snapshots."

At Morningstar.com, you can pull up basic information you'll want to know on U.S. and foreign funds—annualized returns for the past 10, 5, and 3 years as well as returns in the past 12 months, year-to-date, and 3 months. There's also information on portfolio composition: What are the fund's top 25 holdings? How much of the portfolio is invested in tech stocks or utilities or consumer durables? The best part, though, is the reports. Morningstar analysts compile reports (accessible for $12 a month) for nearly every fund—look under "Morningstar Analysis" in the left menu—that include short bites on management, strategy, and risk, as well as a three- or four-paragraph summation of whether the fund is worth investing in.

Where to Screen for Funds

Morningstar.com and SmartMoney.com both have extremely helpful fund screeners. Morningstar's is called "Fund Selector" (see Figure 4.5), and it'll

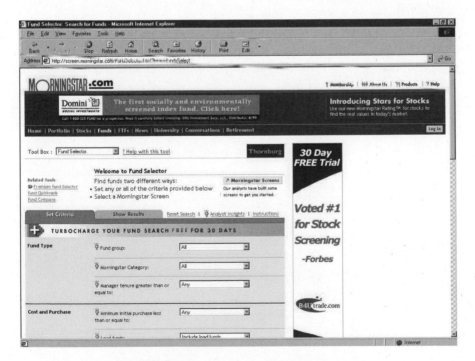

FIGURE 4.5 Morningstar's Fund Selector
Source: Morningstar.com. Reprinted with permission.

walk you through the five points we outlined in our screening strategy. There's "Fund Group" (choose between domestic stock or international taxable bond or municipal bond) and "Morningstar Category," which lets you choose between market capitalization and investment style (large, mid-cap, or small, and value, growth, blend, sector, or region). Move along down the options and you'll see headings like "Manager Tenure," "Cost and Purchase," and "Ratings and Risk." Finally, there's a "Returns" category.

If it sounds complicated, don't worry. You don't have to select a criterion in every category—you can select to screen for only large value funds, for instance, and that's it. But in each category, Morningstar's Fund Selector allows you to either be specific or choose from a preset parameter. In the "Returns" category, for instance, you can choose to screen only for five-year returns if you want (the options are year-to-date, one-year, three-year, five-year, or ten-year). The next step is to set a parameter—"greater than or equal to"—with the options ranging from "category average" or "S&P 500" to fill in the blank. In other words, it's easy to use a screen regardless of whether you're familiar with funds.

At SmartMoney.com, there's a tool called "Fund Finder." There are five broad categories: performance, volatility (things like beta and standard deviation), profile (which includes manager tenure, net asset size, and age of the fund), expenses, and fund family (if you're looking for a fund at Fidelity, for instance).

5

WELCOME TO THE SCREENING ROOM

There are more than 7,000 stocks trading publicly in the United States right now. One of them could be the next Dell, or the next Cisco, or even the next General Electric. The problem is, how on earth are you going to find it?

Well, you could always go on a prowl for hot tips—the kind of stock ideas you get from a neighbor, say, or an analyst you saw on TV. But we wouldn't because that won't work—at least not over the long haul. Sure, you may get a good idea once in a while by trolling for tips, but it's hardly a sustainable method. What you need, as an individual investor, is an efficient way basically to get rid of the companies that are potential bad investments and find your way to the good ones.

At *SmartMoney*, we start nearly every stock-picking effort with a screen—a process of elimination, using electronic databases to sift through the thousands of companies available to investors. This is how we get down to a manageable number of stocks to research, and it's how many of the top pros do it, too. In this chapter we'll show you how to screen for winners yourself.

In any given year, *SmartMoney* writers and editors construct more than a dozen different screens. Though each one is slightly different, their aim is generally the same: to find good values. (See Sidebar 5.1, "The Most Important Screen We Do Each Year.") When we're looking for stocks to buy, our first move is almost always to screen out companies with high price-to-earnings or price-to-sales ratios. (For more on these and other tools for valuing stocks—and how we use them—see Sidebar 5.2, "Our Favorite Ratios.")

'ant Screen

nent outlook for the year, com-
rm the year's "Best Invest-
features, the companies we
are meant for *that* year; we do not
.king investors should hold them for 5 to
it comes to this group, investors must always
adjust to sudden shifts in the market and be ready to
.en the fundamentals of a stock, an industry, or the market
itself take a dramatic turn for the worse.

The basic principle of our Best Investments portfolio is this: Stocks with soaring price-to-earnings ratios are likely to return to their historical norms and thus are probably lousy candidates for buying now. Yet stocks whose P/E ratios have slumped would probably be good candidates for above-average performance.

It's simple, really. If you use a stock's historical price-to-earnings range as a barometer, it's a better bet to buy stocks that are trading below average than above average. Using statistics like this minimizes crystal-ball gazing—it's a disciplined approach that relies on historical data. It also minimizes emotion and other subjective factors that so often get in the way of sound investment decisions.

And over the years it has worked for us.

How have we done? For the first five years, our record was superb. In 1993, our Best Investments stocks were up an average of 9.1 percent, compared to 6.8 percent for the S&P 500. In 1994, a generally miserable year for stocks, our Best Investments portfolio climbed an average of 31 percent, as opposed to the S&P's negative 1 percent return. Our 1995 portfolio rose an average of 53 percent through mid-November, trouncing the S&P's 31 percent return. And in 1996, our top five picks rose an average of 36 percent, besting the S&P 500's gain of 23 percent. Again in 1997, despite a 30 percent gain in the S&P 500, our Best Investments did better and posted a 43 percent return.

No, we're not perfect. In 1998 we faltered. Our selections averaged a 4 percent gain, far short of the 23 percent climb in the S&P 500. But there was one winner that year: DSC Communications, now part of Tellabs and Alcatel, rose 26 percent that year. Two others, Jones Pharma (acquired by King Pharmaceuticals in 2000) and housing company Lennar Corporation, posted positive returns of 13 and 17 percent, respectively. A similar fate befell our 1999 portfolio: Its 15 percent gain did not look good next to a 22 percent climb in the S&P 500. But the department store operator Kohl's Corporation and medical devices firm Guidant both beat the market with 44 percent and 33 percent gains, respectively.

Happily, we redeemed ourselves with our 2000 portfolio, which posted a strong 16 percent average gain, comfortably ahead of the S&P's 4 percent loss.

Our research on all of these articles began the same way: with a hunt for the industries, or sectors, we think will likely outperform in the year ahead.

To find them, we first tap into Zacks Investment Research database, which tracks more than 6,500 companies. As usual, we trim any stocks with less than $300 million in market value or with low trading volume (anything below 40,000 shares traded per day we would avoid). We then screen the market three ways: First for stocks with price-to-earnings ratios that are the furthest off their five-year averages, then for stocks the furthest off their 52-week highs; and finally for stocks with the lowest price-to-earnings-growth (PEG) ratios. That narrows our search down to sectors with stocks that score well on the combination of those measures.

Once we have a list of industries that look promising, we check our impressions with the well-known sector analyst Elaine Garzarelli, formerly of Lehman Brothers, as well as the Leuthold Group, a Minneapolis market-strategy firm known for its detailed sector reports. Each has its own scoring system, but both test for value *and* growth characteristics before deeming a sector "attractive." We reject any sector that doesn't rank on both the Garzarelli and Leuthold lists.

Only then do we go looking for the top individual stocks within the most promising sectors, interviewing analysts, money managers, and company executives to arrive at our Best Investments.

Here's an example from a recent issue of *SmartMoney*. When we started to research our May 2000 cover story, the market had just taken a jolt. It wasn't just high-flying tech stocks that had plummeted from their extraordinary highs; even supposedly safe stocks like the consumer giant Procter & Gamble had collapsed. We saw an opportunity in that collapse. All of a sudden, large, well-known growth stocks were trading at what amounted to a double discount—below both the average price-to-earnings ratio of the market and their own historical P/Es. By taking advantage of the low prices, we figured we could scoop up good, albeit underappreciated, companies at a bargain—what the pros call "buying on the dips." Altogether it made for a low-risk, high-reward proposition.

So that's how we began our "Living Large" screen: We looked for companies trading at or below their five-year average trailing P/E ratios. At the time, this benchmark was a significant hurdle because the typical big company was selling for nearly 40 percent above its five-year average multiple. Even so, we were able to turn up 75 names, and most of them were down 25 percent or more from their 52-week highs. Finally, to get at our beloved "growth at a reasonable price," we deep-sixed any stock with an above-market price-to-earnings-growth (PEG) ratio, which at the time was just over 2. Then the reporting began.

In the end, we settled on eight low-risk, large-cap companies, none of them technology stocks. How have they done? Since we researched them in March 2000, the stocks have climbed 13 percent, trouncing the S&P 500, which retreated to a negative 17 percent return over the same period.

Though those classic value measures are a great place to begin, there's no sense in limiting yourself to them when you're screening. Exhibit A: the companies we profiled in our first cover story, "The 10 Stocks for the '90s." At the time—the beginning of 1992—Wall Street was touting biotech and health-care companies because of their promise for growth over the next decade. But in the end, our list of stocks included a shoe company (U.S. Shoe, now broken up), a mobile-home manufacturer (Clayton Homes), a reclining-chair maker (La-Z-Boy), and Home Shopping Network (now a division of USA Networks). It also included a few tech stocks, like Applied Materials, Cypress Semiconductor, and Communications Satellite (which has since been acquired by Lockheed Martin).

That diverse portfolio went on to absolutely trounce the market. By August 1995—three years after that first issue was published—the 10 stocks had returned an average of 150 percent, nearly six times better than the 27 percent gain in the S&P 500. After nine years, the remaining seven companies on our list still far outpace the market, with a 535 percent gain compared with the 194 percent climb in the S&P 500.

So how did we find this hodgepodge collection of stocks? We began our search for future highfliers by looking backward—at the top 20 stocks of the 1980s. The total returns were astounding, with winners like the Gap and Wal-Mart (both up more than 4,000 percent in the 1980s), the carpet company Shaw Industries (which climbed 5,189 percent), and chicken giant Tyson Foods (3,563 percent) leading the way. What characteristics did these stocks share in 1979—just before their stratospheric rise—that would enable an investor to identify a portfolio of today's stocks with the potential to do the same? We found that all of the stocks were bargains at the beginning of the decade; each traded at a discount to the market based on one or more key fundamental ratios. The Gap, for example, was trading at only 3.6 times its annual earnings at the beginning of the 1980s, while a growth stock at the time typically traded for at least 15 times its earnings. We applied four value criteria—price/earnings, price/book, price/cash flow, and yield—to the universe of stocks. The stocks didn't have to pass every screen. We wanted a cross section, companies that fell below market in some categories but not necessarily across the board.

These purely statistical criteria narrowed our universe to 141 stocks— too many for the average individual investor. So for the final test, we examined first-year performance of the previous decade's top-performing stocks. We were surprised and intrigued to discover that while the stocks did well— an average weighted return of nearly 58 percent—none of them did either extremely well or extremely poorly in the first year of that decade. In other words, they didn't achieve a disproportionate share of their growth in the first year of their 10-year sprint.

How did we translate that data into our stock screen? We decided to examine the previous 12-month performance of the remaining 141 stocks in our universe and apply the same rule. We tossed out any stocks that had done either extremely well (anything that climbed over 79 percent) or extremely poorly (which turned out to be below 39 percent) in the prior 12 months. With that final step, the universe was narrowed to 50 finalists.

After that, it was a whole lot easier to dig in and pick the potential winners from the losers. That is a process we describe in greater detail in

Our Favorite Ratios

No single ratio will tell the entire story about a company's value. Happily, though, the past decade has ushered in reams of research about the predictive value of various ratios using historical pricing data. What it shows is that some ratios are, in fact, better than others. It also demonstrates that using more than one ratio at a time to evaluate stocks is the most useful strategy.

For his best-selling book, *What Works on Wall Street* (Mc-Graw-Hill, 1997), James P. O'Shaughnessy crunched 43 years of numbers in an effort to find the best screening strategy. One of the things he discovered: "Using multifactor models *dramatically* enhances returns." For instance, over those 43 years a $10,000 portfolio based on low price-to-sales ratios as well as the past year's price performance earned $20 million more than a portfolio based on just low price-to-sales ratios.

Josef Lakonishok, of the University of Illinois, Urbana–Champaign, in conjunction with Andrei Shleifer (Harvard University) and Robert W. Vishny (the University of Chicago), did a separate study that came to the same conclusion. They tested the returns of different portfolios—some using just one variable, like cash flow or price to earnings, and others combining two variables—over five-year periods for a study published in the *Journal of Finance*. The conclusion: Using two variables in combination (price-to-earnings and five-year average growth in sales) produces a portfolio with substantially higher returns than using one variable alone. In lay terms: "It's better to use multiple screens than single screens," says Lakonishok.

Here are the ratios and other measures we use most often when screening for *SmartMoney* stocks.

Price-to-Earnings

This is the most common measure of how cheap or expensive a stock is relative to other stocks, hands down. Why? Because earnings growth tends to drive stock prices. To calculate a P/E, you take the current earnings per share and divide it into the stock price. If Microsoft is trading at $40 a share, for instance, and its earnings are $2 a share, then its P/E, or its multiple, is 20 (40/2). Basically, investors are paying $20 for every $1 of earnings.

The traditional P/E—the one you'll find in the newspaper stock tables—is the "trailing" P/E: The stock price divided by earnings per share over the previous 12 months. When you hear a fund manager or analyst talking on TV, though, chances are he or she is talking about "forward" P/E—the stock price divided by earnings expectations for the *coming* year.

Suppose you have two stocks in the same industry—Royal Dutch Petroleum and Texaco—with identical trailing P/Es of 20. Let's say, hypothetically, Royal Dutch has a stock price of $60 and earnings of $3, while Texaco has a stock price of $80 and earnings of $4. They may look like similar investments until you check out the forward P/E. Wall Street is projecting that Exxon's earnings will grow to $3.75 a share—25 percent growth—while Texaco's earnings are only expected to grow by 6 percent to $4.25. In that case, Royal Dutch's forward P/E slips to 16, while Texaco would be valued with a forward P/E of 18.8. Assuming the estimates bear out, Royal Dutch would clearly be the better buy.

There's just one catch: Companies sometimes "manage" their earnings with accounting wizardry to make them look better than they really are. A wily chief financial officer can fool with a company's tax assumptions during a given quarter and add several percentage points of earnings growth. It's also true that the quality of earnings estimates can vary widely depending on the company and the Wall Street analysts who follow it. Some companies may have 20 analysts who track it and make earnings projections. And yet the estimates can vary: More than 30 analysts cover Cisco, for instance. But check out the spread between estimates for its fiscal year 2002: $0.30 to $0.56. Other companies may have just two analysts, and their estimates may vary by as much as 50 cents.

Price-to-Earnings Growth

Who can resist a stock growing earnings at 40 percent? Not many. But this is what drives many stock multiples to astronomical highs: In mid-2001, data-storage software company Veritas Software traded at 67 times trailing earnings and its five-year earnings growth rate was 50 percent. Was it overvalued? Not necessarily. If a stock's growth rate is superior, it may deserve a higher valuation.

The so-called PEG ratio helps quantify this idea. PEG stands for price-to-earnings growth and is calculated by dividing the P/E by the projected earnings growth rate. So if a company has a forward P/E of 20 and analysts expect its earnings will grow 15 percent annually over the next few years, you'd say it has a PEG of 1.33. Anything above 1 means the company is trading at a premium to its growth rate, and anything below 1 means the company is trading at a discount to its growth rate. As always, the key is to compare this ratio with those of the company's peers. Remember Veritas Software? Its 67 P/E versus its 50 percent earnings growth rate means it carries a 1.34 PEG ratio. Sounds expensive, but at the time the rest of the software industry traded at a PEG of just over 2.

The PEG ratio's weakness is that it relies heavily on earnings estimates. Wall Street tends to aim high, and analysts are often wrong. In 1998, some companies in the oil-services sector routinely had projected earnings growth rates in the 35 percent range. But by the end of the year, the crash in oil prices had them swimming in losses. Had you been impressed by their bargain-basement PEG ratios, you'd have lost a lot of money. Our advice is to shave 15 percent from any Wall Street growth estimate when calculating PEG ratios. That should give you a reasonable margin for error.

Price-to-Sales

This was the ratio everyone was using to evaluate dot-coms, because most of them had no earnings. But don't give up on it just because of that unfortunate association. It's a good ratio to track, because sales are much harder to manipulate than earnings; this can make P/S ratios a more reliable measure.

As the name implies, the price-to-sales ratio is the company's stock price divided by its sales (or revenue). But because the sales number is rarely expressed as a per-share figure, it's easier to divide a company's total market value by its total sales for the prior 12 months. (Market value = stock price × shares outstanding.)

Generally speaking, a company trading at a P/S ratio of less than 1 should attract your attention. Think about it: If a company has sales of $1 billion but a market value of $900 million, it has a price-to-sales ratio of 0.9. That means you can buy $1 of its sales for only 90 cents. There may be plenty else wrong with the company to justify such a low price (like maybe it is losing money), but that's not always the case. It might just be an overlooked bargain.

Most value investors set their price-to-sales ratio hurdle at 2 and below when looking for undervalued situations. One important caveat: The ratio is less appropriate for service companies such as banks or insurers that don't really have sales.

Price-to-Book Value

Book value is simple. It's what would be left over for shareholders if the company were sold and its debt retired. To figure it, you take a company's assets (its plants, its equipment, etc.) and subtract its liabilities (how much it owes). The price-to-book (P/B) ratio (market cap divided by book value) measures what the market is paying for those net assets (also known as shareholder equity). The lower the number, the better.

Price-to-book works best with a company that has a lot of hard assets like factories or ore reserves. It's also good at reflecting the value of banks and insurance companies that have a lot of financial assets. But in today's economy many of the hottest companies rely heavily on intellectual assets that don't appear on the balance sheet. That's why high-tech outfits like Microsoft and Cisco Systems have relatively low book values, which give them artificially high price-to-book ratios. The other drawback to book value is that it often reflects what an asset was worth when it was bought, not the current market value. So it is an imprecise measure even in the best case.

But the price-to-book ratio does have its strengths. First of all, like the P/E ratio, it is simple to compute and easy to understand, which makes it a good way to compare stocks across a broad array of old-line industries. It also gives you a quick look at how the market is valuing assets versus earnings. Finally, because assets are assets in any country, book-value comparisons work around the world. That's not true of a P/E ratio since earnings are strongly affected by different sets of accounting rules. In Japan, for instance, price-to-earnings multiples of 100 are common. That can make it hard to compare a Japanese company to its American competitors. In mid-2001, Sony carried a trailing P/E of 100.5; the industry average at that time was just 19.1. On a price-to-book basis, though, Sony traded at a more reasonable ratio of 2.3. That made it appear cheaper than two of its smaller American competitors, Emerson Electronics (P/B of 3.6) and Pemstar (2.7).

Margins

Like return on equity (ROE) and return on assets (ROA) (see Glossary), calculating a company's margins is a way of getting at management efficiency. But instead of measuring how much managers earn from assets or capital employed, this ratio measures how much a company squeezes from its total revenue (sales).

Sounds a lot like earnings, right? Well, margins are really just earnings expressed as a ratio—a percentage of sales. The advantage is that a percentage can be used to compare the profitability of different companies while an absolute number cannot. An example: In the fall of 2000, discount retailer Costco Wholesale had annualized net income of about $632 million on sales of about $31.6 billion. Rival Wal-Mart was earning about $6.2 billion on annualized sales of $191.3 billion.

You could compare $632 million to $6.2 billion, but all that tells you is that Wal-Mart is the bigger company. It doesn't shed any light on which company was more efficient. But if you divide earnings by the sales, you'll see that Wal-Mart was returning 3.3 percent on sales, while Costco was returning just 2.0 percent. The difference doesn't sound like much, but it was worth about $2.7 billion to Wal-Mart shareholders. And it's one of the reasons Wal-Mart trades at a much higher price-to-earnings ratio than Costco.

Viewing how a company's margins grow or shrink over time can tell you a lot about how its fortunes are changing. Between early 1995 and January 1999, Dell Computer's net margin doubled from 4.3 percent to 8 percent even as the cost of a personal computer declined markedly. What does that tell you? Dell was driving down prices and was manufacturing more efficiently. Rival Compaq Computer, meanwhile, went disastrously in the opposite direction—8 percent to negative 8 percent—as the company ran into trouble digesting several acquisitions and began to lose money. That helps explain why Compaq's shares rose only about 500 percent during that time and Dell's roared ahead almost 8,000 percent.

Long-Term Debt

Debt has perilous connotations, but some forms of debt are necessary to the day-to-day operations of a business. And when a company borrows money to make investments that create new opportunities, it can increase corporate returns. Trouble comes when companies take on too much debt or spend the money foolishly. The job of management is to find the proper balance.

How much debt is too much? That depends a lot on the company's earning power, as well as on the terms of its obligations; just like home mortgages, some loans are much more expensive than others. If a company has too much debt, it usually shows up in poor earnings. But even a healthy company can run into trouble for a period of time if business falters in the short term or if interest rates spike, boosting the cost of carrying the debt load. Your hope as an investor is to pick healthy companies with enough margin for error. That's where the debt-to-total-capital ratio comes in.

Total capital is a tally of all the outside investments management has used to finance the business—everything from equity (the amount of stock sold) to long-term debt. Our view is that companies are best off keeping debt below 50 percent of capital unless there is specific reason to carry more—a strategic acquisition, for instance, or a temporary buildup to enter a new business. If you like a company but its debt seems high, the best thing to do is consult Wall Street research to see if any special circumstances exist. Otherwise you might want to look further.

SIDEBAR 5.2

Chapters 7 and 8. But the important thing is that you could have done all of this screening work yourself, from the comfort of your home.

How, and Where, to Screen for Stocks

For our money, there is no better screening tool than the Zacks Investment Research database (see Figure 5.1), which we have installed in the *Smart-Money* offices. Costing roughly $1,000 a year, this remarkable software service is incredibly nimble. It allows you to screen for everything and anything. For example, you can specify that you want to look at only networking companies and software stocks within the Internet infrastructure industry, or the mainframe server companies within the computer hardware industry. But you can also say you want to look at only companies with annual (or quarterly) earnings growing at better than 25 percent a year. Interested only in companies that the analysts like (or hate)? You can screen for that, too. Want to find out what companies are the most efficient? Set a

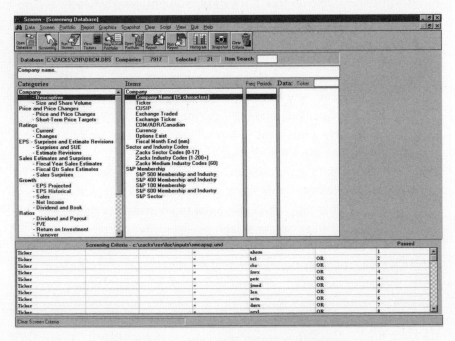

FIGURE 5.1   The Zacks Screening Database
Source: Zacks.com. Reprinted with permission.

parameter for return on equity (greater than 20 percent) or operating margin (better than 10 percent). And of course, you can do simple screens, too: all retail companies with market caps of $5 billion or more and a price-to-earnings ratio of 14 or less.

These days, however, you don't have to shell out a penny for a screening tool—nor should you. Just be forewarned: Not all stock screen tools are created equal. Which one you use really depends on how experienced you are working with ratios and what kind of screen you want to do.

If you're unfamiliar with P/Es and growth rates, try Zacks' web site (www.zacks.com) or the MSN Money web site (www.moneycentral.msn.com). These sites are perfect for investors who just want to look at value or growth stocks, in all industries, but don't want to bother—or don't feel comfortable—with setting all the parameters to find some. They have predefined screens with easy-to-understand names. At Zacks, click on "Top Value" or "Top EPS Growth Stocks" or "Highest Dividend Yields" (see Figure 5.2) and set a market cap (choose from small-, mid-, or large-cap) for a list of 25 stocks.

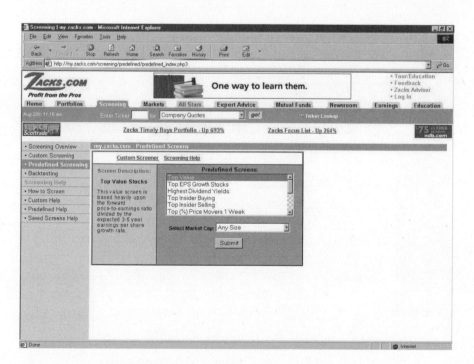

FIGURE 5.2 The Zacks Internet Screening Tool
Source: Zacks.com. Reprinted with permission.

At MSN, choose "Large-Cap with High Momentum" to fetch a list of 25 big growth companies in every sector from insurance to discount stores (see Figure 5.3). Click on "Cheapest Stocks of Large, Growing Companies" and get growth companies that are relatively cheap in price. If you are using Internet Explorer (it is not available on Netscape), you can get even more aggressive: "Great Expectations" will turn up inexpensive small-cap stocks with a lot of potential growth ahead across all sectors. "GARP Go-getters" gets you fast-growing companies that are going at bargain prices. And what about "Distressed Stock Plays"? That screen will present companies that have more than $50 million in market value, stock prices near their 52-week lows, and expected earnings growth of 20 percent or more.

But if you know exactly what you want—a utility company, say, with better than 25 percent earnings growth—then Zacks' and MSN's web sites are not the best choices. A better site for that: Quicken.com (www.quicken.com/investments/stocks/search). In fact, Quicken's stock screen tools (see Figure 5.4) offer something for every investor, beginner or advanced,

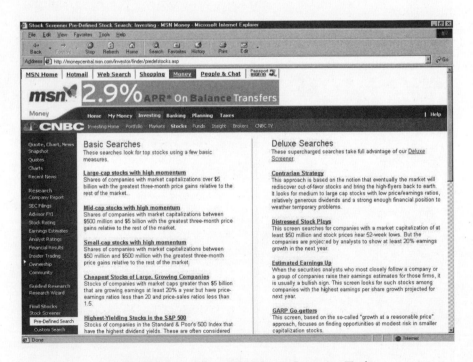

FIGURE 5.3 The MSN Money Screening Tool
Source: msn.com. Reprinted with permission.

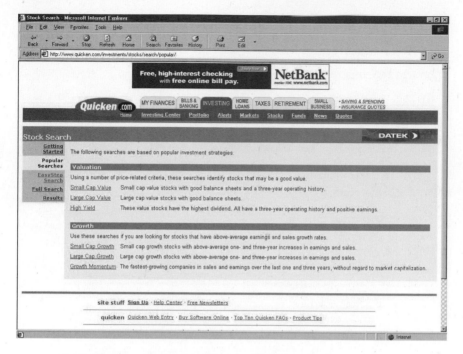

FIGURE 5.4   The Quicken Screening Tool
Source: Quicken.com. Reprinted with permission of Intuit and Quicken.com.

whether someone has a specific request or just wants to do a broad screen. It offers three levels of easy-to-navigate screens. The first level offers beginners preset screens just like the ones we described at MSN's Money web site. It has six predefined screens (small-cap value, small-cap growth, etc.) all under the heading "Popular Searches." Then there's "EasyStep Search," a walk-through screen of the most important variables (industry, market cap, P/E, price-to-book, price-to-sales, and so on) a step at a time. And finally a "Full Search" option, which allows you to set 33 different criteria. If you know exactly what range of P/E you're interested in—for example, above 7 but below 14—plug it in. The "Full Search" tool lets you select the minimum and maximum metric for nearly every ratio, from P/E to return on equity and more.

Check out Yahoo! Finance (http://finance.yahoo.com), too, if you consider yourself an intermediate screener (see Figure 5.5). It's not as thorough as Quicken's site, but you can set up to 16 variables (including one-year stock performance, beta, and estimated five-year earnings growth) by choosing a minimum or maximum from its preset options. One great thing about

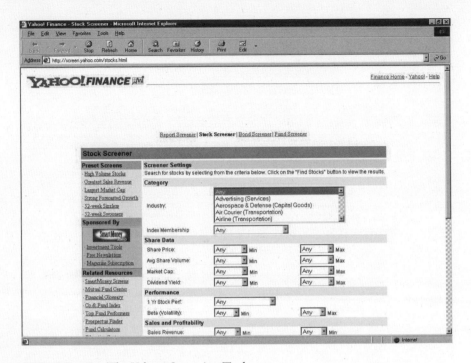

FIGURE 5.5   The Yahoo! Screening Tool
Reproduced with permission of Yahoo! Inc. © 2000 by Yahoo! Inc. YAHOO! and the YAHOO!
logo are trademarks of Yahoo! Inc.

Yahoo! is that you can get good historical price quotes (once you've called up the current price, click "Chart" and scroll down to the bottom of the graphic). What about historical P/E averages? You can get a five-year historical high and low P/E for any company at Multex Investor (www.multex investor.com; see Figure 5.6). Pull up a quote for the company you're interested in and then click on "Ratio Comparison." There, you'll not only get the five-year high and low, you'll also see how a company compares to its industry, its sector, and the S&P 500.

The SmartMoney.com web site also has data on historical highs and lows for P/Es, as well as P/S, P/B, and price-to-cash-flow ratios, among others (see Figure 5.7). To find them, pull up a price quote for any company and then click on the "Key Ratios" tab.

The most important thing to remember about screens is that they're not foolproof. They can lessen your chances of buying an expensive stock—on a price-to-earnings or price-to-sales basis—that has just about hit its peak.

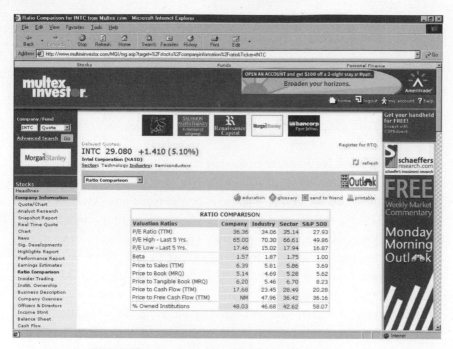

FIGURE 5.6 Comparing Ratios at Multex Investor
Source: Multex. Reprinted with permission.

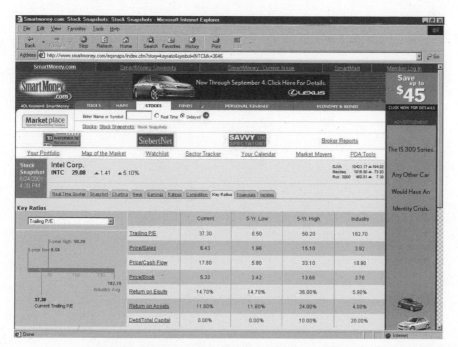

FIGURE 5.7 Historical Data at SmartMoney.com
Source: SmartMoney.com. Reprinted with permission.

But don't assume that every company that's still standing after you've completed running your screens is a squeaky-clean bargain that's poised for spectacular growth. You'd be amazed at how quickly you can find dirt on a company that looks great according to the ratios before you even get knee-deep in research.

In a tech-stock story we researched in late 2000, Yahoo! looked enticing at $25 a share. That was more than $200 off its all-time high. The average rating on the stock by industry analysts at the time was "buy." We were tempted. But after a little research, we felt the stock was an obvious "don't buy." Here's why: Yahoo!, which was then taking in 40 percent of its ad revenue from Internet companies, was surely going to struggle as the dot-com market wilted. And then there was its P/E. Sure, it had plummeted from its previous high of 431, but at 44 it wasn't cheap by any rational measure. We didn't recommend it then, and we're glad we didn't. In the seven months following our rejection of the stock, it dropped another 39 percent.

6

SPECIALTY SCREENS

I t's one of *SmartMoney*'s most popular monthly features—"Stockscreen."
In every issue, the column reveals the latest in stock market research and
then, using readily available screening tools, produces a short list of companies based on that research.

At the risk of sounding excessively promotional, we hope you'll make a
point of reading the column regularly, either in the magazine or at Smart-
Money.com (where you'll also find an archive of past columns). It's simply a
great source of ideas for screens you can do on your own.

To give you a taste of what we mean, here's a look back at some of the
column's more successful screens.

The Payback from Buybacks

Value investors love it when companies buy back their shares. It's a vote of
confidence from management to shareholders—"We're buying, so why don't
you?" It's also a sign the stock might be cheap. And even better, the stock
price typically bumps up following the announcement.

David Ikenberry, a professor of management at Rice University, has
studied the phenomenon. He looked at companies that initiated stock buybacks in the 1980s and found that in the four years following the announce-

ment stock in those companies outperformed those that lacked such programs by an average of 12 percent.

Melissa Brown, at the time the head of quantitative research at Prudential Securities, conducted a separate study in 1997. Her research showed that companies that bought back at least 1 percent of their shares in the four quarters after an announced buyback performed better than those that did not.

The study looked at the stocks of small, medium, and large companies. Brown, now at Goldman Sachs Asset Management, found that stocks of big companies that bought back at least 1 percent had an average annual return of 19.7 percent between 1979 and the first quarter of 1997. The average gain for all large caps was 15.5 percent, and for large caps that issued new shares, the gain was just 14.3 percent. For mid- and small caps, the differences in returns were more dramatic.

We decided to see for ourselves. In our February 1999 "Stockscreen" column, writer Paul La Monica screened for companies that had recently announced buybacks, using names provided by Securities Data (now called Thomson Financial Securities Data), which tracks buybacks among other things. (See Table 6.1. You can compile a similar list by searching news wires or Internet sites for the words "buyback" or "repurchase.") He found 858 companies in the Zacks database.

Then, because Ikenberry's original study showed that *value* stocks with buybacks outperformed the market by 45 percent over four years, La Monica added a couple of layers of value criteria—looking for companies with below-market price-to-book ratios (2.91 at the time) and little debt (less than 38 percent debt-to-capital). After all, the first priority of debt-laden companies should be to clean up their balance sheets, not buy back shares. Finally, La Monica scanned for insider buying (he wanted to see more insiders buying than selling in the previous six months) as a kind of insurance policy against companies announcing buybacks purely for the short-term boost they can provide.

After eliminating several with unique problems or low trading volume, he ended up with 10 stocks, including Boeing Company; two oil companies, Ensco International and Valero Energy; GreenPoint Financial, the savings and loan; and Michaels Stores.

How did they do? Through mid-2001, the average stock in his buyback portfolio had climbed 73 percent, trouncing the 5 percent gain in the

Wilshire 5000 over the same period. The best performer was the energy company Equitable Resources, up 152 percent over the period from early December 1998 to early August 2001. The worst? Insurance company Mercury General; the stock lost 7 percent over that period, and it was the *only* one of the bunch that failed to beat the market.

The Joy of R&D

Since 1975, the level of research and development (R&D) spending has roughly doubled. It now amounts to just under 2 percent of sales of all publicly traded companies. That's a huge number, larger than earnings at many high-tech businesses. But can research and development affect stock prices?

That's what Louis Chan, Josef Lakonishok, both economists, and Theodore Sougiannis, an accountant—all at the University of Illinois Urbana–Champaign—wanted to find out. They took the R&D data for all U.S. public companies during the 20 years between 1975 and 1995 and started crunching numbers. (Corporations must disclose annual R&D expenses if they exceed 1 percent of sales. Over half of all companies don't do enough R&D to meet the threshold, including such industry leaders as Coca-Cola, MCI WorldCom, and Wal-Mart.)

Initially, the professors wondered if firms that do lots of R&D have better returns over time than those that do little—or none. To answer that question, they took the data and separated their universe six ways: into five portfolios of companies ranked from low to high according to their ratios of R&D to sales, and a separate portfolio of non-R&D companies.

As it turned out, the companies that spent more on R&D tended to carry higher P/Es, higher P/B ratios, and minimal dividends compared to the non-R&D crowd. But get this: Over time, there wasn't a measurable difference in the way the two kinds of companies (R&D versus non-R&D) performed. As the authors conclude, run-of-the-mill cement companies and utilities do as well over time as highly touted technology stocks with high R&D budgets.

But within the group of companies that spend money on R&D, the authors made two startling discoveries. First, companies that spend more on R&D relative to sales perform better—to the tune of perhaps 2.5 percent annually—than companies with lower R&D budgets relative to sales. And

TABLE 6.1

The Buyback Screen As It Appeared in *SmartMoney*

Company (Ticker)	Industry	Price 12/4/98	52-Week Hi-Lo	Price/ Earnings Ratio
Boeing (BA)	Aerospace	$32.94	$56–$31	35.80
Ensco International (ESV)	Oil drilling	9.00	40–9	4.33
Equitable Resources (EQT)	Utilities—gas	27.88	35–21	18.58
GreenPoint Financial (GPT)	Savings and loan	37.63	43–25	18.00
MediaOne Group (UMG)	Cable TV	41.13	50–26	N/A*
Mercury General (MCY)	Insurance	42.38	69–33	12.73
Michaels Stores (MIKE)	Retail	19.00	40–17	15.45
Parker Hannifin (PH)	Industrial products	32.94	52–27	11.09
PMI Group (PMI)	Mortgage insurance	53.31	84–35	9.97
Valero Group (VLO)	Oil refining	19.75	36–18	14.96
S&P 500 median				20.23

*Recorded a loss for the previous 12 months. Data as of 12/4/98.
Source: Zacks Investment Research; Securities Data.

Update: The Buyback Screen Two and a Half Years Later

Company (Ticker)	Price 12/4/98
Boeing (BA)	$32.94
Ensco International (ESV)	9.00
Equitable Resources (EQT)	13.94
GreenPoint Financial (GPT)	37.63
MediaOne Group (UMG)[1]	41.13
Mercury General (MCY)	42.38
Michaels Stores (MIKE)	19.00
Parker Hannifin (PH)	32.94
PMI Group (PMI)	35.55[2]
Valero Group (VLO)	19.75
Average	
Wilshire 5000	1,0743.6

[1] AT&T acquired UMG in June 2000; price reflects standard option for UMG shareholders ($36.27 cash and 0.95 in AT&T shares).
[2] Adjusted for a 3-for-2 split.

Price/Book Ratio	Price/Sales Ratio	Debt as Percent of Market Value	Dividend Yield	Value of Announced Buyback (millions)	Market Value (millions)
2.57	0.73	32.55	1.70%	$4,948	$32,909
1.03	1.56	24.41	1.11	65	1,238
1.26	0.48	33.43	4.23	147	1,035
2.02	3.53	18.23	1.70	155	3,560
2.13	4.97	29.43	0.00	1,181	24,959
2.60	2.08	7.70	1.65	200	2,320
1.21	0.39	32.38	0.00	18	564
2.07	0.78	26.85	1.82	140	3,588
1.58	2.95	15.84	0.38	100	1,618
0.94	0.19	25.72	1.62	100	1,103
2.91	1.52	37.55	1.46		7,623

Price 8/2/2001	% Change
$58.81	78.54
20.55	128.33
35.11	151.87
41.11	9.25
55.95*	36.03
39.52	−6.75
42.09	121.53
44.61	35.43
70.16	97.36
35.50	79.75
	73.13
11,296.64	5.15

(drum roll, please) big R&D spenders with beaten-down stocks—so the multiple of market value to R&D budget is relatively low—tend to trounce the market.

The key, then, was to calculate what *SmartMoney* columnist Paul Sturm calls the price to R&D ratio (take the market value of a stock and divide it by the annual R&D budget). Typically, these are stocks that have performed poorly but whose management hasn't slashed its R&D budget a penny. And here's the important part: Over a three-year horizon, these price/R&D laggards beat the market by 6 percent annually.

Would a stock screen be able to turn up these price/R&D laggards? Sturm set out to find out with the following screen: He zeroed in on the roughly 2,000 stocks with market values of more than $500 million. He chucked companies with no reported R&D and ranked the rest by price/R&D ratios. The bottom 20 percent became his potential-winner portfolio, but it included 120 stocks—still too many.

So Sturm winnowed the list by imposing three criteria: He wanted to see consistent R&D spending (that appeals to investment analysts), so companies where spending had grown or diminished by 25 percent in the preceding year got trimmed. He also wanted share prices to be up over the past year, but by less than 100 percent (positive momentum, yes, though not so much that potential gains may already have been realized). And he wanted long-term losers, stocks that were cheaper than they had been three years earlier.

He wound up with nine companies, five of them software companies (where R&D spending is often high). But companies like Callaway Golf and Cabot Corp., which supplies carbon black to tire makers, and autoparts manufacturer Mark IV Industries also made the list. (See Table 6.2.)

In just over a year, this high R&D, low P/E portfolio had climbed better than 40 percent, 36 percentage points better than the Wilshire 5000 over the same period. Two companies—Mark IV Industries and Shared Medical Systems—were acquired at significant premiums. When we checked in with the portfolio again in mid-2001, it was still going strong: Its stocks had climbed an average of 41 percent; the Wilshire was *down* 9 percent.

The best way to recreate this screen at home is sector by sector. Start with a simple screen for software companies or pharmaceuticals, say, with market caps above $1.5 million. Then incorporate a couple of the final screens in reverse: Cut any stocks that have moved up more than 100 percent in the previous 12 months. Once done, you'll probably have a more manageable list to work from. Then focus on the companies with price/R&D multiples of 25 or lower and you'll be looking at above-average spenders. And don't forget Sturm's consistency criteria: Spending has to be consistent from year to year, so if R&D dollars have grown or fallen by 25 percent in the last year, cross the company off your list.

For a practice run, we did exactly that screen (for major drug stocks) using MSN Money's "Stock Screener" (www.moneycentral.msn.com), which requires a quick software download and is well worth it. What it doesn't have is a three-year stock performance option, so we couldn't incorporate Sturm's long-term loser criteria. (Sturm wanted stocks that were cheaper now than three years ago.) But we turned up 13 stocks, a feasible number of companies for which to hunt down annual R&D dollars—and figure out which ones have been long-term losers.

P/S I Love You

Screens based on price-to-sales ratios have generally taken a backseat to those based on price-to-earnings ratios. But the handy metric got a lift a few years ago, thanks to James P. O'Shaughnessy, author of *What Works on Wall Street*.

O'Shaughnessy, a former CEO of a Connecticut investment advisory firm, made headlines when his book, a *New York Times* best-seller, came out in 1997. He had studied 43 years of Wall Street history and discovered that portfolios made up of stocks with low price-to-sales ratios handily outperformed those chosen according to better-known value criteria. We wanted to find out for ourselves how well they worked, so that's what we focused on in our August 1996 "Stockscreen" column.

Of course, no one should invest based solely on P/S ratios or any other single yardstick. So in 1996 we looked for large companies (market value above $500 million) with P/S ratios of less than 0.4 (bargains by almost anyone's standards), below-average levels of debt (to minimize risk), and positive five-year revenue growth (to eliminate the dullards).

The screen, which can be easily replicated on any of the stock screener web sites we've written about, turned up 10 contrarian stocks (see Table 6.3). Apple Computer was one; it was restructuring at the time,

TABLE 6.2 THE RESEARCH AND

The R&D Screen As It Appeared in *SmartMoney*

Company (Ticker)	Industry	Price 9/10/99	52-Week Hi-Lo	Annual R&D Expenses (millions)
Cabot Corp. (CBT)	Specialty chemicals	$23.13	$32–$20	$80.70
Callaway Golf (ELY)	Sporting goods	10.19	17–9	36.50
Cognos Inc. (COGN)	Business software	19.63	28–15	44.50
Informix Corp. (IFMX)	Database software	8.13	14–4	152.80
Lubrizol Corp. (LZ)	Specialty chemicals	26.31	31–18	340.40
Mark IV Industries (IV)	Auto parts	20.88	22–12	54.90
Mentor Graphics (MENT)	Design software	9.61	15–5	116.70
Shared Medical Systems (SMS)	Medical software	57.31	74–40	489.40
Structural Dynamics Res. (SDRC)	Design software	16.75	23–8	63.40
Median for companies with R&D				31.30

NM = Not meaningful; loss in the most recent four quarters. Prices as of 9/10/99.
Source: Market Guide for Windows; Zacks Investment Research.

Update: The R&D Screen Two Years Later

Company (Ticker)	Price 9/10/99
Cabot Corp. (CBT)	$23.13
Callaway Golf (ELY)	10.19
Cognos Inc. (COGN)	9.81[1]
Ascential Software (ASCL)[2]	8.13
Lubrizol Corp. (LZ)	26.31
Mark IV Industries (IV)[3]	20.88
Mentor Graphics (MENT)	9.61
Shared Medical Systems (SMS)	57.31
Structural Dynamics Res. (SDRC)	16.75
Average	
Wilshire 5000	12,347.25

[1]Adjusted for a 2-for-1 split.
[2]IBM bought the database assets of Informix for $1 billion so as a result, Informix adopted a new name and ticker: Ascential Software Co. (ASCL).
[3]In September 2000, Mark IV was acquired by a private equity group (MIV Acquisition) for $23 in cash per share.
[4]Siemens purchased SMS in July 2000 for $71 a share, or $2 billion in cash.

Price/R&D Ratio	Price/ Earnings Ratio	Price/ Book Ratio	Debt/ Total Capital	Est. Annual EPS Growth	Market Value (millions)
18.90	16.10	2.56	0.31	17.00	$1,529
19.70	NM	1.48	0.00	17.20	719
19.10	14.90	5.00	0.01	24.20	849
10.20	NM	6.53	0.00	13.30	1,553
4.20	20.40	1.84	0.33	8.20	1,437
18.70	24.00	1.88	0.54	12.50	1,025
5.50	NM	2.22	0.00	16.80	643
3.10	21.30	3.59	0.28	18.60	1,531
9.50	15.30	2.50	0.00	22.10	601
50.30	23.80	5.42	0.06	22.50	1,574

Price 8/2/2001	% Change
$38.00	64.29
16.31	60.06
16.52	68.40
4.95	−38.11
35.91	36.49
22.94	9.87
18.95	97.19
71.00[4]	23.89
24.75	47.76
	40.98
11,296.64	−8.51

TABLE 6.3

The P/S Screen As It Appeared in *SmartMoney*

Company (Ticker)	Industry	Price 6/14/96	Price/ Sales Ratio
Apple Computer (AAPL)	Computers	$23.94	0.27
Dean Foods (DF)	Dairy, specialty foods	23.88	0.35
FHP International (FHC)	Health-care services	27.00	0.27
Fingerhut (FHT)	Direct mail	16.88	0.37
Hughes Electronics (GMH)	Electronics manu.	60.00	0.39
IBP (IBP)	Beef processing	28.25	0.21
Longs Drug Stores (LDG)	Drugstores	41.76	0.31
SCI Systems (SCI)	Electronics manu.	42.00	0.31
Waban (WBN)	Warehouse clubs	26.00	0.21
Western Digital (WDC)	Disk drives	23.00	0.39
Average company*			1.51

NM = Not meaningful; loss in most recent four quarters.
*Market value exceeding $500 million; excludes financial companies.
Source: Morningstar.

Update: The P/S Screen Five Years Later

Company (Ticker)	Price 6/14/96
Apple Computer (AAPL)	11.97[1]
Dean Foods (DF)	23.88
FHP International (FHP)	27
Fingerhut (FHT)	16.88
Hughes Electronics (GMH)	19.95[2]
IBP (IBP)	28.25
Longs Drug Stores (LDG)	20.88
SCI Systems (SCI)	10.59[3]
HomeBase Inc. (HBI)[4]	25.75
Western Digital (WDC)	11.63[1]
Average	
Wilshire 5000	6,628.95

[1]Adjusted for a 2-for-1 split.
[2]Adjusted for a 3-for-1 split.
[3]Adjusted for two 2-for-1 splits.
[4]Formerly known as Waban (WBN).

Price/ Earnings Ratio	Price/ Book Ratio	LT Debt/ Total Cap. (%)	5-Yr. Avg. Rev. Growth (%)	Market Value (millions)
NM	1.44	30.6	15.1	2,961
15.4	1.59	34.9	5.1	958
NM	.96	24.8	32.5	1,099
18.4	1.44	24.7	10.3	785
21.1	0.67	27.6	6.4	5,862
10.3	2.50	25.4	5.1	2,675
17.7	1.59	7.7	2.8	831
17.8	2.80	40.0	27.2	1,250
11.4	1.53	37.2	9.6	850
11.2	2.33	3.6	22.5	1,014
24.4	3.05	40.1	11.9	

Price 8/3/2001	% Change
19.50	62.91
41.40	73.37
21.00[5]	−22.22
25[6]	48.10
19.36	−2.96
27.42	−2.94
22.66	8.52
30.45	187.43
58.27[7]	126.29
3.80	−67.31
	41.12
11,242.92	69.60

[5]Reflects $17.50 in cash and 0.232 common shares of PacificareHealth.
[6]FHT acquired for $25 cash per share by Federated Department Stores in March 1999.
[7]Reflects one share of HomeBase Inc. (HBI) and one share of BJ's Wholesale Club, an HBI spin-off in 1997.

but we expected a rebound à la IBM. Dean Foods was closing plants and pushing branded products—potentially a big plus, because it's the nation's largest milk producer (market share at the time: 8 percent). IBP, Inc. had an even bigger presence in the beef and pork industries; its stock was well off its 52-week high, but it was increasing its share of the export and food-service markets. Catalog merchant Fingerhut was hurt the previous year by rising costs for paper and postage, as well as by sluggish retail sales.

But did they ever beat the market! When we checked in a few months later, the portfolio had gained 51.5 percent, far better than the market's sturdy 17 percent return. Even five years later, four of the companies were either keeping up with or staying way ahead of the market. Among them: SCI Systems, up 187 percent, and HomeBase (formerly Waban), up 126 percent.

Warming Up to the January Effect

The January effect is one of several calendar-based irregularities, events for which there is no agreed-upon explanation. Stocks tend to go down on Mondays, for example, while they do remarkably well on the last trading day before a holiday. And portfolio returns are better in the first half of the month than in the last half. But the January results are mind-boggling: Based on nearly 70 years of New York Stock Exchange data, the average stock posts a gain of 4 percent in January, while non-January monthly gains are less than 1 percent.

Research has turned up another twist to the January effect: While all stocks do better in January than in other months, small companies—or at least small NYSE companies—do even better. Data show that companies in the bottom 10 percent in terms of market capitalization have January returns averaging better than 12 percent. A study by Tim Loughran of the University of Iowa goes one step further: Small-cap companies with the lowest ratios of price-to-book value are stellar January performers.

The real beneficiaries of the January effect, then, aren't small stocks but small *value* stocks. That's why it's easier to detect the January effect on the NYSE (where small caps tend to be out-of-favor stocks) than it is on the over-the-counter market (which is heavily populated with small *growth* stocks).

Why does the run-up happen? Some economists think institutions trigger it by hunting for bargains in January—and then merely tweak their portfolios for the next 11 months to conform to the benchmark Standard & Poor's 500-stock index. Others say individuals play a big role, as they reinvest the proceeds from tax-loss selling or year-end profit-taking.

Each explanation makes sense, but there are enough troubling facts that leave the mystery unsolved: January gains show up on overseas exchanges, for example, in places where window dressing and tax-loss selling shouldn't play a role. Despite confusion about what causes the January effect, its implications are clear. Conduct your year-end selling as early as possible; November isn't too soon. Then plan to reinvest in December.

With that in mind, back in November 1996 Sturm set out to find companies that seemed particularly well-positioned to benefit from a beginning-of-the-year run-up. (See Table 6.4.) For starters, he zeroed in on small value stocks with market values between $200 and $600 million and price-to-book ratios of less than 2.0.

The key criteria, however, came from a 1985 academic paper on the virtues of contrarian investing. The authors (Werner De Bondt from the University of Wisconsin, Madison, and Richard Thaler, now at the University of Chicago) looked at the performance of stocks with bottom-of-the-barrel three-year returns. On average, these long-term losers rebounded impressively and outpaced the market for nearly 60 months—and, like clockwork, they posted their sharpest gains at the beginning of each year.

So Sturm refined his small-cap value search to include only companies in the bottom 10 percent, based on three-year price performance. To trim the list, he added three hurdles: positive cash flow, debt below 25 percent of equity, and average daily volume of at least 10,000 shares.

The 10 finalists were stocks so beaten down that it would not have taken much to give them a significant boost. Sure enough, a year later they had still outperformed the market: From mid-September 1996 through early October 1997, the 10 stocks had climbed 74 percent. By contrast, the Wilshire 5000 was up 40 percent. We checked in again with the group in mid-2001 and found that four of the companies were beating the market or keeping pace with it.

To recreate his screen on MSN Money, we set a market-cap limit of $600 million, a price-to-book ratio below or equal to the S&P 500, trading volume over the past year of 10,000 or more, and a debt-to-equity ratio of

TABLE 6.4

The January Effect Screen As It Appeared in *SmartMoney*

Company (Ticker)	Industry	Price 9/13/96	3-Yr. Price Decline (%)
Arctic Cat (ACAT)	Snowmobiles	$ 9.13	44
Burlington Coat (BCF)	Specialty retail	10.63	37
Carter-Wallace (CAR)	Personal products	11.75	61
Dress Barn (DBRN)	Specialty retail	10.00	24
Franklin Quest (FNQ)	Time-mgmt. products	17.50	37
Gibson Greetings (GIBG)	Greeting cards	13.50	39
Giddings & Lewis (GIDL)	Machine tools	12.25	48
Information Resources (IRIC)	Market research	13.00	69
National Presto (NPK)	Small appliances	38.38	27
J. M. Smucker (SJMA)	Food products	17.75	22

NM = Not meaningful; net loss for the most recent four quarters.
Source: Morningstar U.S. Equities; Telescan ProSearch 5.0.

Update: The January Effect Screen Five Years Later

Company (Ticker)	Price 9/13/96
Arctic Cat (ACAT)	9.13
Burlington Coat (BCF)	8.85[1]
Carter-Wallace (CAR)	11.75
Dress Barn (DBRN)	10.00
Franklin Covey (FC)[2]	17.50
Gibson Greetings (GIBG)[3]	13.50
Giddings & Lewis (GIDL)[4]	12.25
Information Resources (IRIC)	13
National Presto (NPK)	38.38
J.M. Smucker (SJM)[5]	17.75
Average	
Wilshire 5000	6,671.11

[1]Adjusted for a 6-to-5 split.
[2]Franklin Quest merged with Covey Leadership Center in May 1997 and the ticker changed to FC from FNQ.
[3]Gibson Greetings was bought by American Greeting for $10.25 cash per share in 1999.
[4]Giddings & Lewis was acquired by Thyssen AG, a German company, for $21 a share in July 1997.
[5]Smucker ticker changed to SJM from SJMA.

Price/Earnings Ratio	Price/Book Ratio	Price/Sales Ratio	Price/Cash Flow Ratio	Debt/ Equity	Market Cap (millions)
12.3	1.73	0.63	9	0	270
20.5	1.05	0.27	8.6	21	438
34.1	1.6	0.83	17	18	545
12.9	1.17	0.44	6.7	2	225
9.1	1.51	1.1	7.2	2	362
NM	0.9	0.41	22	19	217
43.3	0.83	0.53	13	22	424
NM	1.57	0.95	3.4	7	361
15.6	1.2	2.36	14	0	284
9.4	0.93	0.48	17	22	256

Price 8/3/2001	% Change
14.69	60.90
14.81	67.34
20.13	71.32
23.22	132.20
5.13	−70.71
10.25	−24.07
21	71.43
7.7	−40.77
27.66	−27.93
27.13	52.85
	29.25
11,242.92	68.53

25 percent or less. How did we deal with the three-year loser screen? Unfortunately, that's not an option with MSN Money's screening tool, so we chose to look for the stocks with a 12-month return that was as "low as possible." (You can also set a specific number, like greater than or equal to negative 10.) Our screen turned up more than 100 finalists—the maximum number on the stock screen tool—but we eliminated 91 because the market cap for those companies fell below $200 million. (MSN's tool doesn't let you set a minimum-maximum limit for market cap.) That left nine, a manageable list with which to start our fundamental analysis.

7

Collecting Information—and How to Analyze It

Reporters might spend up to a week or even two researching a single stock for *SmartMoney*. In that time, you can bet they've read everything about the company they can get their hands on: the annual report, the company's most recent Form 10-K or Form 10-Q (maybe even both), analyst reports, recent headlines, the company web site. They've also talked to someone at the company (ideally the CFO, if not the CEO) and to numerous equity analysts and fund managers. And often they've interviewed experts at data research firms like Gartner Inc. or Forrester Research or Dell'Oro Group and maybe even talked with some of the company's competitors (or read their Form 10-Ks, annual reports, analyst reports, recent headlines, etc.) to get a read on the rest of the industry.

If it sounds like a lot of work, that's because it is. But this is the most crucial part of stock picking. Sure, the screens are fun, and lots of books have been written about how quantitative winnowing alone can turn up good stocks. Take that narrow an approach, however, and you might as well judge a book by its cover. Bottom line: There's no substitute for fundamental analysis.

Let's say you start with a simple stock screen, looking for companies that carry price-to-earnings ratios below their long-term growth rates. You might turn up a company like Callaway Golf, the maker of the famous driver Big Bertha. A little while ago it was trading at $18.46 a share, carrying a P/E of

13.7, and earnings for the next five years were expected to grow 16.8 percent. Meanwhile, the rest of the sector was trading at 37 times earnings with expectations of 13.5 percent earnings growth over the next five years. Not only did the stock sound like a bargain, it was practically a slam dunk. But if you did just a little digging you'd discover that a fair amount of uncertainty clouded the stock. For starters, there was the company's new ERC II driver, which the U.S. Golf Association (USGA) said was nonconforming and which therefore had been banned by the USGA from professional tournaments. The company had a new CEO (outgoing CEO Ely Callaway, the founder, had retired). Three analysts downgraded the stock around the same time. And then the company lowered its revenue and earnings expectations for the upcoming quarter, citing bad weather, poor market conditions, heavy discounting, and the slowing economy. Still think it's a sure thing? Again, there's no substitute for thorough research.

SmartMoney reporters, we'll admit, do have some advantages when researching stocks. We might be able to pick up the phone and get the top semiconductor analyst to talk to us about Intel (after some dogged phone tag of course). You probably won't. But you can most likely download the analyst's recent research report on the company. And while we may be able to get an expert on the UNIX server market to tell us which company is gaining the most market share in units sold, chances are you can find a story on a news database that gives you an idea about the answer. It takes only a good Internet connection and some spare reading time.

Where to Go

One place: the Web.

Chances are you've already scoped out the company on www.smart-money.com or Yahoo!'s finance page, so you know the gist of what the company does and what its recent earnings and revenue history looks like. If not, this is a fast way to figure out at the very least what a company does. Then, it's time to get on to the nitty-gritty.

Start with the company's own web site. You'll be amazed at how much you can learn about not just the company, but also the industry. On the web site of kidney dialysis kingpin Fresenius Medical Care (a German company that trades on the New York Stock Exchange), you will discover that there are only two options for people suffering from kidney failure: dialysis and a transplant. But only 5 percent of all dialysis patients ever receive a transplant. When we researched Fresenius in 2001, not even the analysts covering the company knew that factoid. But we did because we had scoured through the company web site.

After you've trolled the web site for general information (products, customers, the "about us" section, etc.) click onto the investor relations site. There you'll find financial reports: the annual report, quarterly reports, and the Form 10-K and 10-Q. This is mandatory reading for investors trying to research a company. The annual report to shareholders is the principal document used by most public companies to disclose corporate information to their shareholders. It is usually a state-of-the-art, four-color report, including an opening letter from the chief executive officer, financial data, results of continuing operations, market segment information, new product plans, subsidiary activities, and research and development activities on future programs. The Form 10-K, which companies must file with the Securities and Exchange Commission (SEC), typically contains more detailed information about the company's financial condition than the annual report. (It's worth noting that the Form 10-K is also called an annual report. But for our purposes, we'll refer to the glossy four-color as the annual report and to the SEC-regulated form as the Form 10-K.) One last thing: Before you leave the company web site, be sure to click on the page that includes any recent news about the company, be it through company-issued press releases or news stories.

Your next stop: your brokerage firm's web site. You're looking for independent research reports from company analysts, who scrutinize every little twitch a company makes, rate each stock they cover a "buy," "sell," or "hold," and set targets for 12-month earnings, sales, and price movements. (These days they almost invariably say "buy," a problem we'll get to in a moment.)

Many brokerage firms—full-service and discount—offer access to equity research reports. At a place like Merrill Lynch or Salomon Smith Barney, for instance, you'll get the in-house equity research reports (many of them from top-ranked analysts) for free. Discount brokerage firms don't have in-house equity research analysts, so they don't generate in-depth research reports. But most have aligned themselves with a larger firm that does. Fidelity Investments offers its clients Lehman Brothers reports as well as S&P Stock Reports (which are a lot like reports from investment research firm Value Line) and Argus Research. Also, there are web sites, like www.multexinvestor.com, that act as research report warehouses: Search for a ticker and pull 20 to 100 reports from different brokerage firms (some offer a 30-day free trial) across the country. (See the web site directory starting on page 206 for more information on other sites.)

Finally, read the business sections of newspapers and financial magazines. They provide the easiest way to keep up with your companies on a day-to-day basis, and often offer more details on the business than is possible in a 10-K or an annual report.

Annual Reports

If you're like most investors, that annual report (often wrapped in dark blue plastic sheeting) you get in the mail once a year from every company you own stock in sits unopened on your desk—or worse, it gets tossed in the trash the minute you come in the door.

That's understandable. After all, who wants to slog through a chronicle of all 24 divisions at General Electric (including aircraft engines, plastics, and commercial-equipment financing)?

But here's the thing: Annual reports are as much about where the company wants to go next year as they are about what happened last year. They're also about corporate culture. As such, these reports are one of the best ways to keep track of a stock you already own. And if you don't know anything about a company, the annual report is the best place to start.

These reports typically open with a letter to shareholders from the chairman. It is a recap of significant events in the past fiscal year—a kind of Cliffs Notes to the more formal "management's analysis of operations" that follows (as well as the Form 10-K). But whereas the management's analysis of operations is empty of all emotion—very dry—the chairman's letter reads more like an impassioned speech.

Take IBM's annual report for the technology nightmare year of 2000. Chairman Louis Gerstner wrote a long letter, the ending of which is as inspiring as Henry V's rousing speech to his troops at Agincourt in Shakespeare's play. Chin up, his message says, because the next two years will be far more important—and involve more hard work—than the past two:

"This is fun. I find myself relishing this work as never before. There's simply nothing like working as hard as you can with an extraordinary group of people to hit your targets, to prove yourself against tough odds, to build something entirely new, even to change the world. For me, it's the most satisfying feeling there is. We'd better not blink. These next couple of years are going to go by in a flash."

Where do we sign up?

That's not the only thing IBM's annual report will tell you. "In markets we once led—high-end storage, UNIX servers and database software—we're battling back and making up lost ground." Earth-shattering news it isn't. But it's the kind of information you wouldn't necessarily pick up reading the daily business pages.

Who knew that for the eighth straight year, IBM earned more patents than any other company (more, in fact, than its eight closest competitors combined)? And that fully one-third of those patents had already made their way to the marketplace? And who knew that IBM is already one of the world's largest Web hosting companies? If you read the 2000 annual report, you would.

But a word to the wise: Don't get too carried away with it all. If you've already read through a few annual reports, then you know some of the rhetoric is just one big pep talk. Flip through First Union's annual report, for instance. The second page reads like a resume, ticking off the North Carolina–based bank's best attributes: "Superior asset-gathering franchise. Asset management powerhouse with $171 billion in assets under management. Niche capital markets business. Multi-channel distribution network." You'd never know that the stock has basically been on a downhill path since 1998; that its disastrous 1998 acquisition of the Money Store has finally been cast aside (it closed the lender down, writing off $3.8 billion in the process, one of the most expensive write-offs by an American company ever) and that earnings fell off a cliff in 2000 (to 12 cents a share from $3.33 in 1999).

Form 10-K

The annual report is like a big snapshot of the company; the Form 10-K is all the financial details. Unfortunately, it looks like a legal document and reads like one, too. But you won't find a better source of information on your company—and sometimes its competitors, too—than the Form 10-K. This is the report that publicly traded companies must file with the SEC on an annual basis within 90 days after the end of the company's fiscal year. (The Form 10-Q is filed quarterly, 45 days after the end of each fiscal quarter.)

Some companies don't bother with a glossy, four-color annual report and just send shareholders a 10-K. The two are often distinctly different, though. The annual report is more or less a sales pitch for the company, but it often includes—in less glamorous form—an analysis of business last year. The Form 10-K is a detailed explanation of its business as well as an accounting of what's happened throughout its past fiscal year.

The problem is, you have to slog through a lot of business jargon and repetitive information before you get to the good stuff. Never fear: Once you get the hang of reading these documents, the lingo won't seem as foreign and you'll know what to look for. In time, you'll be flipping through them in minutes.

Be forewarned, however, for not every Form 10-K is as informative as the next. In fact, some will seem practically bare-bones next to others that are chock-full of information (Merck's 10-K for instance, is replete with information about the company's drugs—what each ones does, how much revenue each one pulls in a year, when its exclusivity patent expires. But Johnson & Johnson's will leave you wanting.) Nevertheless there are a few core topics that each company's 10-K must cover (the extent to which they cover them, again, can vary).

Description of Business

Short of having an insider tell you a company's strengths and weaknesses, this is the only place you'll find that stuff on your own.

This is because the SEC requires that companies discuss the general development of business during the past five years in this section—Part One, Description of Business. You'll get the lowdown on things like whether the company has changed significantly the way it does business; whether it needs to raise money in the next six months to cover expenses; and whether any segment of the business is dependent on a single customer. All of these are red flags that might deter you from buying the stock—or at the very least warrant a little more research before you do.

Plus, you're bound to find some nuggets of interesting information: Clayton Homes, the manufactured housing company, explains in its Form 10-K, for instance, that its homes range from 500 to 2,400 square feet in size and in price from $10,000 to $75,000. Look, too, for some industry background: The Form 20-F (same as Form 10-K but for foreign companies) for French oil company Coflexip is a veritable primer on the subsea oil field services industry and its major products.

Competition

Don't expect to find a list of all competitors—most companies simply describe the kind of competitor they face (retail or oil services); but other times, you'll find more information. In the Form 10-K of Internet consulting firm Modem Media, for example, the company outlines that it has three kinds of competitors and in some cases offers examples: Internet professional services firms (Sapient, Razorfish); traditional technology services firms (Accenture, Electronic Data Systems); and internal Internet services, technology, market, and design departments. And R. J. Reynolds Tobacco Holdings, the cigarette company, discloses in its Form 10-K that its biggest competitor, Philip Morris, commanded an overall retail share of 50.4 percent in 2000 while Reynolds had just 23.6 percent.

Customers

If the company sells a product or service, it must within Part One identify the markets and kinds of companies it counts as its customers. In some cases, the company will list its major customers. Here's where you'll find out whether the company is too dependent on one customer for revenue. Wipro, an Indian consulting firm, comes clean in this section of its 10-K, for instance, about General Electric: The U.S. conglomerate is its biggest client, and in 2000 GE accounted for 9 percent of Wipro's revenue.

Risk Factors

This is one section of the form that always succeeds in scaring off someone who has never read a 10-K before. It's easy to understand why: The risk section of Yahoo!'s recent Form 10-K lists 23 items and runs on for 10 pages!

Read through a treatise like that—it runs longer than the section titled "Management's Discussion and Analysis of Financial Condition and Results of Operations"—and it most certainly will quell any desire you ever had to buy the stock. But once you've skimmed through two or three of these Form 10-Ks, you'll recognize that while some factors do point to a real risk to the company's fortune, others are included just to cover the company's butt.

Companies are required by law to declare any circumstances that might negatively affect a shareholder's investment—a safeguard, no doubt, against frivolous shareholder lawsuits. But that can include even natural disasters, catastrophic events, and the volatility of the stock market. One of Yahoo!'s factors for instance, goes like this: "Our stock price has been volatile historically, which may make it more difficult for you to resell shares when you want at prices you find attractive." Duh.

Some factors are industry specific. In any clothing retailer's Form 10-K, for example, you'll most certainly find weather is a risk factor—fewer people shop when the weather is either too good (warm and sunny) or too bad (snowy and wet)—as well as the unpredictable whimsy of fashion trends. And the restaurant chain Applebee's mentions that its dependence on fresh produce and meats subjects the company to the risk that shortages or interruptions in supply, caused by severe weather or other conditions, could adversely affect the availability, quality, or cost of ingredients. All are valid concerns, ones worth paying some attention to. But these are industry-wide risks—not risks particular to one firm. The latter are the ones you want to watch for.

Like this one: "Our ability to continue as a 'going concern' is uncertain." That's the first risk factor listed in Covad Communications Group's 2000 10-K. The company's problem is money—not enough of it—which you can figure out by reading the sentence that follows. Clearly, the smart move would be to wait *at least* until the company gets an influx of more cash before you think about buying any shares.

Then there's Modem Media. Sandwiched between all the predictable risks (like its ability to attract and retain "qualified personnel"), you'll notice some red flags: "Our dependence on a limited number of clients," for instance, is a potential problem. Here's another: "Our ability to fulfill the CentrPort Commitment." Who knows what that means, right? Well, before you buy the stock, you should know what the CentrPort Commitment is and whether you think the company can fulfill it.

Legal Proceedings

Obviously, it's better if the company isn't involved in any lawsuits. But often companies juggle several legal actions that—most likely—will not have a negative effect on the company's financial position. Maytag, for instance, has what it calls "contractual disputes, environmental, administrative and legal proceedings and investigations of various types." You don't need to worry about those.

So which ones do you need to worry about? A Department of Justice antitrust suit, as in Microsoft's case, is one obvious instance. So, too, are the various legal actions against the tobacco industry. As of December 2000, R. J. Reynolds had 1,664 such active cases pending. (And those are just the claims involving smokers. There are 3,074 passive-smoking suits.)

Probably the worst-case scenario is a shareholder class action lawsuit, because that points to major problems—perhaps even illegal goings-on—within the company. But chances are, if a company is in that much trouble, you'll know way before you get to legal proceedings that something is amiss. Covad Communications, for instance, faces several shareholder class action lawsuits that could cost the company some $142 million in damages, a fact disclosed in its most recent 10-K: "The complaints in these matters allege violations of federal securities laws." Serious items like this will close with a sentence that reads something like: "While we do believe that we have strong defenses in these lawsuits, the ultimate outcome of these litigation matters is inherently unpredictable, and there is no guarantee we will prevail." The lawyerly lingo may put you to sleep, but it should be taken seriously. If other shareholders have filed suit against a company, why would you ever want to buy stock in it?

Management's Discussion and Analysis of Financial Condition and Results of Operations

The whole point of this section is to explain the events of the past fiscal year and analyze how it compares to the previous year. What segments of the business did better than last year? Which ones did worse? What segments contributed more to revenue and earnings? Were there any significant expenses or write-offs? There aren't any specific red flags we can point to here, but we would say this is probably the most important part of the 10-K.

Why? Because even though you think you know everything there is to know about Microsoft, for instance, which gets so much press coverage, unless you have read through its discussion of financial condition you wouldn't know that the company has changed its distribution methods. Nowadays, some select products are being shipped straight to retail customers, a move that saved the company $250 million in product returns in 1999. You might also not know that while revenue grew 16 percent in 2000, that is nearly half the rate at which it grew the year before (29 percent). This kind of news could make or break a decision to buy the stock. Bottom line: Read the management's discussion, no matter how well you think you know the business.

Equity Analyst Reports

It used to be there was a "Chinese wall" separating stock researchers from investment bankers at most firms. Neither group was to know what the other was doing, in order to eliminate conflicts of interest. (How would it look if the stock analysts were saying positive things about companies that just *happened* to be paying big fees to their investment banking arms?) Well, guess what. The Chinese wall seems to have broken down. Now firms are unabashedly throwing everything they can into generating banking fees—including the promise of upbeat coverage from their analysts. "Most [banks] would say, 'Our analysts are here just to do great research and follow companies,' " says Mickey Misera, head of equity capital markets at Wachovia Securities, formerly First Union. "But that's not the reality. They have a lot of responsibilities—and investment banking is becoming more essential."

Does that mean you can't trust anything a stock analyst says? Not at all. The best analysts—such as the ones highlighted every year in the *Wall Street Journal*'s "Best of the Street" report—routinely pick better stocks and have more accurate earnings forecasts than their peers. The average computer software stock on Rehan Syed's recommended list at SG Cowen Securities, for instance, performed 149 percentage points better than his rival's picks in 1999. Internet analyst Fred Moran, now at Jefferies & Co., can top that. His portfolio—up 492 percent in 1999—smoked his rivals' gains by 218 percentage points.

The trick is to know the difference between information in reports that's strictly data—facts about the company's business—and what falls under the analysts' realm of "analyzing." We're not saying you can't believe any opinions analysts put forth in their reports. All we're saying is, don't gulp it all down. The analyst has taken some of it, sifted it, and repackaged it.

For starters, there's the analyst's recommendation—buy, sell, or hold. It's probably the biggest reason you picked up the report in the first place. We're not saying you can't trust the analyst's rating of the stock. But flip to the last page and read the fine print at the bottom. Do you see a clause that says, "The firm, including its parent, subsidiaries, and/or affiliates, has acted as manager or comanager of a public offering of the securities of this company"? If there is something to that effect, it may mean the analyst has to publish a somewhat rosier view of things because his or her firm is getting millions of dollars in investment banking business. Some analysts, for instance, will refuse to talk to reporters about a company if their firm is currently representing it, or if their firm was involved in the initial offering of shares.

Then there's the problem of deciphering those recommendations. Rarely do firms stick to just "buy," "sell," or "hold." They use a swarm of different phrases that seemed designed to just muddy the water: outperform, market perform, accumulate, neutral, strong buy. (See Sidebar 7.1, "Five Things Stock Analysts Won't Tell You.")

Take an A. G. Edwards report on the Missouri furniture manufacturer Furniture Brands International. It's labeled "accumulate/aggressive." That means buy, right? It says aggressive, right? Read further into the report, however, and you'll see, in bold, language that signals a more cautious approach:

"Current conditions very ugly—sales and costs."

"Consumer rebound is anybody's call."

"The short run is very choppy."

All of which is hardly the kind of language you'd expect for an "accumulate/aggressive." What, in the end, does that mean exactly? You'd be better off paying more attention to the rest of the report than to the rating. Here's what we thought after reading the report: Unless you're willing to withstand some not-so-good news over the next three quarters and other bumps as the company gets going on a major restructuring plan—which will no doubt

Five Things Stock Analysts Won't Tell You

1. "Sell."

Securities analysts make their living by feeding investment advice to brokers and investors. But there is one suggestion you'll seldom hear them make, especially about a stock they've been bullish about in the past: "Dump it." Instead, they're almost always urging you to buy, or at worst, "hold" your shares. (Many times "hold" is code for "sell"—particularly if an analyst has been bullish for some time and suddenly changes his or her mind.) During late 1999 and most of 2000, less than 1 percent of 28,000 recommendations issued by brokerage analysts called for investors to sell stocks.

Why? When an analyst slaps a sell recommendation on a stock, "You've just destroyed your relationship with the company," says one New York analyst. Many times the company will simply cut off the analyst, failing to keep him or her up-to-date and not returning telephone calls. That's a serious problem for someone who is charged with following a company's every move.

2. "I'm anything but objective."

Every securities firm has a "Chinese wall." This is a theoretical barrier separating the firm's corporate-finance department, which helps corporations raise money through stock and bond offerings, from the researchers who analyze those companies for investors. That's supposed to keep the analysts objective.

In fact, analysts often climb over the wall at will. Analysts regularly help drum up new banking business for their firms. They help new clients set reasonable prices for their offerings, and they pitch in when it's time to write the offering prospectus. Analysts even go along with the bankers on nationwide "road shows" to talk up their clients' new offerings among institutional investors.

Should you trust analysts who work with their firms' bankers? These days you have little choice. So many of them do it. But keep this potential conflict of interest in mind when you sort through research reports. Look for disclaimers noting the firm's business with the companies it follows, usually found in small type at the bottom of the first or last page. That ought to make you skeptical.

3. "I know what's going on, but I can't tell you."

When a company is making an offering or some other deal, the only information most analysts will get is in the prospectus. They're stuck, because the company is legally prohibited from talking while the deal is under way.

Now, some analysts—the ones who worked with the company on its deal—know full well what's going on. But they're expected to be every bit as quiet as the company. Even if the CEO suddenly dies, they can't comment on its significance for the stock. (At least not publicly. You can be sure that big institutional clients get some inside dope from time to time. At the very least, the analysts will discreetly lead them to another analyst who shares their view.)

Analysts aren't fond of this quandary. "It's probably the most frustrating position in the world," says one. "You've put people into a stock, and then suddenly you have to say, 'You're on your own.' "

4. "My firm likes me to change my mind."

Most individual investors pay commissions on every share of stock they buy or sell. Much of that goes to their broker, the rest to the brokerage house.

What does this mean to you? "A lot of firms encourage analysts not to have neutral ratings," says former Morgan Stanley Dean Witter analyst Todd B. Richter, now with Banc of America Securities. "They push analysts to take an actionable position." In other words, they urge them to change their ratings regularly to crank up the commission volume. That usually means you get buy ratings on stocks when the right move is simply to hold.

5. "I'm often wrong—but who cares?"

The line that old-time analysts like to throw around is that they only have to be right 51 percent of the time. In fact, they don't even have to be that good.

Say an analyst recommends 10 stocks at $10. The first nine go from $10 to $8. But the last one hits $100. This analyst was 90 percent wrong, but he's 100 percent hero. "What's important," says Richter, "is that my rights are bigger than my wrongs."

If a broker calls you up with a tip from a hot analyst, it may be your lucky day. But first ask about the analyst's track record—and not just within the industry. You need to know how the analyst has done with this company specifically. If the stock has been climbing, what was the analyst's take on the company before the rise? What was the analyst saying when the stock was in the dumps? This way, you'll decrease your chances of following the advice of a one-hit wonder.

rattle the stock—don't buy. But all of this doesn't help us with the larger question of whether we even want to invest in a furniture store—and this particular one at that. We'd have to do more research to answer that one.

Reading reports like these, a lot of investors are tantalized by the analyst's 12-month target price. It's a nice guideline for how much higher the analyst thinks the stock can go in the near future, but the way it is calculated is subject to the analyst's opinion and thus can be awfully arbitrary. Back in late 2000, when we researched Yahoo!, among others, for a feature on tech stocks, we found that two analysts—one at US Bancorp Piper Jaffray and the other at UBS Warburg—had come up with wildly different target prices for the stock: $135 and $65, respectively. (The actual price of the stock on that day in mid-November, by the way, was just over $41 a share. And six months later, the stock had slid to just over $18.) Needless to say, we ignored them. After all, a price target is just a projection. We need only remember the laughable $1,000 price target of Qualcomm back in early 2000 to know that there's no guarantee. (The stock was trading in the $50s as of this writing.)

The only thing that should interest you about the 12-month price target is where it is in relation to the current trading price of the stock. If it's just a few dollars higher, that's maybe a sign the stock has had a good run lately and you'd be wise to hold off picking up shares. If, on the other hand, the analyst's target price is a good 40 to 50 percent above the current price of the stock, that's good reason to look even more closely at the company.

In October 2001, the median 12-month target price for JDS Uniphase hovered around $8. Meanwhile the stock was at $9. Wal-Mart, at just over $52, had a median 12-month target price of $61, a 19 percent jump. And the target price on Intel in mid-October was 63 percent above its trading price at the time.

Finally, a word about earnings estimates: You'd like to think that analysts have meticulously pored through balance sheets and income statements and come up with—all on their own—company earnings estimates. That may happen some of the time, but it doesn't happen most of the time. In most cases, companies have given analysts so much guidance about their earnings that the numbers are basically being spoon-fed. Companies will actually tell analysts during quarter-end conference calls that they expect $1.25 in earnings this year and $1.30 next. And the next day, five different analysts will issue reports saying they expect the company to report $1.25 in earnings this year and $1.30 next. The moral: Take what an analyst says about projected earnings with a big grain of salt.

To get the most from reading analyst reports, you need to have a strategy. You can't just read one random analyst's report—suppose you happen to hit on the only person with a bullish point of view? Collect thorough reports from at least three different firms on each company you're investigating. Check web sites such as Zacks (www.zacks.com) to find out how many brokers are optimistic and pessimistic on the company.

That's the kind of approach you should take whenever you read an analyst report, whether it be a company update—a one- or two-page report issued in response to firm-related news, like a merger or an earnings warning (these reports are useful because you get a feel for whether the breaking news is good or bad for the company and thus the stock)—or, even better, the in-depth 10 to 20 or even 30 pagers. In these reports, you'll get a breakdown of each segment of the company business, where the company is going with each one, and how each contributes to the firm's overall revenue and earnings.

In June 2001, Juniper Networks issued a dramatic earnings warning for the second quarter. The move sent the stock reeling almost 18.5 percent or nearly $9 a share. US Bancorp Piper Jaffray analyst Frank McEvoy issued a research note the next day.

"The fundamental outlook is not good," McEvoy wrote. "Nevertheless, we believe that the slowdown is not Juniper specific and that its products offer a compelling long-term opportunity. They continue to maintain several advantages over younger startups that are at their heels for market share. Specifically, Juniper is profitable and can continue to fund and grow its R&D resources, they have more than $1 billion in cash and marketable securities, and they maintain a strong customer base, including some of the largest backbone providers. For these reasons, we believe Juniper is well positioned to weather the storm and emerge stronger than it entered."

As promising as that sounds, McEvoy lowered his earnings estimates for 2001 and 2002 by 48 and 56 percent, respectively. He also cut his 12-month price target to $44—at a time when the stock was trading at $40 a share. Meanwhile, the rating on the stock: a buy/aggressive.

So what do you do as an investor?

We would stay away from this stock—for the time being. It's not that we didn't believe McEvoy's argument that Juniper was a market leader with huge advantages in its niche. We did. But the "fundamental outlook is not good" sentence stopped us in our tracks. And he cut his earnings projections for 2001 to 47 cents from 90 cents, and 2002 earnings to 44 cents from $1 a share. That's a dramatic cut—one that means earnings growth will decline for two years in a row (the company posted a net profit of 53 cents a share in 2000). With the stock at $40, McEvoy slashed his 12-month price target to $44 from $60—a real indication that the stock, for the time being, was trading at close to fair value. Since earnings growth tends to drive stock prices, there was a good chance that Juniper's stock might be what the Street calls "dead money" in the near term. We'd wait three to six months before taking a serious look at the stock again.

8

THE LAST STEP—PUTTING IT ALL TOGETHER

Okay, so now you have all your numbers and you've read through all your reports and 10-Ks. How do you take the last step? How do you decide whether to buy a stock you've got your eye on?

At this point you've got to step back, take a deep breath, and assess all the data you've collected. It's a daunting task, we realize. That's why we find it helpful to start with these Nine Essential Questions.

1. Why is this company's stock so cheap?
2. What's next for this company?
3. What about the rest of its industry?
4. What's up with this company's earnings?
5. How do its numbers compare with its peers'?
6. Is its management a bunch of clowns?
7. Does it have the urge to merge?
8. What is this company's biggest weakness?
9. How does the current economy affect this company?

Let's walk through each of these Nine Essential Questions.

Why Is This Company's Stock So Cheap?

Most of the time, the stocks that make it through to our final screens have been beaten down, a function of *SmartMoney*'s value-oriented philosophy. Sometimes they're cheap because they're truly in bad shape. But there are, in fact, acceptable reasons for a slumping stock price, just as there are plainly bad reasons.

The bad ones are relatively easy to spot. They usually have to do with crummy management decisions, like a major accounting irregularity from which it'll take years to recover (think Cendant or Sunbeam) or legal entanglements (think tobacco or asbestos litigation). But other times, a company is taken down for reasons far outside its control—reasons that, in retrospect, seem to be an overreaction and that represent excellent buying opportunities for investors.

Some examples:

A Sinking Tide Lowers All Ships

A market correction can be a healthy thing, pulling an overvalued stock market back into line with its historical average. But sometimes stocks that *deserve* higher valuations are dragged down along with the overinflated ones. Take Nokia, which fell by nearly 24 percent in August 1998—some 9 percentage points further than the S&P 500—on fears of Asian exposure and decreased consumer spending. Investors who stuck with the wireless phone giant got their reward: Nokia's stock finished the year 38 percent above its July 31 price, almost four times the S&P's gain.

Nobody Likes Surprises

Intel seemed to have a real disaster on its hands. The new version of its Pentium chip, which had just hit the market, was flubbing certain types of mathematical equations and the media were having a field day with the story. Stunned, investors walloped Intel's shares as the news broke back in 1994. The company's stock slid 13 percent in a matter of days, purely based on the Pentium fiasco.

But when Intel announced a simple peace offering—all Pentium customers could exchange their chips for free debugged ones—its stock rebounded. Investors who were able to tell that the chip debacle would blow over quickly watched their investments double within six months.

Misery Loves Company

Sometimes all it takes is the whiff of a potential problem to send an entire industry spiraling downward. Such was the case with personal computers (PCs) back in 1997. Fears of slowing computer sales triggered a massive sell-off, pulling down even well-positioned companies. In less than three months, Dell slipped 25 percent; Compaq and Hewlett-Packard, 31 and 15 percent, respectively. Yet by January 1998 most computer stocks had come roaring back—kicking off a five-month, 28 percent rally in the Nasdaq index. Dell climbed 18 percent in January alone.

A similar buying opportunity came along when Bridgestone had to recall 6.5 million of its tires in August 2000. Naturally Bridgestone's stock got creamed, but nervous investors apparently decided that tire maker Goodyear was guilty by association, as its stock dropped 27 percent over the next three months as well. Did you buy in? If you had, your investment would have been worth 75 percent more within just seven months.

Someone Got Left at the Altar

More often than not, a failed merger is the trigger for a wholesale sell-off. A prime example is Tellabs, an optical networking company. Its plans to merge with Ciena, another optical networker, fell apart in late 1998, not long after Ciena had failed to win a $100 million contract and AT&T temporarily dropped the company as a supplier.

The market basically hung up the phone on Tellabs, sending its shares down 62 percent. But it was *still* posting 30 percent revenue and profit growth and its margins were *still* in the 50 percent range. A year later, Tellabs' stock was up 350 percent.

What's Next for This Company?

By the early 1990s, Wal-Mart had pretty much covered most of the United States. The discount retailer had more than 1,500 stores, and over the previous five years it had grown sales and earnings by better than 25 percent a year. At the time, it was the sixth most admired company in the country, according to *Fortune*, and everyone wanted to buy founder Sam Walton's book, *Made in America* (Bantam Books, 1993). But critics claimed the company's growth story was over. What else could Wal-Mart do to revolutionize the discount store format? And where else could it expand? In other words, what could possibly be next for Wal-Mart?

Once a Wall Street darling whose stock consistently posted double-digit gains, Wal-Mart turned into a dog in 1991. From 1993 through 1996, the share price went nowhere, bouncing between $11 and $13 (split-adjusted).

But as it turned out, the company did have an answer to the question "What's next?" It spent the rest of the decade reinventing retail all over again with its supercenters, essentially discount and grocery stores wrapped into one. Earnings at those outlets surged more than 30 percent from 1996 to 1998, a remarkable pace for any retailer, let alone one with $150 billion in annual sales. Wal-Mart became a threat to every category of merchant, from 7-Eleven and Toys 'R' Us to Circuit City. What's more, the company had been expanding overseas. It had 10 foreign stores in 1993. By 2000, it had 1,004, and international sales had grown more than 50 percent for three years in a row. Overall company earnings rose 20 percent for two consecutive years, and the stock quadrupled in a span of three years from late 1996 to late 1999.

The lesson? At some point, it's not enough for a company to keep doing what it's doing. It has to grow and change. It has to evolve. A good company will change in step with its competitors. A great company will lead the way.

Again, Dell serves as a good example. When we recommended the PC maker in March 1998, it was not what you'd call a hidden gem. In fact, investors knew all too well the story of the direct, custom-fit-to-order business; it was so familiar that many thought the company had gone as far as it could with it. That same month, in fact, *Money* magazine advised its readers to sell the stock. By then, the stock had already climbed 13,166 percent since its initial public offering, and to be honest, the story was getting a little old.

But Dell was already one step ahead. It was making headway, however small, into the enterprise systems business: servers and workstations. While everyone was ready to cross off this company as a PC seller that had seen its best days, Dell already had 4 percent of the world's server-system business and 1.5 percent of the workstations market. Granted, it wasn't much. But at the time it was the company's fastest growing business; sales grew 340 percent in the third quarter of 1997. All of this information, by the way, was plainly written in the company's annual report.

We bet that the company would succeed in grabbing market share, given its direct-to-order custom-fit service and its lower prices. And we were right. The company, at the end of its fiscal year, announced that it ranked No. 2 in the server market (with three times the growth rate of the market leader) and No. 1 in workstations. From the time we recommended the stock in our March 1998 story, at a split-adjusted price of $11.59, to July 2001, Dell stock climbed 1,209 percent—and that includes the 70 percent drop the stock suffered when the technology sector imploded in 2000.

Of course, now we're wondering—as all smart investors should—what's *next* for Dell?

What About This Company's Industry?

Sometimes a company can be barreling along with everything just going great, only to have a rival step in and completely change the competitive landscape. (See Sidebar 8.1, "Dueling Stocks.") Case in point: Toys 'R' Us. In the 1980s, this was the category-killer of the toy-store scene, putting mom-and-pop stores out of business. But in the mid-1990s the company faltered, and earnings fell 71 percent in 1996.

The problem? Its monopoly was over. Discount stores like Wal-Mart stole chunks of its huge market share by offering products for lower prices (knowing they could make up the difference on other items). In 1997, Toys 'R' Us had 18.4 percent of the market; Wal-Mart had 16.4 percent. Toys 'R' Us was too slow to jump into electronic retailing, but that wasn't its biggest problem. The store was also having trouble keeping up with toy trends; kids were demanding high-tech toys and electronics, and parents couldn't find them in Toys 'R' Us stores.

As you might expect, Toys 'R' Us got pummeled. From late 1995 through late 1999, its share price was cut in half. Struggling to find a decisive "what's next" strategy, and after running through three CEOs and three overhauls, the company finally hired John Eyler away from FAO Schwarz in early 2000 to turn things around.

Dueling Stocks: How to Compare Two or More Potential Investments in the Same Industry

How does a company compare to its competitors? Which one—regardless of size—is able to squeeze more profits from its sales? Which one pays the bigger dividend relative to stock price? Which one has the better balance sheet? At *SmartMoney*, we typically employ the following ratios when we compare rivals.

Efficiency Ratios

If one group of managers was able to squeeze more money out of its assets or capital than another you'd go with the first one, right? Of course. That's why accountants and stock analysts long ago began looking for a reliable way to measure management efficiency. Return on equity (ROE) and return on assets (ROA) are what they came up with. Both ratios are an effort to measure how much earnings a company extracts from its resources. Return on equity is calculated by taking income (before any nonrecurring items) and dividing it by the company's common equity or book value. Expressed as a percentage, it tells you what return the company is making on the equity capital it has deployed. Return on assets is income divided by total assets. It gives you a sense of how much the company makes from all the assets it has on the books—from its factories to its inventories.

As measures of pure efficiency, these ratios aren't particularly accurate. For one thing (as we've mentioned elsewhere), earnings can be manipulated. It's also true that the asset values expressed on balance sheets are (for various reasons) not entirely reflective of what a company is really worth. Microsoft and an investment bank like Goldman Sachs rely on thousands of intellectual assets that, as the saying goes, walk out the front door every day.

But ROE and ROA are still effective tools for comparing stocks. Since all U.S. companies are required to follow the same accounting rules, these ratios put companies in like industries on a level playing field. They also allow you to see which industries are inherently more profitable than others.

Inventories

Manufacturers have warehouses filled with raw materials, component parts, and finished goods to help fill orders. Retailers have stock waiting to be sold. For every moment any of it sits idle on the shelves, it costs the company money to store and finance. That's why managers strive to have as little inventory on hand as possible. Certain types of companies (manufacturers, retailers) by nature carry more inventory than others (software makers, advertising companies).

As an investor you want to look for two things: First, does one company in a given industry carry more inventory as a percentage of sales than its rivals? Second, are its inventory levels rising dramatically for some unexplained reason?

You can't look at inventory in isolation. After all, if a company's inventory level increased 20 percent but sales grew at a rate of 30 percent, then the increase in inventory should be expected.

The warning sign is if inventory spikes despite normal growth in sales. In 1997, the stock of high-flying apparel maker Tommy Hilfiger got nailed when its inventories suddenly rose 50 percent—spooking Wall Street analysts, who figured the popular menswear maker had lost its edge among teenage boys. Tommy eventually righted the situation (it had more to do with inventory management than fashion sense), and the stock recovered. But a lot of investors lost money along the way.

A helpful number to look at is the inventory turnover ratio—annual sales divided by inventory—which reflects the number of times inventory is used and replaced throughout a year. Low inventory turnover is a sign of inefficient inventory management. If a company had $20 million in sales last year but $60 million in inventory, then inventory turnover would be 0.33, an unusually low number. It would take three years to sell all the inventory. That's obviously not good.

There's no rule of thumb when it comes to turnover. It's best to make comparisons. If a retailer had a turnover of 4, for example, and its closest competitor had turnover of 6, it would indicate that the company with higher turnover is more efficient and less likely to get caught with a lot of unsold goods.

Current Assets/Liabilities (Current Ratio)

Naturally, a strong company will have more assets than liabilities. One ratio between the two is called a current ratio, and many analysts use this measure as a quick way to assess a company's financial situation. Current assets are things like cash and cash equivalents, accounts receivable (money owed the company by customers), and inventories. They are defined as anything that could be sold quickly to raise money. Current liabilities are what the company owes in short order—mostly accounts payable and short-term debt.

A ratio of 2 or higher is desirable, but exceptions are made if assets are mostly cash. A ratio of greater than 5, however, could mean that the company isn't deploying its assets to their best advantage.

The other thing to look for: trends. Are current assets growing quickly from quarter to quarter? It could mean the company is accumulating cash—a good thing. Are accounts receivable trending up? Could mean the company is having trouble collecting bills from its customers—a bad thing. A big climb in current liabilities is rarely a good thing, but it might be explainable due to some short-term corporate goal.

If you see a spike in either category, it's worth further exploration. Check the analyst research and news reports, or get the financial statements and read the notes. Management is required to explain changes in the company's financial condition.

Dividend Yield

A dividend is a payment many companies make to shareholders out of their excess earnings. It's usually expressed as a per-share amount. When you compare companies' dividends, however, you talk about the "dividend yield," or simply the "yield." That's the dividend amount divided by the stock price. It tells you what percentage of your purchase price the company will return to you in dividends. Example: If a stock pays an annual dividend of $2 and is trading at $50 a share, it would have a yield of 4 percent.

Not all stocks pay dividends, nor should they. If a company is growing quickly and can best benefit shareholders by reinvesting its earnings in the business, that's what it should do. Microsoft doesn't pay a dividend, but the company's shareholders aren't complaining. A stock with no dividend or yield isn't necessarily a loser.

Still, many investors—particularly those nearing retirement—like a dividend, both for the income and for the security it provides. If your company's stock price falters, you always have a dividend. And it is definitely a nice sweetener for a mature stock with steady but unspectacular growth.

But don't make the mistake of merely searching for stocks with the highest yield—doing so can quickly get you into trouble. Consider the stock we mentioned with the $2 dividend and the 4 percent yield. As it happens, 4 percent is well above the market average, which is usually below 2 percent. But that doesn't mean all is well with the stock. Consider what happens if the company misses an earnings projection and the price falls overnight from $50 a share to $40. That's a 20 percent drop in value, but it actually raises the yield to 5 percent ($2 divided by $40). Would you want to invest in a stock that just missed earnings estimates because its yield is now higher? Probably not. Even when searching for stocks with strong dividends, it's always crucial to make sure the company clears all your other hurdles.

Payout Ratio

This is similar to the dividend yield (percentage of the stock price the company will pay out in dividends), but instead it tells you what percentage of *earnings* the company will dole out to shareholders in dividends. If the number is above 75 percent, consider it a red flag—it might mean the company is failing to reinvest enough of its profits in the business. A high payout ratio often means the company's earnings are faltering or that it is trying to entice investors who find little else to get excited about.

Relative Price Strength

This is just buying on price momentum—if the price is moving up, the theory goes, it will continue to rise. We've all been guilty of doing this at one time or another—maybe not on purpose. Given the market's climb in recent years, how could you not? But in this context, some investors actually use momentum to screen stocks. Critics claim buying on price strength can be dangerous because it doesn't take into account any company fundamentals. Furthermore, as has been drilled into our heads time and time again: Past performance is no indication of future earnings. But fans insist the measure works as an investment tool because stocks with strong and improving relative strength tend to continue to outperform.

Enterprise Value

This doesn't really fit in as a growth or value screen. And it's not really a ratio per se. It's a proxy for market value, and we don't use it as a metric for our screens. But it gets a lot of press, and many analysts these days, especially the folks at Goldman Sachs, love it. So we figured we'd explain it to you.

Some would say it's a more accurate way to value a company: To arrive at a company's enterprise value, you take the company's market capitalization, add debt, and subtract cash on the books. Simply put, it's how much you would have to dig out of your pocket to buy the company at its current market price, and then pay off all the debt.

Here's how it works. In mid-2001, Juniper Networks had a market capitalization of $9 billion, debt of $1.1 billion, and cash of $1.1 billion. The company's enterprise value: $9 billion.

Fyler set a course that would lift the company out of its warehouse, low-priced, supermarket-style format to more interactive stores, with cordoned-off sections targeted by gender and age (baby dolls near the displays of glittering nail polish and steps away from Barbie's corner) and more exclusive products. In his first two and a half years on the job, the stock more than tripled.

What's Up with the Company's Earnings?

"The bottom line"—that overused phrase—means net earnings, the number that actually resides on the bottom line of a company's income statement. It's the net profit or loss at the end of a quarter or a fiscal year. Like the last line on your paycheck, it's what you—or the company in this case—will take home.

Here at *SmartMoney*, one of the first things we examine when researching a company is the annual earnings *trend line*. This is different from the long-term earnings growth rate, which is analysts' estimate of the company's future profits. What we're talking about here is actual earnings posted by the company over the past five years or more. Is it trending steadily upward—always the best-case scenario? Or are earnings shrinking from year to year? Or are they jumping around like a heart monitor?

No, this isn't rocket science. Who wouldn't rather bet on a company with steady 15 percent growth in earnings year after year than one that has seen its earnings shrink 10 percent in the past two years? Past performance may be no indication of future results, but all the same a good track record is certainly better than a bad one.

Your next question has to be whether that kind of growth is sustainable. A company may have posted torrid earnings growth for two to three years running, but what was behind it? Can it keep going?

Let's go back to Wal-Mart for another good example. We wrote about the retailer in a November 1999 cover story. The company had been on a roll at the time: Earnings had risen 25 percent for two consecutive years. And its stock had done even better, quadrupling since 1996. But we wondered: Can this retailing juggernaut continue at this pace? Our conclusion: probably not.

The company's big growth driver had been the supercenters, whose profits were growing at more than 30 percent a year. But analysts were saying that growth was going to slide back down to the 20 percent level and the company's traditional discount stores were increasing their earnings a measly 5 percent per year. Plus, though international sales were a second source of company growth, profits were down in that business because of its heavy investment overseas.

It was a good call. A year later, the stock had barely budged.

One last thought on this subject: As with everything when it comes to analyzing a stock, earnings trend lines are relative. So we also look at sales trend lines. If sales and earnings are growing at an even, complementary pace, then in all likelihood everything is in order. But if sales are shrinking, you can bet that earnings are going to, too, eventually.

In 1998, H. J. Heinz Company posted a tiny 2 percent decline in revenue (caused mainly by the strong dollar, according to the ketchup maker), yet earnings soared 165 percent. Strong sales of ketchup and tuna helped offset the decline in revenue, but so did a sweeping restructuring plan that called for 2,500 job cuts and the sale or closure of 25 plants by year's end. The next year, sales were still largely flat (up 0.1 percent), but net income plummeted 40 percent. The stock? It went into free fall for 15 months—down 46 percent—from late 1998 to early 2000.

How Do This Company's Numbers Compare with Its Peers?

During the steamy summer of 2001, Intel was looking like a relative bargain. The stock was down 61 percent from its 52-week high and it was trading at a trailing P/E of 37—well below its five-year trailing P/E high of 50. Ditto its price-to-sales ratio: At 6.4, Intel stock was trading smack in the middle of its median five-year range.

But put all that aside for a minute. How does the company measure up to its competitors as a business?

Look what happens in Table 8.1 when you compare Intel with Advanced Micro Devices (AMD), Analog Devices, and Texas Instruments.

Well, it beats everyone by size, certainly. The company's $5.4 billion in 2000 net earnings eclipsed its competitors by five times or more. That helps explain why on a PEG ratio basis, Intel was trading at a premium to its peers (Intel's PEG registered 2.93; Advanced Micro Devices carried a much more modest—and inexpensive—PEG ratio of 1.17). But the 23-plus percent return on equity at Analog Devices and AMD made Intel, at 14.6 percent, look shabby. What's more, Intel's net margins of 18 percent were just average for its industry. Analog Devices had a net margin of 24 percent. Finally,

TABLE 8.1   WHICH CHIP COMPANY MAKES THE BEST INVESTMENT?

	Company			
	Advanced Micro Devices	Analog Devices	Intel	Texas Instruments
Market Value (millions)	$5,754	$16,859	$195,287	$60,625
Revenue (millions)	4,556	2,880	30,444	10,749
Net Earnings (millions)	752	685	5,383	1,374
5-Year Sales Growth (%)	17.27	18.05	10.56	0.25
5-Year Earnings Growth	N/A	23.37	11.48	46.68
Net Profit Margin	16.50	23.80	17.70	12.80
Est. EPS Growth Rate	17.10	25.00	18.40	21.90
Forward P/E	20	36.2	53.8	52.2
PEG Ratio	1.17	1.45	2.93	2.38
Price/Sales Ratio	1.3	5.8	6.4	5.6
Price/Cash Flow Ratio	N/A	19.3	N/A	16
Price/Book Ratio	1.8	6.4	5.3	4.8
ROE	22.90	25.90	14.60	10.80
ROA	12.50	14.30	11.60	8.20

Source: SmartMoney.com; data as of late July 2001.

earnings growth at Intel didn't beat the average, either: Analysts were expecting Texas Instruments' and Analog Devices' earnings to grow by more than 20 percent over the next five years, yet they pegged Intel's long-term earnings growth rate at just 18 percent. By nearly every measure, Intel appeared less efficient, more expensive, and slower growing.

Are we saying you should sell Intel? Hardly. But we *are* saying that, if you wanted to invest in a chip company in the summer of 2001, there might be better places to put your money than the obvious choice.

For more on how to value stocks in this sector, see Sidebar 8.2, "Chip Shots."

Is Its Management a Bunch of Clowns?

Spending face time with CEOs and other top executives is a huge part of the job for many professional money managers. They want to get right up close and see what these people are made of.

Sam Stewart, who runs the top-performing Wasatch Core Growth fund, meets with management from every company he owns stock in—or is considering. After 25 years of running his own investment shop, he says, "You start to get a feeling as to whether the executives are straight shooters. Are they making sense? Does their strategy? Does their story add up?"

Stewart tells the story of a meeting he once had with a top executive at Provant, a workforce training and efficiency consulting company. The guy wouldn't make eye contact with him, Stewart recalls, and he was evasive when asked questions about the integration of recent acquisitions. So Stewart unloaded the stock. Within three months, Provant's profitability began to shrivel, and the stock fell 74 percent over the next 14 months.

Chances are you won't be able to meet personally with management, but there's no reason you can't keep tabs on its track record. Have executives delivered on promises to analysts and shareholders? Do they routinely keep Wall Street apprised of what's going on in their business?

The fact is, Wall Street rewards good management. Look at General Electric. In the 20 years former CEO Jack Welch ran GE, he never disappointed his investors. Welch led GE through a multidecade string of 8

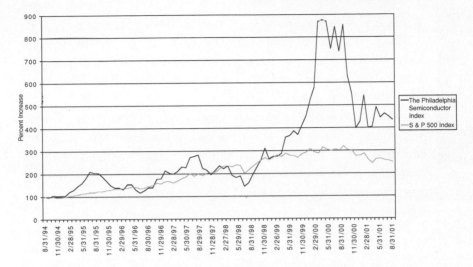

FIGURE 8.1   Chips Ahoy: The Rollicking Semiconductor Index
Source: SmartMoney.com. Reprinted with permission.

Chip Shots: Making Money on Semiconductor Stocks

Intel is easily the most famous—and the biggest—chip company in the world. And in the past 10 years, the stock has climbed an astounding 1,867 percent, or an annualized 112 percent a year. Many investors have made fortunes off the stock, or at least managed to place a down payment on a house, cover college tuition for their children, and maybe even fund a few trips to Europe and the Far East. But truth be told, the ride has been anything but smooth, and there were times when the downdrafts lasted longer than the upswings. (See Figure 8.1.)

"I think this is one of the toughest sectors to invest in. It's extremely volatile," says Shannon Reid, who heads the Evergreen Select Strategic Growth fund. "If you pull up a chart, over time [semiconductor stocks] have done very well, but boy do they jerk you around."

The problem is simple: supply and demand. Waves of demand drive the stocks upward just as waves of excess supply push them down. It happens over and over again and is as reliable a cycle as the change in seasons. As demand rises, supply works hard to meet it until eventually supply exceeds demand. An inventory glut hits and the industry spends months, sometimes years, using it up before the cycle starts all over again.

When it comes to picking a good semiconductor stock, knowing where we are in the cycle becomes just as important as understanding what the company actually makes—whether it is a computer processor chip or a memory chip or a high-tech telecommunications chip. For the downward cycles, as history has shown, always turn out to be excellent buying opportunities.

In our premiere issue, for instance, nobody had chip stocks on their minds. It was the middle of 1992, and the semiconductor industry had just finished a devastating year. That's when we recommended Applied Materials. "The business of this company is so technical that it has scared off investors," we wrote. What does it do? It builds the equipment that make chips. Over the next five years, its stock returned more than 800 percent, or an annualized return of 55 percent a year.

"It's counterintuitive," says Reid. "The best time to buy is when things look the bleakest and the best time to sell is when things look the strongest."

Here's what you should keep in mind when the time comes.

Inventory Levels

In June 2000, Reid and his team of portfolio managers attended a Bear Stearns tech conference. "Things could not have looked stronger," he says. Because demand had outstripped supply, companies were having to double and triple order just to ensure they got what they needed. "That's what happens when the cycle peaks." Indeed. By August or September, says Reid, "demand started to roll over and end-user customers ended up with way more supply than they had anticipated. That was the peak." It was also a signal to Reid to start selling.

There are two ways to go about this: You can measure the inventory levels of the chip manufacturers, and you can track what's happening to their end users. Why end users? Because they drive sales. Intel, for instance, makes microprocessor chips for computers. It counts all the computer companies as customers: Compaq, Dell, Gateway, and more.

Let's look at what happened with Dell and Intel stock in 2000. Both companies kicked off the year with double-digit gains in earnings and sales. But during the previous year, inventories had jumped even higher. Dell's leaped 43 percent; Intel's increased 52 percent. In none of the previous five years had such a sizable increase in inventory been recorded. A jump that high is a clear signal that the cycle is taking a turn and that the stocks are about to retreat a little. And that's exactly what happened. In 2000, Intel stock slumped 27 percent and Dell stock was a real dog that year, down a whopping 66 percent.

Valuation

It's an obvious cause-and-effect situation: When demand within the semiconductor sector begins to sink, pinching sales and earnings, the stocks sink, too. So one way to gauge whether a chip company has hit bottom is to look at the stock's trailing 12-month price-to-sales ratio relative to historic valuations. In mid-2001, the programmable logic device maker Xilinx traded at what looked like a very low price-to-sales ratio of 8.2. That's a mighty fall from its P/S ratio in 1999, when the stock was trading at 17 times the previous 12-month sales. But relative to its *historic* price-to-sales, 8.2 is huge. If you go back to 1998 and before, the highest Xilinx stock ever traded was 7.7 times sales; the lowest was 2.5 or 3 times sales. Knowing that, you can guess that it might be a while before that stock hits bottom.

Price-to-earnings ratios, by the way, won't offer a good picture of a chip company stock valuation. "You're best off buying when things look bleakest, and at that time the earnings might not be there, so the P/E looks high," says Reid. Conversely, when earnings are peaking—and thus the cycle is, too—chances are that's when the P/E appears low.

Position along the Food Chain

In the 1980s, chips were made for one thing: personal computers. In the next decade, however, the market exploded. Now chips are made for consumer electronics, cars, industrial equipment, and telecommunications equipment. The evolution of this sector hasn't changed the cyclical nature of the market, but it has made picking chip companies—and understanding all the various chips they make—a little more challenging. Here's what you should know:

At the bottom of the food chain you'll find the commodity-chip makers, like the dynamic random access memory (DRAM) maker Micron Technology. "These are very low-cost chips, which add very little value," says Reid. From there you work your way up the chain as the chips get more complicated and offer greater value, from computer microprocessor chips (the Pentium or Celeron, for example) to the communications chips made by PMC Sierra and Applied Micro Circuits. "These are proprietary products that require a lot of research and development," says Reid. "They command much higher prices and thus higher margins."

Each section of the semiconductor market, however, can suffer its own supply–demand hiccups. You have to understand what stage of the cycle your company's market is in before you invest—and that point may differ from where the rest of the semiconductor market is. Just as telecommunications chips were taking off in the first half of 1999, the DRAM market was in a total glut. So DRAM market leaders like Micron Technology were watching their stocks decline, while Applied Micro Circuits recorded a gain of 142 percent.

Product Cycles

Just as you want to keep an eye on chip company customers' inventory levels, you should watch their product cycles, too. For instance, Microsoft's newest operating system (Windows XP, launched in late 2001) could drive personal computer sales. Historically speaking, at times like that, Intel and AMD stock tend to do well (incidentally, Intel's Pentium 4 chip also should goose PC sales). And should the much-hyped 3G (third-generation high-speed) cellular phone technology ever take hold, we will most certainly see a boost in new handset sales. According to Merrill Lynch global telecom analyst, Adnaan Ahmad, the switchover to 3G phones could push handset sales up 15 percent in 2002, up from 9 percent in 2001.

percent-plus annual sales growth and consistent 13 percent-plus annual earnings per share growth. And of course there's the stock, which returned more than 3,500 percent under Welch.

As you try to assess the quality of a company's management team, look for clues in the company's performance. Is it consistent, like GE, or sporadic? Does it follow through on what it tells analysts after every quarterly report?

Another tip-off: How does it deal with a crisis? Johnson & Johnson's Tylenol tampering scare was way back in 1982, but it's still held up as the gold standard for how management should respond to a crisis—full disclosure, everything up front. The company issued an immediate recall, informed everyone about its investigation into the tampering, and worked with government to design a tamper-proof container. Shareholders rewarded the company for the deft way it handled the crisis: That year, in spite of the tragic incident (seven people died), J&J's stock climbed by 35 percent.

By contrast, when 42 Belgian schoolkids got sick after drinking Coke in June 1999, critics say Coca-Cola dragged its feet—which is one reason its stock declined 31 percent over the next 12 months. Coke issued a recall, but a top official didn't visit Belgium to apologize until 10 days later, and the company continued to downplay the situation for months. The fiasco was a contributing factor to the abrupt retirement of then-CEO Douglas Ivester six months later.

Does This Company Have an Urge to Merge?

There are times when even just a whiff of a merger and acquisition (M&A) rumor can send stocks soaring. In early 1998, when word got out that Netscape was in talks with several companies—the rumor included Sun Microsystems, America Online (AOL), IBM, and Oracle—shares rose as much as 25 percent in a single trading day. Netscape is now owned by AOL.

But over the long term, what does a merger really mean for investors? Usually nothing very good, especially when it comes to the company that's been acquired. Ultimately, most M&A transactions are just wheel spinning, according to a study by Timothy Loughran, an associate professor of finance at the University of Notre Dame. After examining the returns of M&A deals completed from 1979 through 1989, he found that the typical merger or acquisition didn't add to share value in the least. "It's a zero gain," says Loughran. "There's no effect."

Still, *some* merged companies actually do improve in value over time. Here are some indicators that, based on the historical evidence, should help you separate the good mergers or acquisitions from the bad ones.

Cash Is King

Stock is the currency of choice for deal makers these days; each of history's 10 largest transactions was a stock deal. But that doesn't mean it should be *your* currency of choice. The fact is, takeovers paid for with cash do much better for shareholders, Loughran found. In his study, shares in companies that engaged in friendly stock mergers lost 25 percent of their value within five years. When companies did hostile takeovers using cash, their shares gained an average of 62 percent in the same period. "If you were a manager and you felt your stock was undervalued, the last thing you would do is go out and use it to buy other companies," Loughran observes.

Welcome Hostility

Loughran and other students of the M&A business have concluded that, on the whole, hostile deals tend to work out better for shareholders than do friendly deals. What's behind their findings? "It's all about expectations," explains Mark Sirower, an M&A adviser at Boston Consulting. The market expects bigger changes and improvements when an unfriendly management comes in, and "major changes can signify long-term benefits." A hostile acquirer "is more prone to get rid of product lines, plants, and people that aren't creating value," adds Loughran.

High Premiums Suggest an Early Exit

The day AOL said it would buy Time Warner, shares of the latter stock jumped to $90 from $65, a 38 percent gain. Should investors have locked in those gains by selling? Probably.

"Just because you got a premium [over the market price] doesn't mean you're going to keep it," says Sirower. Indeed, a little more than a week after the announcement, Time Warner shares had dropped to $82. And AOL? Its shares had sunk all the way to $61, nearly a 20 percent fall.

As a rule, the more an acquirer pays over a stock's current market price, the more likely investors should take the money and run. "The higher the premium, the more management has to do to prove it was deserved and to keep it," says Sirower. Every quarter the expectation will be for the firm to increase savings or post larger earnings as a benefit of the merger. Even though former Booz-Allen vice-president John Harbison (now president of Raytheon Commercial Ventures) points out that there is no magic premium at which to bail out, current trends are making the decision easier: The average premium paid to shareholders in an acquired company has jumped to 82 percent, from 36 percent in 1990. In many cases—as with an overheated initial public offering (IPO)—you can buy shares later at a cheaper price if the merger is working.

Beware the International Merger

While going global may make sense on paper—remember all the hoopla surrounding Chrysler's merger with Daimler-Benz?—real benefits and savings often turn out to be elusive. Since those two automakers joined forces, the combined company's earnings have taken several hits from higher-than-expected integration costs. "Just putting together a collection of brands doesn't immediately create new value," explains Sirower. A study of 700 cross-border deals from 1996 through 1998 backs him up. Fifty-three percent of the deals resulted in lower share prices, according to international consulting firm KPMG. Thirty percent had no effect, and only 17 percent actually benefited investors.

Practice Doesn't Make Perfect

Plenty of today's best companies have built themselves by buying other companies. Again, let's use GE as an example. It has gotten so big in part because of the many takeovers it has engineered over the past 20 years. But that doesn't mean investors can go on autopilot because management has a few acquisitions under its belt. For every GE, there are plenty of managements that claim to be old hands at M&A but get their lights knocked out trying to pull off another deal. Cases in point include Cendant and Conseco, both of which have suffered huge share price declines due to acquisition hangovers.

What Is This Company's Biggest Weakness?

Every company has some kind of Achilles' heel. Your job as a stock picker is to figure out what it is and whether the company has made any moves to address it.

Sometimes a company's weakness is easy to pinpoint because it has to do with the company's industry: Gateway and Dell Computer are vulnerable to PC demand. Intel has to grapple with the semiconductor cycle. Pharmaceutical companies like Merck and Pfizer have to keep an eye on product pipeline and patent expirations. And occasionally the vulnerable spot is something internal: At GE, for instance, can new CEO Jeffrey Immelt *ever* live up to Jack Welch's reputation?

There will be times when you have to really dig to find a company's Achilles' heel. In the mid-1990s, for instance, HFS (later renamed Cendant) was buying everything in sight, and CEO Henry Silverman was considered a high-finance wizard for building—acquisition by acquisition—the hodgepodge group of brand names like Century 21 real estate company and the Days Inn lodging business. Earnings exploded 76 percent in 1996 and 100 percent in 1997. And the stock flew from $4 at its IPO in 1992 to $73.88 in late 1997. But the phenomenal growth—in early 1997, HFS posted its 18th consecutive record quarterly profit since its IPO—proved to be the company's Achilles' heel.

The problem was that to maintain that incredible growth, Silverman had to continue the pace of his acquisitions. At some point he would make a mistake. And he did—famously. For in early 1998, he closed an $11 billion deal with CUC International that proved disastrous after accounting irregularities forced the company to restate its earnings and shareholders filed suit against the company.

How Does the Current Economy Affect This Company?

Knee-jerk reactions to interest rate movements can be extreme: Witness the market action in early January 2001, when the Federal Reserve unexpectedly slashed the federal funds rate to 6 percent from 6.5 percent. Shares of investment banker Lehman Brothers shot up 17 percent, Goldman Sachs stock jumped 15 percent, and Citigroup shares rose 9 percent. That explains the old axiom: When interest rates fall, buy financial stocks. (See Sidebar 8.3, "Take It to the Bank.")

But what about other sectors? What kinds of stocks do well when interest rates rise? What kinds do better when rates fall? Here's a road map to investing with interest rates. Keep in mind, however, that being long-term investors, we wouldn't advise that you sell or buy a stock solely because rates are falling or rising. This is just another thing to take into consideration, along with the many others we've explained in this chapter, when you are buying a stock.

Falling Rates

A study of Fed rate cuts from 1980 to 1998 shows that, on average, health care companies gained 25 percent in the year after the initial rate cut. Retail and technology stocks rose 26 percent. The real slingshot? Broadcast and media stocks, up 28 percent. By contrast, the study shows that on average, a year after the initial rate cut banks had a respectable but less exciting gain of 15 percent.

Surprising? It shouldn't be, according to Lance Stonecypher, a senior equity sector strategist at Ned Davis Research, who conducted the study. "Look, a friendly Fed environment is bullish for the stock market because when rates come down, the cost of borrowing capital declines," he says. "The economy does better and growth stocks do better." The effect increases when rates are cut more than once.

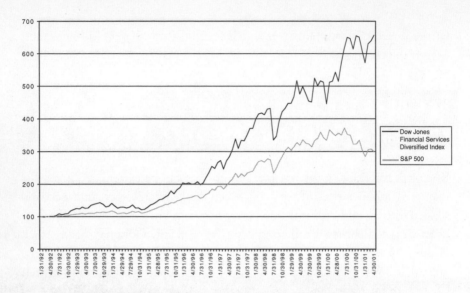

FIGURE 8.2   Where the Money Is: Financial Services Stocks

Take It to the Bank: Investing in Financial Services

SIDEBAR 8.3

It's been hard to lose money in financial services stocks over the past few years (see Figure 8.2)—and some of the industry's leaders have been nothing short of astonishing. Charles Schwab gained 330 percent from mid-1996 through mid-2001; Morgan Stanley Dean Witter was up 355 percent. Citigroup's shares soared 368 percent. You'd think we were talking about a bunch of high-tech company stocks.

Chalk it up to evolution. The landscape has changed a lot in the financial services sector in recent years. No longer are consumer banks limited to taking deposits and making loans, brokerage firms to just trading, investment bankers to corporate finance. Ever since Citibank merged with Travelers in 1998 and Congress dropped all barriers between banking and securities underwriting in 1999, it's been open season for consolidation. And it's not over yet.

It's basically a race for money. Baby boomers are in the wealth-generation phase, and that means there will be more money that needs to be managed. At the same time, there's the worldwide movement toward self-funded, 401(k)-type retirement plans (and away from government pension funds) as well as the growth of the capital markets. In the United States, 70 percent of all corporate funding comes from the capital markets, not bank loans. In Europe, it's the other way around—for now. "The capital markets are starting to open up," says Sean Aurigemma, manager of the top-ranking Morgan Stanley Financial Services fund. "Europe will look like America a couple of years from now."

Even so, it's important to remember that despite the move to merge, each subgroup of the financial services sector is different. Some, like credit card issuers and trust banks, fare better when the economy is growing. Others, lenders like thrifts and mortgage bankers, tend to rally during an economic downturn—and vice versa.

For that reason, we'll discuss the criteria for different kinds of financial services companies separately. But before that, there are some general things we can say about earnings growth for financial services firms as well as their valuations.

Growth

When it comes to financial services companies, there is such a thing as too much growth. "You want to be very careful when you see financial services companies growing rapidly," says Aurigemma. "You want to see strong growth, but you want to see that it's controllable." A bank growing its loan portfolio by 30 percent a year will most likely face severe credit risk down the road. He points out, "There hasn't been one that has grown loans 30 percent that has not blown up eventually." The average bank, including regional or diversified financials like Citigroup, tend to post earnings gains of 8 to 12 percent. Specialty finance companies, like American Express or Household International, grow at about 15 percent. Life insurance companies tend to grow about 10 to 15 percent a year (other insurance companies, like property and casualty, tend to be more cyclical, with 2 percent growth in some years and 20 percent growth over the next one or two years). And, finally, asset management firms—the ones with the best prospects, as it stands now, for long-term growth—generally post 15 to 16 percent annual earnings growth.

Valuation

"Across the board, most financial services companies have a hard time trading at a premium to their growth rate," says Aurigemma. On average in mid-2001, the entire financial services sector traded at 1.35 times its growth rate. But the typical bank stock traded at 1.43 times its five-year earnings growth rate—a premium that's basically the same for insurance companies. Specialty finance companies, however, trade at a slimmer premium: 1.26 times their long-term growth rates. In short, rare is the financial services company that trades at 2 times its earnings growth rate.

Now on to the smaller groups within the financial services sector.

Banks

This group includes everything from diversified financials (huge banks like Citigroup) to regional banks like Wells Fargo and Mellon Financial to mortgage lenders like Countrywide to savings and loans or thrifts like Dime.

Reserves

Every time a bank writes a loan, it has to keep a reserve in its cache in case the loan goes bad. It's like a rainy-day fund. But banks can get tricky with this money. Because a company has to take from its net earnings pile to add to its rainy-day fund, building a reserve account sometimes comes at the expense of earnings—or vice versa.

Some banks—in the interest of goosing earnings—will underallocate for their reserves. From the looks of Wachovia's second-quarter earnings growth for 2001, you might conclude the company is in fine shape: Diluted earnings per share climbed 74 percent to

$1.22 a share from 70 cents the year before. But in the meantime, its nonperforming loans have climbed 34 percent. And its net charge-offs have climbed 120 percent. Its reserves account? It's up only 13.4 percent.

Generally speaking, companies with a high reserve account—sometimes called the "provision for loan losses" or "allowance for loan losses" in the 10-K—will make a better bet, all other things being equal, than one with a low reserve account. The key is knowing how to measure the size of the loan-loss account. How do you tell if a reserve account is big enough? Read on.

First, how big is the bank's reserve account compared to its loan account? Look for the year-end reserve account balance—"allowance for loan losses" or "provision for loan losses"—within the 10-K tables. You'll want to check the total loan balance (or the average loan balance) in the 10-K as well. A bank holding $100 billion in loans and $2 billion in its reserve account has a reserve-to-loan ratio of 2 percent ($2/$100). And, all other things being equal, if Bank of America has a 1.2 ratio of reserves to loans and Wells Fargo has a 2.5 percent ratio, then you'd rather own Wells over BOA.

Second, how much has the bank set aside each quarter (or year, depending on whether you're looking at the 10-K or 10-Q) to build up its reserves? A bank builds its reserves through provisions—it's actually itemized in the balance sheet as "provision for loan losses"—a quarter at a time. If a company in a given quarter has set aside $5 million in provisions, but is writing off $5 million charges, then it has added nothing to its reserve account. This isn't a problem if it hasn't added any loans to its book. But if loan growth was $2 billion in that quarter, that means the company isn't covering its loans.

Alarm bells were raised at St. Paul Bancorp in 1999 when the bank's coverage of nonperforming loans fell from 399 percent to 227 percent. Meanwhile, nonperforming assets climbed 58 percent to $19.9 million from $12.6 million, and the bank hadn't made any provisions for loan losses in 1998. In fact, it even reversed $640,000 of previously booked loan-loss reserves and added it to income. Needless to say, the bank wasn't doing very well; that year earnings failed to meet analysts' expectations.

Keep in mind: The "best reserved" companies, as Aurigemma puts it, often trade at high P/E multiples because they are pouring money into reserves rather than writing them off as earnings.

Net Charge-Offs

Every bank has some delinquent loans on its books (called nonperforming). So every quarter, a bank has to write off a portion of its nonperforming loans. To find the net charge-off in the 10-K or 10-Q, look for a table that starts with "Allowance for Loan Losses." Beneath that you'll find "Loan Losses" and then "Loan Recoveries." Don't pay attention to the figure that reads "Total Loan Losses"—that doesn't include payments that the bank has received on its nonperforming loans. What you want is the figure that reads "Net Loan Losses."

Okay. How much is the bank charging off quarter-to-quarter or year-to-year? Is the sum trending higher or lower, or is it the same? The net charge-offs at First Union, the nation's sixth largest bank, grew 8 percent in 1999 and more than 9 percent in 2000. It's no wonder: The bank's nonperforming assets grew 51 percent over that two-year period (the biggest chunk of which was a large problem credit to a single borrower). Was the bank in trouble? Well, it certainly had a lot of work to do. Earnings fell off a cliff in 2000 (to 12 cents a share from $3.33 in 1999).

Next, compare the net loan losses to the total balance of the reserve account. How many years (or quarters if you're looking at the 10-Q) in charge-offs will the reserve account cover? (Take the balance of the reserve account and divide it by the net charge-offs.) You want a reserve account that covers about 2.5 to three years' worth of loan losses, says Aurigemma. For example, at the end of 2000, Bank of America had $6.8 billion in reserves, about the same amount it had at the end of 1999. But net charge-offs in 2000 ($2.4 billion) climbed 20 percent from 1999 ($2 billion). As a result, the balance of the allowances for loan losses compared to the net charge-offs from year to year dropped to 2.85 from 3.41 the previous year ($6.8/$2.4 and $6.8/$2, respectively).

On an absolute basis, that doesn't look good for Bank of America. And compared to its competitors, BOA looks even worse. At

S I D E B A R   8 . 3

Wells Fargo, for instance, the ratio of reserve balance to net charge-offs climbed to 3.04 in 2000 from 2.99 in 1999. And Firstar, now U.S. Bancorp, has an impressive ratio of 4.03, down slightly from 4.3 in 1999.

Also, what's the ratio of the net charge-offs to the total loan portfolio? (Some banks do this calculation for you, and you'll find it in the annual report, again with the table that lists "allowance for loan losses.") You can use the ratio to compare one bank to another.

U.S. Bancorp, formed when Firstar acquired U.S. Bancorp in February 2001, reported a ratio of net charge-offs to total loans of 0.35 percent for its 2000 fiscal year. That's nearly half the ratio of Wells Fargo, which clocked in at 0.76 percent, and much better than Bank of America, which reported a ratio of 0.61 percent in its 2000 10-K.

Management

"With financial services companies," says Jim Catudal, the manager of the top-ranking Fidelity Select Financial Services fund, "management has the discretion to decide how much they'll put in reserves and how much to treat as earnings in a given quarter. So in some respects, management competence is very, very important because a financial company can hide problems for a long time and then all of sudden they surface. That might be true of all companies, but it's especially true in financials."

It all boils down to how aggressively managers treat the numbers. Catudal offers this tip: Look at reserves to get a clue about how aggressive or conservative management is. "If reserves are stable or increasing, that can be a sign of conservatism," he says. "If management is being aggressive to make earnings—they're taking money out of reserves to make current earnings," he adds, then you have a more aggressive management team on your hands.

Where Are We in the Economic Cycle?

Bank business can rise and fall in step with the economy for obvious reasons: When times are good, people's wallets are fatter. So they're saving money (and stashing it away in a savings bank) or they're spending more money on a new car or a new house (and they'll need loans). A slowdown may not mean problems, says Catudal, "but if we move into a bad recession, credit is going to be a problem." As the country settled into a recession in 1990, for example, the Dow Jones Money Center Bank index dropped 32 percent.

Interest rates can pose a problem, too. Bank stocks tend to closely track interest-rate movements—albeit in the reverse; when rates rise, bank stocks fall and vice versa—because of the effect rates can have on credit quality, capital market business, loan originations, and net interest margins (the spread between interest-earning assets and a bank's borrowing costs), all of which affect bank earnings.

The more diverse a bank's assets, the better protected it is from market swings and interest rate moves. This is what makes one-trick ponies, like subprime home or auto lenders, more volatile than, say, a savings and loan, which is making all kinds of loans—school, home equity, auto—as well as accepting deposits for savings accounts. In the early 1990s, stocks in subprime lenders were red-hot: In 1995, stock in the Money Store quadrupled in nine months. Aames and United Cos., both subprime mortgage lenders, climbed 300 and 250 percent, respectively. But all they do is originate one kind of loan—to borrowers with credit problems—bundle them together, and sell them to larger companies. In 1998, when Russia defaulted on part of its debt and the hedge fund Long-Term Capital Management blew up, many went bankrupt. "About 20 companies closed down all at once," says Aurigemma.

Insurance

"Insurance companies are even more complicated than banks to analyze," says Catudal, "and it's really a black box because what they do when they write an insurance policy is make assumptions over the next 60 years. And those assumptions can be good or bad." Nevertheless, there are a few aspects of an insurance company's year-to-year or quarter-to-quarter business that you can examine on your own—in conjunction with the typical fundamental analysis you'd do for any other company, of course.

Combined Ratio

"For an insurance company, this is probably the most important thing," says Catudal of the combined ratio. That's because the combined ratio—sometimes referred to as the combined loss ratio or the loss ratio—is a picture of the company's health. It takes into account the premiums a company has taken in over a given period, minus the claims and expenses it's had to shell out, plus any money it has made from investment income. "It's basically your total income," says Catudal. Calculating it yourself is possible, but it's a dreadful task. You'll find the ratio computed for you in the 10-K or 10-Q. A combined ratio below 100 is good because it means the company is taking in more premiums than it's paying out in claims or expenses.

Meadowbrook Insurance Group, the parent company of Star Insurance and Savers Property & Casualty, saw its combined ratio deteriorate to 112.1 percent in the first six months of 1999 from 91.7 percent during the same period in 1998. Meanwhile, Meadowbrook's pretax income fell to negative $1.1 million in the first six months of 1999 from positive $9.7 million the year before. The stock slid steadily in 1999, moving down 52 percent over that 12-month period.

Where's the Bond Market?

When an insurance company pulls in its premiums in a given year, it typically sets aside a chunk in reserve against any future claims it may have to pay, just as a bank would set aside reserves against its loans. Most of the reserve gets invested in bonds. "In general the bond market is more important to investment income than the stock market," says Catudal. So watch out.

In 2000, junk bond defaults rose to 5.7 percent of the $600 billion outstanding—the highest rate since 1991. And in the insurance industry, life companies are most at risk because they tend to invest more in junk. The average life insurer had 4.8 percent of its $37.6 billion investment portfolio in junk at the end of 2000, according to Salomon Smith Barney. Some companies carried even higher exposure. American Express had 11 percent of its portfolio in junk. Lo and behold, in its first quarter in 2001, AmEx took an 18 percent hit in earnings because of a $185 million loss in its insurance unit's investment portfolio, mostly because of junk bonds.

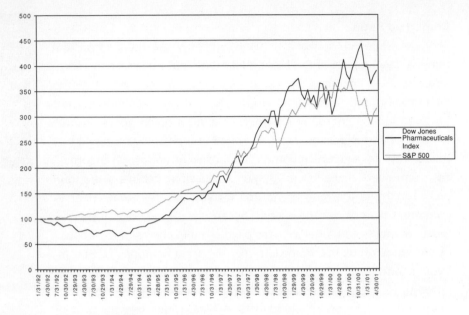

FIGURE 8.3   Drug Stocks: High Risk, High Reward

On Drugs: Cashing in on Pharmaceuticals

They may lack the glamour or the hyper-growth of some biotechnology firms, but even so, pills are big business.

Gross profit margins for the top five U.S. companies average 90 percent, and sales and earnings have climbed by nearly 10 percent in recent years. What's more, despite the slowdown in annual increases in drug prices—to just 3 percent a year from 7 to 8 percent in previous decades—innovative new drugs have driven up per capita prescription drug spending 125 percent in the past decade. With an aging population expected to drive health care expenditures even higher, national spending on prescription drugs is predicted to more than triple to nearly $366 billion in 2010, according to the Health Care Financing Administration.

"The outlook is strong for the health care sector. There is no doubt," says Liu-Er Chen, who manages the top-performing Evergreen Health Care fund. "We've accumulated in the last 10 years a great deal of knowledge about genomic, antibody technology, and we have a much better understanding of important diseases, like cancer and Alzheimer's. It is just a matter of time before a lot of new products will come from pharmaceuticals."

Before you jump in, however, it helps to understand from the get-go that drug stocks suffer from a bit of a split personality. They're part defensive in nature. People always get sick. No matter what the economy is doing or whatever else is going on in the world, we'll still need medicine. But they're growth stocks, too. Pharmaceutical company earnings are expected to grow by 25 percent for the next few years, according to Zacks. That's faster than the average 13 percent earnings growth expected for the S&P 500. As a consequence, drug stocks tend to trade at a premium to the market (in mid-2001, the industry carried a price-to-earnings average of 33; the S&P 500, 24), and they tend to be more volatile as well. But as you can see from Figure 8.3, that volatility has been rewarded with huge gains.

Choosing the best drug companies to buy at any given time is not easy, but if you know what to look for in a drug company—in addition to all the other fundamentals that go into stock picking—you can do it, too. We suggest you start with four basic elements:

1. *A strong new-product pipeline*. Drug stocks have traditionally moved in tandem with expectations for new drugs in development, sometimes even when it's just one hot new drug in the works. We'd stay away from these companies. A few years ago, investors bid up the company Vivus in anticipation of its impotency drug Muse. But when a production snag hit in 1997, the stock fell by 31 percent in a single day. Instead of gambling on the regulatory and testing process, choose companies with enough new products in the works that one or more of them are likely to succeed.

2. *Few patent expirations.* Stocks tend to anticipate patent expirations. In the middle of 1997, Merck's stock was beset by anxiety over the loss of patent protection for Vasotec and Mevacor, two of the company's most successful products. That year, the stock finished up 33 percent, but it spent most of the 12 months bouncing between $45 and $50—and it sorely underperformed its rival Pfizer, which finished the year up 80 percent.

Some drug companies—like Bristol-Myers Squibb—try to get around patent expirations in court by issuing the drug in a new dosage or by claiming it cures another illness as well. But this is just putting off the inevitable. If the company has one or two new products in its pipeline that promise to be big sellers, that can cushion the blow of a blockbuster about to lose its patent. However, if there's a one- or two-year lag between upcoming patent expirations and new products hitting the market, the company could be looking at sagging earnings until sales pick up again.

3. *Strong research and development*. Research scientists create the product pipeline—and the better the scientists, the greater likelihood of successful new products. While it can take an average of 12 years to go from discovery to Food and Drug Administration approval, stocks move much more quickly in anticipation of a successful new drug. Investing in a scientific team backed by strong R&D spending is the best way to get out in front of the product pipeline. In 2000, Pfizer and Eli Lilly both spent in the range of 15 to 18 percent of sales for research and development, but when you look at the actual sum of money expended, the difference is astounding. Pfizer, a much bigger company, spent $4.4 billion; Eli Lilly spent $2.0 billion.

4. *Market power*. "No matter how good a product is, if a company doesn't have the sales force, or market power, to sell it, then no one will buy it," says Liu-Er Chen, the Health Care fund manager for Evergreen Investments.

These days, you can't open a magazine or even turn on the TV without spying an advertisement for some new drug. This was unheard-of 10 years ago. But increasing competition has changed the game. Today, a strong consumer brand name isn't enough. A drug company has to have the sales force to sell its products. Pfizer, for instance, has more than 8,100 sales representatives in the United States alone—about one rep for every 85 physicians, according to Merrill Lynch. If each rep makes eight sales calls per day, Pfizer can theoretically reach every physician in the country in two weeks.

Okay. So where are you going to find all of this information?

You're going to want to keep on top of the news with this sector. Not only are things always changing, you can make some big money by staying ahead of the curve. In mid-1996—two years before Pfizer's blockbuster sex pill Viagra became widely available—every paper from *USA Today* to the *Buffalo News* and the *Arizona Republic* was buzzing about the impotency cure-all. Alert investors who snapped up shares then would have seen their investment climb 238 percent by the time the drug hit the market in mid-1998.

Besides just reading the news, you'll want to keep up with the company's announcements. Johnson & Johnson, for instance, has a web site that's pretty helpful. You'll find an updated list of products it has in the pipeline, as well as how far along they are in clinical trials. And Merck's 10-K is a great source of information. Not only does it have a helpful history of the drug industry, but the company will also tell you which products are losing their patents in upcoming years as well as how much revenue each drug generated in the latest fiscal year.

Rising Rates

Common sense will tell you that the kinds of stocks that do well when rates are falling—growth stocks like technology—will do badly when rates rise. That's exactly what happened in 2000, when rates were on the rise: According to the Russell indexes, technology stocks plunged almost 35 percent in 2000.

But why is that?

Look at it this way: When rates are on the rise, it usually means that the economy is slowing down. So growth sectors suffer, as do stocks that rely on consumer confidence, like home builders, specialty retailers, mortgage lenders, and savings and loans.

What kinds of stocks outperform? So-called defensive sector stocks that generally resist stock market declines (although they ordinarily move up more slowly in a bull market): utilities, energy stocks, pharmaceutical companies and drugstore retailers (see Sidebar 8.4, "On Drugs"), and consumer cyclicals (like apparel). For instance, consumer staple companies rallied 20 percent in 2000, as investors looked for companies whose earnings might hold up in an economic downturn. After all, people need food no matter what the economy does.

9

SPECIAL TOPICS FOR TODAY'S INVESTORS

At its core, the *SmartMoney* style of stock picking is all about hunting for undervalued companies. As we've noted, this is simply the best way to build wealth. But we also recognize there are going to be times when you've already *found* the stock you want to buy—and it seems hopelessly overpriced. Should you throw caution to the wind and jump in anyway? Or should you wait?

In this chapter, we'll share one strategy for picking the right time to get into a stock. We'll also touch on three other investing strategies you may come across as you wade into the market: options trading, buying stocks on margin, and selling a stock short (that is, betting it will go down, not up).

Bull's-Eye: Setting Target Prices

It's too late. That's what you tell yourself time and again as yet another great stock soars to yet another record high, and all the while you've been sitting on the sidelines, thinking you've missed the boat. Microsoft at $93? Too expensive, you decided in early 1998. Nine months later it was at $150. Intel selling for $110 in the fall of 1996? No way it could sustain that price, especially during the biggest slump to hit the semiconductor industry in years. But two years and a 2-for-1 stock split later, it was up 136 percent.

With some stocks—great, well-managed companies operating in a growth industry—it's almost never too late. Even if you missed getting in on the ground floor of the past decade's most powerful performers (Dell, America Online, and Cisco Systems) and bought them instead when they were well into their upward climb, you could have done pretty well.

Of course, you would have done better still if you had kept a close watch on these stocks and bought them when they took periodic dips. Even the best stocks have their bad days, and if you believe in the underlying strength of a company, those bad days are the times when you should jump in.

In the mutual fund business, this process is sometimes called setting a target price (and not, as some cynics might charge, wishful thinking). A number of top managers do it, albeit informally. Bill Miller and his team of analysts at Legg Mason watched Silicon Graphics for nearly a year before they bought it after waiting to get in at the right moment. When they first noticed the workstation and supercomputer company in turnaround (its computers created the dinosaurs used to make *Jurassic Park*), the stock was trading at around $14 a share. "We were interested, but not enough to buy it," says the firm's Lisa Rapuano, a portfolio manager and director of research. A few months later, new management stepped in, and the price was up to $16. The folks at Legg Mason backed off the stock once more. But when the market correction hit in the fall of 1998, Silicon Graphics dropped to $8 a share. Rapuano promptly bought the stock. The stock climbed all the way to $20 in the next year.

Of course, hindsight is 20/20, and it's easy to look back at these stocks and tell what the optimum time was to play catch-up if you had missed out at the beginning. It's much harder to project that process into the future.

So how does one figure out when—at what price—to step into a hot growth stock? One approach is to look at the historical trading pattern of each stock—its price movement, as well as its trailing price-to-earnings ratios—relative to the S&P 500.

First, the price movement. Ask yourself this: Over the past five years, whenever the stock took a hit, how far did it tend to fall? Ten percent, 15 percent, or 20? You'd be surprised how consistent some stocks are when they fall (outside of fundamental reasons or a long-drawn-out downturn in the market). The drug company Merck tends to fall between the high teens and the mid-20s, and in the past five years it has never dropped more than 33 percent (see Figure 9.1). General Electric usually gives back anywhere from 10 to 25 percent (see Figure 9.2). Intel's range hovers typically around 30 percent, but in the tech crash in late 2000 it dropped nearly 53 percent (see Figure 9.3).

FIGURE 9.1   Merck—Daily Closing Price

FIGURE 9.2   General Electric—Daily Closing Price

FIGURE 9.3   Intel—Daily Closing Price

You can analyze each company's P/E ratios over the past five years and compare them with the five-year P/E history of the S&P 500. At what premium to the S&P 500 did each company trade on average? What was the maximum premium? What was the minimum? Starting with the average premium for each stock—and after adjusting for any bad years that would have brought the multiple to a deceptively low level—you can calculate a multiple that would lead to an ideal target price.

To do this on your own, you'll first need a three-to-five-year historical pricing list, which you can do on www.siliconinvestor.com or Yahoo! Finance. Keep in mind the major market corrections over that time. How has the stock reacted to these crises? How far has the stock, on average, fallen?

When we looked at the trading history of Microsoft, we noticed that it tends to fall 30 to 40 percent. It fell 33 percent in late 2000, for instance, as the Nasdaq took its record 60 percent plunge, and it fell nearly that much in late 1998, as well, during the tech sell-off. (See Figure 9.4.)

Then you'll need the five-year trailing P/E range, which you can get from the stock screener tool on MSN's Money (moneycentral.msn.com). You can look up the P/E five-year average, as well as the high and the low through its stock screener database. As of midsummer 2001, its P/E was 48, well below its five-year high. Sounds like Microsoft stock is a relative bar-

FIGURE 9.4   Microsoft—Daily Closing Price

gain, right? *Whoa.* Before you jump in, figure out when in the past five years Microsoft has traded with a P/E as low as 20.4. How does that time compare to this time?

The stock most recently carried a low-20s P/E back in 2000 (something we figured out by taking yearly trading highs and lows, and the annual actual earnings posted by the company). At the time, interest rates were falling and the economy was slowing down precipitously. What's more, using Standard & Poor's Stock Reports, which include a table that reports the P/E highs and lows in each calendar year, we noticed that the stock has traded in the low-20s range five times in the past 10 years—in the years 1993 to 1996 and in 2000. All of which means a low-20s P/E is not unusual for Microsoft stock, especially when the economy is slowing down and interest rates are falling. Given the economic situation in mid-2001, we'd be buyers if the P/E were anywhere between 25 and 35, or $48 to $67 a share.

Here's how we arrived at our target price range: In mid-2001, analysts expected the company to post $1.92 in earnings for its current fiscal year ending June 2002. A 25 price-to-earnings multiple would put the stock at $48 ($1.92 multiplied by 25). A 35 P/E puts the stock at $67 ($1.92 multiplied by 35).

What Are Your Options?

When you hear the phrase "stock options," what's the first image that pops into your head? Some people think of goateed tech moguls who parlayed generous employee stock-option grants into millions of dollars. Others think of goateed tech moguls who were burned when their once-valuable stock options suddenly became worthless.

But employee stock options are only one kind of stock option—and a relatively minor one at that. While employee stock ownership plans (ESOPs) are private contracts negotiated between companies and their employees, there's an entire class of stock options that trade on public exchanges just like stocks. And you don't need a Fu Manchu to buy them.

More than 500 million options contracts change hands every year at places like the Chicago Board Options Exchange (CBOE), the American Stock Exchange, and the International Securities Exchange. Since each option contract is worth at least 100 shares of an underlying stock or index, you get a sense of the staggering size of the U.S. market. And it's expanding all the time.

The trouble is, options are expensive, complicated, and risky. They've gotten a bad name because individual investors too often wade into these markets without enough experience and get thoroughly soaked. The CBOE, the world's largest options marketplace, has been teaching individual investors the nuances of options trading for years via an educational effort called the Options Institute. In most cases, its students are far from investing novices. "Our research shows that the average investor will spend somewhere between eight and 10 years trading equities before they become comfortable enough to step out into equity options," says Terry Haggerty, a senior staff instructor.

Under certain circumstances, however, options can be beneficial. And our intent here is just to get you familiar with how these financial instruments work. So, let's go over the basics.

Options, Not Futures

First of all, some people confuse options contracts with futures contracts, since they're both derived from underlying commodities, currencies, or financial instruments like Treasury bonds or stocks. But there are important differences. A futures contract is a legal pact in which the purchaser agrees to buy or sell a certain amount of the underlying instrument at a set date in the future. That makes them incredibly risky, because the holder is required to live up to the contract no matter what's happened in the market.

For instance, a soybean farmer might agree to sell 5,000 bushels of beans in November 2001 for $50 a bushel using a futures contract from the Chicago Board of Trade. The upside for the buyer could be great, but the downside could be devastating. For example, if the market price were to sink to $45 by the time the contract expired, the person who agreed to buy soybeans from our farmer at $50 a bushel in November 2001 would lose $5 a bushel for a total of $25,000. We advise individual investors to stay away from futures altogether.

Option contracts, by contrast, give buyers the option of exercising the contracts at their own discretion. In other words, they offer a choice. There are options on stocks, bonds, commodities, interest rates, and currencies. For our discussion we'll stick with stock options, since that's what most individual investors are interested in.

When you purchase an option, it gives you the right to buy or sell a certain number of shares of the stock in question at a predetermined price (the "strike price") before or at the contract's expiration date. For this right, you pay the seller a fee, called a "premium," which is a tiny fraction of the shares' market value. During the life of the contract, you control the shares in question. Contracts can last anywhere from one month to three years. (Options more than nine months in duration are called long-term equity anticipation securities, or LEAPS. They trade just like options.)

Puts and Calls

There are two kinds of option contracts: a put and a call. A put is an option that gives the buyer the right to sell the underlying stock; a call is an option giving the buyer the right to buy the underlying stock.

People generally use puts to hedge their bets. They're paying money now for the right to sell a certain number of shares later at a price agreed on today. Say, for instance, that in mid-2001 you bought 100 shares of General Electric at $41 a share, and you wanted to protect against a big drop in that price. You could buy a January 2003 put at a strike price of $30. That would give you the right to sell 100 shares of GE at $30 at any time until the contract expires, thereby minimizing your potential losses on the stock you bought at $41.

The premium on that contract in mid-2001 would have been about $145. If GE were to fall to, say, $15 by December 2001, you could exercise the option and get out of the position at $30. You'd still lose $1,100 on the stock ($41 minus $30 for 100 shares) and $145 on the option premium, but without the option you would have lost $2,600 on the stock alone ($41 minus $15 for 100 shares). Of course, the reverse could happen, too. If the stock goes up to $95, you wouldn't want to exercise the option at all, and it would expire worthless. In that case, you'd have spent $145 on unnecessary protection.

Call options are contracts in which the buyer pays for the right to purchase shares at a certain date in the future. These are often used to take a long position in a stock without actually buying the shares now. For instance, say you think General Electric is going to climb but you're not sure you want to bet everything on that possibility. In mid-2001, you could have bought a January 2003 call option with a strike price of $55 for around $180, giving you the option of buying 100 shares for a fraction of their market price.

If General Electric were to shoot up to $100 in December 2002, you could exercise your option and buy the 100 shares of stock for $55, then turn around and sell them at $100, earning a profit of $4,320 ($4,500 in stock market gains minus the $180 option premium) on your $180 investment. It would be a different story, however, if the stock sank below $55 and stayed there until 2002. In that case, your option would expire worthless (you wouldn't want to exercise it and take a big loss), and you'd have lost your $180 premium.

Are They Worth It?

Our feeling is that puts and calls are generally too expensive to do individual investors much good by themselves. But there are some strategies that make sense if you want to manage your risk in certain short-term situations.

If you still think you have what it takes to venture into the market, we recommend you spend some time checking out the CBOE's Options Institute and the Option Industry Council's web site (www.optionscentral.com).

There you can read about puts, calls, straddles, strangles, and all sorts of exotic options plays in detail.

We can't emphasize it enough, however: Options are incredibly complicated and can be highly risky. They're not for the faint of heart. Novice investors should stick with stocks, plain and simple. Buying your average tech company is risky enough.

At the Margins

Double your profits, double your fun. That's what margin trading is all about. You borrow some money, add it to your own, put it on a stock that's going up, and—presto! You're rich!

Unless, of course, the stock goes down. Then you find yourself doubled over in pain—not unlike that time you crapped out in Vegas.

Margin trading isn't gambling per se. And the fact is, a margin strategy executed prudently can pay off big. But you have to know what you're doing and accept a huge amount of risk. What follows is an introduction to get you started.

What Is Margin Trading?

Think of margin as a loan from your broker. It allows you to purchase more shares of a stock than you'd be able to with the paltry sum stashed away in your own bank account. When you open a margin account (it doesn't matter whether you trade online or off-line) your broker will ask you to sign a contract called a margin agreement. Usually you'll be required to make an initial investment of at least $2,000 (though some brokerage firms require higher minimum investments). And once you've opened the account, you can then borrow up to 50 percent of the purchase price of a stock, as long as you have enough money in your account to cover the balance.

Here's an example. Let's say you want to buy $20,000 worth of Microsoft stock, 50 percent of it on margin. That means you need to have at least $10,000 cash in your account, allowing you to borrow the other $10,000. Just like a bank, your broker will charge you interest on the loan. Rates vary between firms and can depend on the balance in your account.

You can usually keep the loan out as long as you want—with a couple of provisos. First, when you finally sell the shares of stock in your margin account, you'll immediately have to pay back the money you borrowed plus interest and any trading commissions. (You keep the remaining profits.) Second, if the value of your portfolio falls below a certain threshold, the brokerage reserves the right to "call" the loan, meaning you have to pay back enough of what you borrowed whether you want to or not. This ominous event is referred to as a "margin call." We'll talk more about that later.

For now, though, let's focus on the fun part—exaggerated profits. Imagine Microsoft suddenly skyrockets. Overnight, the $20,000 in stock you bought jumps 30 percent to $26,000, and you're feeling flush. If you decided to sell those shares and book profits, you'd be sitting on $16,000 in returns. You'd owe the brokerage the $10,000 (plus fees and interest) you borrowed, but you'd get to keep the extra $6,000. That's double the $3,000 profit you would have earned had you bought just $10,000 worth of Microsoft stock. See what we mean? Double your pleasure.

The Grim Reaper

Now you know why buying stocks with borrowed money has become so popular. You juice your profits, and your broker earns interest. When the market is rising, buying on margin is a win-win scenario for investors and brokers alike. But what about when the market is falling? Does that mean you lose money twice as fast?

Correct.

Let's say PC sales grind to an absolute halt and Microsoft plunges 30 percent in a day. Your $20,000 stake dwindles to about $14,000 in the blink of an eye. If you were to sell those shares, you would be forced to pay back the $10,000 loan (plus interest and fees), leaving you with just $4,000. Had you invested $10,000 only (and avoided the margin loan) that 30 percent loss would have left you with $7,000. Not good, but not devastating, either.

It gets worse, much worse. With a normal investment gone sour you can at least take comfort in the notion (however thin) that your losses are paper losses, at least until you sell the stock. Maybe your $10,000 has become $7,000, but so what? If you wait long enough, Microsoft stock is likely to recover, and you'll be back in business.

With margin investing, though, you may not have that choice. As we mentioned, your brokerage reserves the right to call your loan if the value of your equity falls below a certain threshold of the account's total value. The minimum maintenance requirement established by the National Association of Securities Dealers (NASD) and the exchanges is 25 percent of the current value of the account. But most brokerages use a higher number—maybe 30 percent—and it can go even higher than that if you buy some very volatile stocks like Yahoo! and Amazon.com.

In our example, that means you have to sell your shares and pay back your brokerage immediately. Here's why: Say your firm's margin requirement is 30 percent. That means your equity in the margin account (the account's market value less whatever you owe on your loan) must be 30 percent of the account's current value. When that Microsoft stock fell 30 percent, your total account fell to $14,000 and your equity (measured as $14,000 minus the $10,000 you owe) dropped to $4,000. Since that $4,000 is only about 28 percent of the $14,000, you would be subject to a margin call, meaning you have to either liquidate your account to pay off the loan or put up more money to satisfy the margin requirement.

But beware: When the markets are tumbling quickly, you may not get a margin call at all. Your broker might just liquidate your account for you. Most margin agreements give brokers the right to sell off a customer's margin account without notice if such a move is necessary to protect the broker's capital. In fact, that scenario happened quite frequently during the big tech sell-off in April 2000. Many brokerage firms like TD Waterhouse didn't wait the customary three-day period for investors to deposit additional money into their accounts. Instead the firms liquidated accounts without warning.

More Than 100 Percent?

The worst-case scenario (and not a rare one) is when you lose more than 100 percent of your original equity. Consider the case of this New Jersey investor, who asked to remain anonymous. The very first time he bought stock on margin, his broker had recommended he buy shares in a computer hardware and software marketer called Multiple Zones, now called Zones, Inc. The company had just signed an agreement with Amazon.com to be one of the charter merchants on its auction web site, and the future seemed bright.

It wasn't. "I bought it high and it went straight down," the investor says. He snatched up $16,500 worth of the stock for $16.50 a share—$8,250 of his own money, $8,250 on margin. He then watched the stock plummet 62 percent, to $6.25, in a matter of months. The $16,500 shrank to $6,250. That means he had to sell the stock and pony up another $2,000-plus just to pay back the $8,250 he borrowed and pay all the interest.

"It is the one investment you can make where you can lose more than 100 percent of your principal," says Joe Grunfeld, a financial consultant with Merrill Lynch.

Crafting a Strategy

So if margin investing is so perilous, should average investors simply avoid it altogether? Not necessarily. But as with any investment, you have to know what you're getting into and whether you can afford it—both financially and psychologically.

Steve Kaye, a financial planner with New Jersey–based American Economic Planning Group, says an investor who buys stock on margin must always be mindful of the downside risk, even when the markets seem to be heading straight north. You have to be able to "withstand a worst-case scenario," which means you can afford to lose everything. He suggests that you calculate exactly how much you stand to lose before making any investment. Then you should keep some cash on the side to cover any potential deficiency. (Sounds pretty much like the old casino strategy: putting $200 in your pocket and playing until the sun comes up or your money's gone.)

It goes without saying that you should never put money you need for anything from retirement to the down payment on your house in the account. Restrict yourself to "risk money," or money you can afford to lose. The key is to remember that margin is a tool, not a winning lottery ticket. In good times, it can help you make a little more money and buy some of those stocks you've been eyeing for a while. But in bad times, it can cost you a bundle.

The Short End of the Stick

Leave it to Wall Street to figure out a way to profit from a falling stock. It's called "selling short," and it's becoming increasingly popular among individual investors. It works like this: Say an investor analyzes Intel and decides that all signs point to a decline in the stock price rather than an increase. Intel is trading at $100 a share, so the investor borrows shares of the stock at that price—typically from his or her broker—and immediately sells them. After the stock falls to maybe $80 a share, the short seller buys it back on the open market to repay the debt. But since the price is lower, the short seller pockets the difference—in this case $20 a share.

Of course, if the price goes up from the original price, the short seller loses big time. And that's the real danger of selling short. If you buy a stock and hold onto it (that's called being long a stock, in Wall Street parlance), the most you can lose is what you paid for the stock. But if you sell it short, your losses are theoretically unlimited! The higher the stock goes, the more you lose since you have to repay the debt eventually at the market price. So we would suggest most individuals stay away from short selling, tempting though it may be when you come across a stock that's obviously overpriced.

That said, it is worth keeping an eye on professional short sellers, and here's why. There are entire companies devoted to selling stocks short and they make it their job to seek out companies that are in trouble. They pore over financial statements looking for weaknesses. But sometimes they merely think a company is too highly priced for its own good. The stock exchanges track "short interest" in a stock and report it each month so other investors can see what these short sellers are up to. You can see the short interest for any company by pulling up its stock snapshot at SmartMoney.com.

A high (or rising) level of short interest means that many people think the stock will go down, which should always be treated as a red flag. Your best course is to check the current research and news reports to see what analysts are thinking. But high short interest doesn't necessarily mean you should avoid the stock. After all, short sellers are very often wrong.

The short interest ratio, meanwhile, tells you how many days—given the stock's average trading volume—it would take short sellers to cover their positions (i.e., buy stock) if good news sent the price higher and ruined their negative bets. The higher the ratio, the longer they would have to buy—a phenomenon known as a "short squeeze"—and that can actually buoy a stock. Some people bet on a short squeeze, which is just as risky as shorting the stock in the first place. Our advice is this: Use the short interest ratio as a barometer for market sentiment only, particularly when it comes to volatile growth stocks. If you really want to gamble, you're probably better off in Vegas.

10

LESSONS FROM THE PROS

oday it's easier than ever for individual investors to manage their own portfolios, right in the comfort of their own homes. We hope that's a message that comes through loud and clear in these pages.

But there's no denying that the great professional money managers have resources we individuals can't ever hope to share (not the least of which is simply their experience). So your goal, as a nonprofessional, should be to learn as much from these pros as you can.

In the following pages, we'll profile a handful of the most extraordinary money managers today—the great Warren Buffett, Bill Miller of Legg Mason, Bill Nygren of Oakmark Funds, Kevin Landis of Firsthand Funds, and the team behind most of the Janus funds.

You'll notice that while all of them seek quality companies with good management and strong growth prospects, none of them tackle stock picking in exactly the same way. Yet they all do share one characteristic: Over time, they beat the market.

Warren Buffett

The Manager

Buffett, 71, has been managing money since the mid-1950s, when value master and mentor Benjamin Graham hired him, for $12,000 a year, to work for the Graham-Newman fund. But he's most famous for building Berkshire Hathaway, a business best described as a holding company with subsidiaries in diverse enterprises like insurance and reinsurance (GEICO and General RE), newspapers (the *Washington Post*), and food companies (See's Candies and Coca-Cola), among others. In that sense it's like a mutual fund, except that the shares trade on the stock exchange, and some of the companies in the portfolio are privately held, while others trade publicly.

His Track Record

Since 1965, Berkshire Hathaway stock has outpaced the S&P 500 in all but four years (1967, 1975, 1980, and 1999). In that time, per-share book value—the difference between assets and liabilities divided by the number of outstanding shares—has grown from $19 to $40,442, a gain of 23.6 percent compounded annually. The overall gain over that time: 207,821 percent; in the S&P 500, 5,383 percent. The Omaha, Nebraska, company ended 2000 with $3.3 billion in net income, a debt-to-equity ratio of 0.07 percent, and $5.2 billion in cash. (See Figure 10.1.)

His M.O.

Given his unrivaled track record, you'd think it would take a genius to understand his methodology. Not so. The basic approach, which he learned from Benjamin Graham, is to look for companies that are so cheap that they are free of risk—like buying $1 worth of stock for 50 cents.

Buffett did better than that on some deals. In 1973, for instance, when he first started buying shares of the *Washington Post* (of which he still owns 1.7 million shares), he figured the company's assets—the *Post*, four television stations, *Newsweek* magazine, and newsprint mills—were worth $400 million. But the stock market was valuing the entire company at

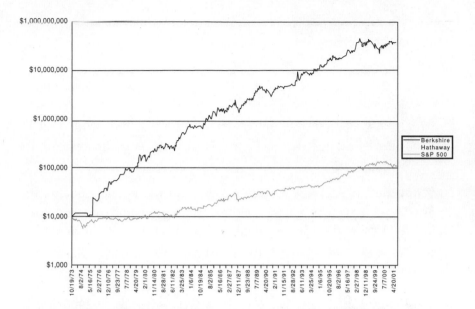

FIGURE 10.1   Capital Appreciation of $10,000 Invested in Berkshire Hathaway versus S&P 500, 1973–2001

$100 million. His investment in the company has climbed 9,590 percent in the past 28 years.

Over the years, Buffett would stretch the theory a little. For instance, when Buffett made his first investment in Coca-Cola—he acquired $1.02 billion worth of stock in the spring of 1988—a Wall Street analyst termed it "a very expensive stock," according to *SmartMoney* contributing editor Roger Lowenstein in his book, *Buffett*. But Buffett recognized that Coca-Cola—a simple business—had an asset that wouldn't appear on its balance sheet. It had a brand name. And he was right. Within three years, his investment had more than tripled to $3.75 billion. (And in the past 13 years, despite its misadventures in recent years—New Coke, the Belgian schoolkids disaster—Buffett's investment has climbed 8,382 percent.)

These days, value isn't at the top of Buffett's list. Here's the list of six criteria that he published in Berkshire Hathaway's 2000 annual report:

1. Large purchases (at least $50 million of before-tax earnings).

2. Demonstrated consistent carning power (future projections are of no interest to us, nor are "turnaround" situations).

3. Businesses earning good returns on equity while employing little or no debt.

4. Management in place (we can't supply it).

5. Simple businesses (if there's lots of technology, we won't understand it).

6. An offering price (we don't want to waste our time or that of the seller by talking, even preliminarily, about a transaction when price is unknown).

Still, Buffett is clearly a value player. And the recent economy has spurred Buffett to go on a shopping spree lately; he completed eight acquisitions in 14 months. Two economic factors played a role in this: First, many managers and owners experienced near-term slowdowns in their businesses. It's a near-term outlook that doesn't scare Buffett. "The declines make no difference to us, given that we expect all of our businesses to now and then have ups and downs," Buffett wrote in the 2000 annual report for Berkshire Hathaway. "We don't care about the bumps; what matters are the overall results." But it scares other people, "which can both spur sellers and temper the enthusiasm of purchasers who might otherwise compete with us."

That said, Buffett was able to make some great deals in 2000. He spent $8 billion (97 percent in cash, the rest in stock) for the eight businesses, and all told they generate $13 billion in sales. Talk about a bargain hunter. And truth be told, he didn't have to go looking very hard: "Our acquisition technique at Berkshire is simplicity itself," he wrote in the annual report. "We answer the phone." Or they check the fax machine.

In November 1999, Buffett received a one-page fax from a face from the past (an airplane broker who had sold Berkshire a jet in 1986 and who, before the fax, had not been in touch with Buffett for 10 years). Attached was a *Washington Post* article that described an aborted buyout of Cort Business Services, a leader in rental furniture, primarily for offices but also for temporary occupants of apartments.

Buffett knew nothing about Cort. But he immediately printed out its SEC filings and, as he puts it, he liked what he saw. The company had a net worth (assets minus liabilities) of $206 million at the end of the third quarter in 1999; sales grew at 11 percent in the first nine months of that year, net income at 26 percent. In the previous year, Cort had $318 million in sales and $25 million in net income. Plus, it was throwing off $90 million in net cash from its operating activities.

At the time, Cort was in trouble. It was a small-cap (Cort had a market cap of about $250 million in November 1999) old-economy stock—the opposite of what investors wanted back then. Since it peaked in April 1998, Cort stock had dropped nearly 60 percent to about $20 a share. In an attempt to revive the stock price, in March 1999 the company entered an agreement with an investor group and some Cort top executives to buy out the company for $24 a share. But that deal fell through in early November. Enter Buffett.

Six days after the fax came through, Buffett was sitting down with Cort CEO Paul Arnold. "I knew at once that we had the right ingredients for a purchase: a fine though unglamorous business, an outstanding manager, and a price (going by that on the failed deal) that made sense." He was willing to pay $28 a share for the company—about $384 million—a premium to the stock price at the time, which still hovered around $20.

Less than three months later, the deal was done. Buffett purchased Cort for Wesco Financial Corporation, a Berkshire Hathaway 80 percent–owned subsidiary, for about $386 million in cash. (But not before an 11th-hour offer from a rival furniture company whose previous bid earlier in the year had been rejected by Cort's board. The new offer, for $29.50 a share, tempted Cort's board and they wanted Buffett to raise his bid. But Buffett refused.) It's the fourth furniture retailer in Berkshire's portfolio.

How much will Cort add to Berkshire's bottom line? As with most Buffett acquisitions, it will take some time before anyone knows for sure. But it's worth noting that in the 15 months following the acquisition, stock in Berkshire Hathaway's Wesco Financial unit was up by 40 percent.

The Last Word

"We like to do business with someone who loves his company, not just the money that a sale will bring him (though we certainly understand why he likes that as well)," Buffett wrote in his latest annual report. "When this emotional attachment exists, it signals that important qualities will likely be found within the business: honest accounting, pride of product, respect for customers, and a loyal group of associates having a strong sense of direction."

Bill Nygren

The Manager

Nygren was head of research for Harris Associates, which runs the hugely successful Oakmark fund family, when he was given his own portfolio, Oakmark Select, in March 1996. He was so successful that when former star manager Robert Sanborn left the flagship Oakmark fund in 2000, Nygren stepped in. All told, Nygren, now 41, oversees $7 billion in assets. He's been with Harris Associates since 1983, when he joined as an analyst two years after getting his master's in finance from the University of Wisconsin.

His Track Record

Nygren has led the Oakmark Select fund to an annualized 31 percent five-year return. Since he took over the top position at the family's core fund, Oakmark, it has regained its position among the top 2 percent of all value funds. (See Figure 10.2.)

His M.O.

Like other value managers, Nygren seeks companies that have fallen out of favor. But that's where many of the similarities end. Using conventional value measures, for instance, Nygren would have surely skipped Chiron, a biotech firm that specializes in vaccines and blood testing. Trading at a P/E of 45 in mid-1999, it looked expensive. But Nygren found that earnings were depressed because Chiron was spending heavily on research and development. Since Nygren started buying it at $25, the stock has jumped 96 percent. "Despite our price sensitivity," he explains, "we're looking for growing businesses, not decaying or distressed business with low P/Es."

If a company can fulfill three criteria, it will eventually find its way into one of Nygren's funds: It has to be a value, it has to be growing, and management has to have a strong record of success and of putting shareholder interests first.

Nygren's definition of value hinges on what he calls a company's "business value." To calculate this number, he'll divide a company's so-called enterprise value (the market value of the company, plus its debt, minus its cash) by its

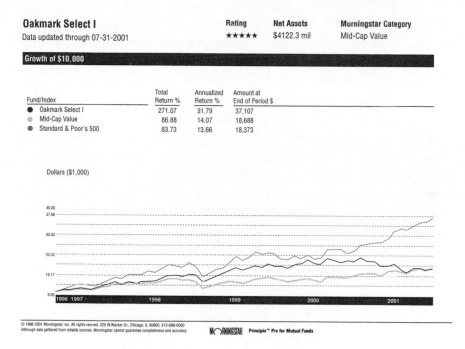

Oakmark Select I
Data updated through 07-31-2001

Rating	Net Assets	Morningstar Category
★★★★★	$4122.3 mil	Mid-Cap Value

Growth of $10,000

Fund/Index	Total Return %	Annualized Return %	Amount at End of Period $
● Oakmark Select I	271.07	31.79	37,107
● Mid-Cap Value	86.88	14.07	18,688
● Standard & Poor's 500	83.73	13.66	18,373

Dollars ($1,000)

FIGURE 10.2   Oakmark Select I Fund
Source: Morningstar. Reprinted with permission.

earnings before interest, taxes, and amortization (EBITA). This gives him, in his view, a more accurate price-to-earnings ratio. "The P/E ratio is so highly influenced by a company's balance sheet—how much debt or cash it has," says Nygren. "The methodology we use levels the playing field." For Nygren to buy a stock, it must be trading at less than 60 percent of its business value.

On the growth side, Nygren looks at sales and earnings growth—though that's "just the starting point," as he puts it. What he really wants to see is growth that's being produced efficiently (i.e., without spending a lot of cash to get there). "Some companies will have to raise money to finance the growth, and that will reduce the growth rate of their business value," he says. "On the other hand, some generate heavy per-share cash. That boosts the per-share earnings."

Got all that? Here's an example that should help. Back in mid-1992, Nygren was taking a close look at Kendall, an old-line hospital supply company (famous for Curad bandages) that had suffered serious financial problems in 1990. But now, a turnaround was in the works: It hired a new, capable CEO with a good track record at two other companies. And it was, by Nygren's definition, a value trading at just six times forward earnings.

The only question was growth in business value. Nygren felt that sales could grow steadily at 6 or 7 percent. "Nothing very exciting; it was Curad—not a lot of new demand for bandages." But because of better expense management, Nygren had a hunch that EBITA would grow at better than 10 percent because of margin improvement. He also figured that better control of inventory and receivables would mean the company could support its sales growth without having to reinvest earnings back into the business. Instead, it could pay off the company's $300 million debt. "Our belief was that the [debt level] over three years would fall to $175 million." The combination of improving EBITA and a stronger balance sheet meant an estimated long-term EBITA growth of 20 percent. Nygren bought the stock in August 1992 at $16, and in July 1994 Tyco International acquired the stock for $55. Nygren's total gain in less than 24 months: 244 percent.

The final measure is management. "Everyone says, 'We want a strong management team running the company.' And we do, too," says Nygren. "But just as important to us is seeing its economic goals: Is it in line with shareholders? Do its stock options and incentive plans focus on driving equity value?" Nygren would be much happier with an incentive plan dependent on seeing an improvement on return on capital within a business division than one that's focused on getting top-line sales growth. "That doesn't help the shareholder."

So Nygren and his team of researchers will examine a manager's track record—even go as far as looking at previous job performance. They'll also pore over proxy statements to see what kind of "economic" commitment the management has: How much company stock do they own? How many options? What's the exercise price on the options? What kind of incentive plan is in place—what variables is it measured on and what levels do they have to achieve? All of this information, by the way, is public information that's filed with the SEC.

One of the reasons Nygren loved Kendall, for instance, was the new CEO, Richard Gilleland. When he joined, he instituted a new rule on purchase orders: Each one had to come across his desk. "He felt if it was inconvenient enough that if it weren't really important [his employees] would find a way not to have to do that." What's more, his own fortunes were tied to the firm: "He made a comment to me," says Nygren, "my all-time favorite from any CEO: 'My daughter and I own 6 percent of this company. At a P/E of 17 times, each dollar that Kendall wastes is a dollar off our net worth.' That appealed to us because we highly value management being aligned with shareholders."

Even today, Nygren won't buy unless he sees that kind of commitment. He had rejected buying shares in the troubled toy store Toys 'R' Us until recently primarily for one reason: "It wasn't that the stock was too expensive. It was a lack of confidence in the people," says Nygren. "We could never get comfortable that management was either solving problems or had interests that were in line with shareholders." Then along came John Eyler from FAO Schwarz. Here was someone who had a track record (he had masterminded a turnaround at FAO Schwarz). And Nygren felt he understood what needed to be fixed. Even better, he had a big options package and even personally purchased more stock when he joined the company. That's when Nygren bought the stock—in early 2000—and through mid-2001 it had gained nearly 90 percent.

The Last Word

"If all three criteria line up, then we can have the benefit of a very long time frame," says Nygren. "We'll expect to hold a stock for five years or longer knowing not only is the stock cheap today, but also its business value is growing and management is going to make decisions in the shareholders' interest. Then it doesn't matter when the market recognizes the value. Over the long term, we'll make money."

Kevin Landis

The Manager

Landis, 40, launched his first mutual fund, Interactive Investments Technology Value, in May 1994 with his then-partner Ken Kam. That fund, now called Firsthand Technology Value, is just one of six in the Firsthand Funds family, five of which fall under Landis' purview. Before that, Landis had never managed money; he was a new-products manager at chip maker S-MOS Systems and previously had worked at Dataquest, the research firm, as an analyst.

His Track Record

By the time the Firsthand Technology Value was old enough to have a three-year record (in mid-1997), its average annual return was 56 percent, better than any other mutual fund in existence at the time. But like everything else in technology, it has stumbled recently, with a three-year record of 27 percent in mid-2001; but still, that was better than 87 percent of all other tech funds. And it remains wildly popular—it has $4.6 billion in net assets, which makes it the third largest tech fund in the country (after T. Rowe Price Science & Technology and Fidelity Select Electronics). (See Figure 10.3.)

His M.O.

Landis starts out by identifying trends he thinks will be most powerful over the next four to five years.

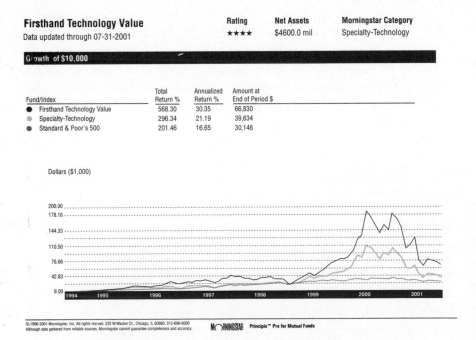

FIGURE 10.3   Firsthand Technology Value Fund
Source: Morningstar. Reprinted with permission.

Like cell phones: "These days it seems like everybody has a cell phone, but they're just using them to talk to each other. Over the next five years, people will use their cell phones for much more than talking to one another," says Landis. "A good strong trend can be stated that easily."

Or digital cameras: "Sometime over the next five years, it will be really hard to find a store that sells you film," says Landis, "because so many people will switch over to digital cameras."

Once the trend has been identified, Landis gets the lay of the land. "We ask ourselves what does the emerging ecosystem and the food chain look like, who's involved and at what levels?" In the cell phone business, for instance, you'll have the companies that build the handsets, obviously. But also there are the companies that provide components that go into the handsets, the software that runs inside the handset, the networking technology, and services to the service providers. "When technology is commercialized, it involves a lot more companies working together than you might think at first glance."

Naturally, one trend might have 10 or more different offshoots. That's why Landis starts "peeling the trend." Within cell phones, for instance, there soon will be location-based services. Call 911 almost anywhere in the United States and an emergency operator will be able to pinpoint where you are. Or a buddy list—your phone alerts you if you're within proximity to someone on your list. "We might come up with two or three more—say voice recognition—and each one has different companies involved in that technology."

But which of those companies has the most attractive position? Consider the early days of the personal computer. "I can recall working at Dataquest and listening to analysts argue about which was the best PC company to buy," says Landis. "The answer was to buy Intel and Microsoft—not any of the PC companies."

So once Landis and his Firsthand team have targeted the trend and the players within it, they try to zero in on the company with the most leverage. "Who's got the negotiating power?" he asks. "Who's the Microsoft and the Intel?" Defensibility is another issue: "Who has the ability to hang onto what they've won?"

At this point, they have a list of companies to work with. They cull the list further by focusing on companies with strong management teams. And they still have to do the conventional analysis, running through the companies' numbers while asking themselves: How big can this company get? How much can the company cash in on? How much in revenue and profits can this company generate a year or two out? This requires a fair amount of projecting, but says Landis, "This doesn't have to be precise. Whatever you come up with will be wrong a little bit. You have to make the best effort to guess what they're capable of."

The key is to find companies that are growing but don't cost a fortune. "We're not that much different from anyone else once it comes to looking at numbers," says Landis. "We like growth at a reasonable price. We're trying to get them before they're everyone's darling."

Getting in early is Landis' forte. One of his current favorites, for instance, is a California chip company named Zoran. In the three-plus years he has owned the stock, he has made 76 percent on his investment. "It's been out there quite a while," he says, "and it's never gotten any attention." Only five Wall Street analysts cover the stock, according to Zacks. And that's just how he likes it.

Landis first picked up the scent of Zoran back in the mid-1980s, when an investment banker friend who had worked on the IPO told him about it. But the company was a military applications business—specifically radar. Landis wasn't interested—he wasn't managing money, either.

Ten years later, when another friend suggested he take another look at it, Zoran, which had just been motoring along, suddenly looked poised to hit the jackpot. The Santa Clara, California, company had moved into the consumer market selling its chips to be put into DVDs and digital cameras. At the time—1996—both of those markets were modest growth stories. Landis saw potential but wasn't going to pounce until mainstream players like Disney started really pushing DVD titles.

"It was all just a matter of Zoran standing at the plate and swinging until they hit a home run," says Landis. "They were supplying the basic building blocks to all consumer electronics companies, which were going to eventually have products in the sweet spot. As soon as that happened, Zoran was going to go along with them for the ride."

That time came in the fall of 1998. Zoran started shipping its DVD chips in volume—counting Fujifilm, Lucent, and Sony Electronics as some of its customers—and Landis made his first purchase of Zoran in February 1999 at $19.50 a share. It was a bargain when you backed it up against Firsthand's expectations: According to Ken Pearlman, Firsthand's director of research, they expected at least 35 percent earnings growth— "to be conservative, assuming no market share gains and severe pricing pressure"—with upside to as much as 100 percent. "For the upside, we were looking at the potential to gain share, the penetration of the China market, and the expectation of them entering the rapidly growing digital camera market." Even as the stock hit lows of $8 in 1999, Landis continued to pick up shares.

They were right: The DVD market (in units sold) doubled in 1999 and 2000. In 2000, the stock traded into the mid-$70s.

It has faltered lately (what hasn't?), and the stock was trading in the mid-$30s in mid-2001, but Landis still sees 50 to 60 percent growth over the next two years. Only 12 percent of all American households had DVDs in 2001, whereas video VHS machines had a 92 percent penetration. And Zoran's share of the chip market has grown to 35 percent from roughly 25 to 27 percent in 1999.

"You can see the opportunity there," says Landis. "I don't think anyone is buying videotape machines anymore. They'd better not be." And don't forget Zoran's digital-camera chip business, he adds, which isn't as big as the DVD market, but it's growing just as fast—in the neighborhood of 60 percent this year.

The Last Word

"Don't swallow somebody else's idea," Landis says. "Go out and rent *Boiler Room* if you want to know why. You're going to have to dig deep on your own. You're looking for players that are well positioned in a powerful trend. Great technology companies do something that's essential, unique, and therefore defensible."

Bill Miller

The Manager

Bill Miller manages the five-star Legg Mason Value Trust, and he is the CEO of Legg Mason Funds Management. After college (Washington & Lee, class of 1972), Miller served as a military intelligence officer overseas, then pursued a Ph.D. in philosophy at Johns Hopkins University. Before joining Legg Mason in 1981, he was treasurer of the J. E. Baker Company, a manufacturer of products for steel and cement companies. At Legg Mason, Miller served as director of research from October 1981 through June 1985. In late 1999, he assumed overall responsibility for management of the firm's equity funds. The Value Trust fund opened in 1982, and Miller comanaged it for two years until late 1990, when he took over as lead manager. He also runs the Legg Mason Opportunity Trust fund, which opened in 1999. All told, he manages over $24 billion in mutual funds.

His Track Record

On an annualized basis, Legg Mason Value Trust's 10-year return of 18 percent sounds impressive, even enviable. But the consistency of his returns is what's truly awesome: Miller's Legg Mason Value is the only fund in the country that has outpaced the S&P 500-stock index every single year from 1991 to 2000 (plus the first eight months of 2001). (See Figure 10.4.)

His M.O.

How does he do it? The truth is, he doesn't. He and 17 other analysts do it together. Relying on a team that's heavily staffed is the only way Miller's way would work, because it is incredibly research-intensive. On a basic level, Miller looks for undervalued businesses that trade at significant discounts to what he thinks they are worth. But the way they arrive at that worth is multifaceted. You've read already about how some top value investors establish their estimate of a company's intrinsic value using a favorite valuation tactic—enterprise value, or book value, or acquisition value. Miller's way is to employ all of them—and every other methodology he can think of—to assess a company's intrinsic value before he'll invest.

Part of Miller's edge may be his keen understanding of the S&P 500. It is an index, and thus passively managed in that the stocks in it don't change very often. And its stock-selection criteria are fairly simple: adequate trading liquidity, at least three years' operating history, companies that are largely representative of one industry. But why is it, then, that active managers, on average, fail to beat it? That's the question Miller figured out long ago.

"It's the implicit rules they use when they make additions to the index,"

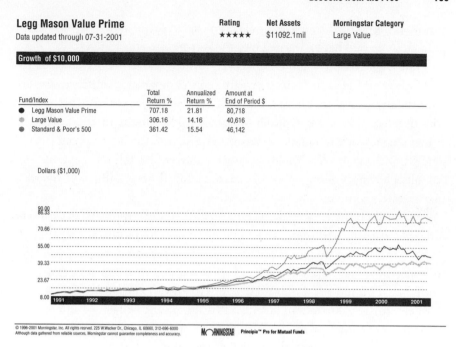

Fund/Index	Total Return %	Annualized Return %	Amount at End of Period $
● Legg Mason Value Prime	707.18	21.81	80,718
◌ Large Value	306.16	14.16	40,616
● Standard & Poor's 500	361.42	15.54	46,142

FIGURE 10.4   Legg Mason Value Prime Fund
Source: Morningstar. Reprinted with permission.

says Mary Chris Gay, a senior vice president at Legg Mason who has worked with Miller for 13 years. Rather, it's that there aren't any rules.

For instance, macroeconomic factors never influence decisions about what companies are included in the index. If the Fed is raising rates, the S&P isn't going to purge the index of its utility companies. (Many retail fund managers, on the other hand—some very successful—will make multiple portfolio moves based on what's going on in the economy.)

In addition, there aren't any constraints on investment style (growth or value), nor are there limitations on the size of a position—so a single company can make up 20 percent of the index if it grows that big. Plus, the index, despite its 500 companies, is heavily concentrated on the largest stocks. Fifty names make up more than 60 percent of the index," says Gay. What's more, turnover has averaged a slim 7 to 10 percent since 1957. "The average fund manager has turnover of over 120 percent," she says.

Having surmised this much about the S&P 500 index—what Miller considers his competition—it should come as no surprise that he has incorporated some of what he learned into the way he runs his funds.

The Legg Mason Value fund has very little turnover—an average of 10 to 15 percent a year. It focuses on large-cap companies that are leaders in their industries and that have a competitive advantage over their peers. It is concentrated: There are typically only 35 to 50 stocks in the portfolio. When a new stock is added, Miller makes a significant bet of about 2 to 3 percent of the portfolio. Finally, as stock analysts, the folks at Legg Mason will observe what's going on in the economy, but it never influences the way they research companies or select stocks.

When it comes to actually picking stocks, Miller's approach is very traditional. Starting with companies that have shown profitability, earnings growth, and strong balance sheets, it begins in most cases with a screen tied to historical valuations. "We try to identify a group of companies that look cheap based on historical measures," says Gay, using P/E, P/B, price to cash flow, enterprise value to EBITDA, and ROE, among others. "The past is a guide to the future," says Gay, "but it's more important for us to try to understand where the future value is of the company."

This is where Miller and team move into the qualitative stage of their research: They build elaborate models in an attempt to come up with a company's intrinsic value—the underlying value of a business separate from its market value or stock price. And it's safe to say they don't have one tried-and-true method.

They are perhaps most well-known for analyzing companies on a discounted cash flow basis. That is, they build financial models that estimate annual free cash flow for two periods—a forecast period (say the first five years) and a final year's cash flow, which is then assumed to recur annually or grow at a particular rate into perpetuity. Then they take each yearly cash flow and discount it back to the present (given that a dollar today is worth more than a dollar tomorrow). Because the analysis is based on a series of assumptions about the future, Miller's analysts will map out different scenarios, each of which has a set of assumptions and a particular probability, to determine the "central tendency" of valuation.

But in truth, discounted cash flow isn't the only way they analyze companies. They employ as many other methodologies as they can think of. What's a company worth if it were to be liquidated? If it were sold off in parts? What is it worth if you were to own the entire company privately? What would another company pay to acquire it or merge with it? "We try to minimize the number of things that could go wrong," Gay explains. "We want to understand the bear case as well as the bull case. We truly focus on the difference between the potential for outsized gains and the potential for losses."

What they want is a company that's able to generate excess cash flow, earn high returns on capital, and allocate its capital efficiently. Many studies have shown, says Gay, that "there's a very high correlation between companies that can earn and sustain returns on invested capital relative to their cost of capital and a subsequent rise in the market value of that company.

If a company's stock trades 50 percent below the "central tendency" of its intrinsic value, then Miller is a buyer. "That's to incorporate a margin of safety of what we believe the company is worth on a three-year time horizon and what we think it's worth today," Gay says. Once a stock makes its way into the portfolio, it usually stays in for 7 to 10 years. But the truth is, it often takes a little time before it starts to pay off. Many times, in fact, the stock keeps heading south.

Waste Management, for instance, was a stock Miller first picked up in early 1999, when it was trading in the mid-$40s. But that year, the stock kept dropping—to around $17 by December—and Gay says, "We were heavily criticized." In 2000, however, the stock rebounded 60 percent and became one of the best-performing stocks in the portfolio last year. As of mid-2001, Waste Management was the company's largest holding.

Of course, in the process, numbers aren't everything. Part of Miller's strategy hinges on a subjective take on the company's story as well. When most of the companies you're analyzing are Wall Street's rejects, that's only natural.

When Miller came upon Waste Management, the company was totally on the outs. Amid an accounting-irregularity scandal, the entire management team had been dismissed and the stock dropped 56 percent between April and July 1999. But when Miller and his team analyzed the company, they realized that it was well-positioned—No. 1—in an industry that had high barriers to entry. And in a meeting with the company, the new management team laid out plans to improve its return on invested capital: They were going to sell off unprofitable units. "The company's strategy piqued our interest," says Gay.

And then there's AOL. First of all, it's hardly what you'd call a value stock; in many ways, it's the quintessential growth stock. But when Miller started eyeing the company, the stock had fallen more than 60 percent. This was back in the fall of 1996, when the company changed to its one-price structure and a flood of subscribers logging on stalled the servers. Critics predicted the demise of AOL, claiming that soon the time would come when people wouldn't pay for the services anymore—they wouldn't have to—and the problems with logging on were like the company's deathblow. But Miller's analysts discovered that despite the complaints and the gloomy forecast for AOL's services, its customers weren't quitting the service. "The churn rate among the customers was low," remembers Gay. "And 80 percent of the traffic stayed within the service—they weren't getting on the Internet. This led us to believe that the type of services AOL offered online were very attractive to customers. They were providing a lot of value."

That's why the analysts decided to break apart the company's numbers. And instead of looking on a per-subscriber basis—as all the Wall Street analysts were doing—Miller and his team looked at the advertising revenue. "Companies were paying to place their banner ads on AOL, and those carried 100 percent margins and had grown 100 percent in one year," says Gay. Realizing this could drive returns at the company, they bought the stock. In a relatively short period of time (about a year), AOL's advertising revenue came to represent 80 percent of its cash flow. Miller's investment in AOL grew 4,700 percent before he cut back his holding in the stock significantly—to less than 4 percent of the portfolio from 12 percent—in late 1999 and early 2000.

Getting out is another Miller forte. (In the 18 months after he trimmed his AOL shares, the stock dropped 40 percent.) Maybe that's because he brings the same thoroughness and discipline to selling stocks as he does to buying them. "Our sell discipline is how we control risk in the portfolio," says Gay.

Miller will sell when a stock has reached its Legg Mason–derived intrinsic value. Or if a better investment comes along—something that offers a better risk-adjusted rate of return. Or as Gay says, "When there's a misjudgment on our part, or when something external changes, say legislation that affects the business or the valuation."

In late 1999 and early 2000, many of the fund's tech holdings—stocks it had acquired in 1995 and 1996—began to hit their estimated intrinsic value, and Miller sold them. AOL was one; Dell was another. Miller bought the Texas computer company in the first quarter of 1996 and watched his investment grow by 15 times by 2000. But that's when the stock, close to $60 a share, started to hit the top of Legg Mason's estimated fair value of between $45 and $60. So Miller started shedding shares. "It went from 6 percent of the portfolio to 0.9 percent of the portfolio," says Gay. And it was perfect timing. The stock hit a high of just over $59 in March 2000 and started to sink from there—it hit $30 in September. (When it fell below $20 in December, that's when Miller started to get back in. Nine months later, Dell stock had climbed nearly 50 percent.)

The Last Word

"We do not believe that carving the world into 'value' or 'growth' is a sensible or useful way to think about the investment process," Miller wrote in a recent letter to his shareholders. "Growth is an input into the calculation of value. Companies that grow are usually more valuable than companies that don't. If a company earns below its cost of capital, though, then the faster it grows, the less it's worth. Companies that earn returns on capital above their cost of capital create value; those that earn below it destroy value."

The Janus Team

The Manager

It'd be easier if there were one single star at Janus whom we could highlight. But truth be told, this Denver fund family, arguably the most successful growth house in the country, is chock full of them. Among its most celebrated managers: Helen Young Hayes of Janus Overseas and Janus Worldwide, Scott Schoelzel of Janus Twenty, Warren Lammert III of Janus Mercury, David Corkins at Growth and Income, and Blaine Rollins at the flagship Janus fund.

Their Record

For a time in the late 1990s, fewer than 14 percent of all domestic equity funds beat the S&P 500, yet every single Janus domestic equity fund was among them. Even with the spill that growth stocks have undergone recently (some of the funds had negative returns in the 20 to 30 percent range for the 12 months ending mid-2001) that statistic still holds. Over the past three years, most of Janus' equity funds (those old enough to have three-year records) have outpaced the S&P 500. Even the international portfolios. What's more, fully 7 of the 12 funds in Janus' stable with three-year records fetch four or five stars from Morningstar. No other fund family comes close to that kind of record. (See Figure 10.5.)

Their M.O.

The secret to Janus' modus operandi is team research. The team—including portfolio managers and analysts—numbers somewhere over 50, according to Lammert, and each member contributes every step of the way. Think of Janus as a giant investment club. "Because we work as a team, there's a lot of collaboration," says John Schreiber, who was an analyst for three years be-

FIGURE 10.5   Janus Mercury Fund
Source: Morningstar. Reprinted with permission.

fore he began running the Janus Fund 2 in 2000 (he was an analyst at Fidelity for two years before that). "And the communication is very natural because all of the analysts are interested in learning more and making good stock picks and helping the portfolio managers succeed."

It's typical, says Schreiber, to have one analyst say to a neighbor in the office, "Gee, one of the companies I called today is a supplier to one of your companies, and did you know . . . ?" Of course there are other places analysts go to generate ideas: They read the financial press and analysts' reports, trade journals, attend industry conferences, and talk to analysts, company managers, suppliers, and customers. Basically they pay attention.

There's not much magic in that. But Janus sets itself apart when it starts digging. "It might be neat to sit down with the CEO, but the information he's giving us is so filtered and watered down and spun that he might not have a good sense of what's happening in the trenches," says Schreiber. "We'll often try to talk to the salesmen of a company, someone who can't provide a picture of how the company's doing, but can tell us how effective their management is and what information they're getting from their customers," adds Lammert. This is a ploy that Janus has used again and again with companies like EMC and Cisco and insurance companies like UnumProvident.

Naturally, they'll also talk to a company's suppliers, customers, and competitors. "Many times because we spend so much time talking to customers and suppliers, we can get a better viewpoint of what's going on with a company than the company managers themselves," says Schreiber. So, with every company Janus is even considering, an analyst will build a web of contacts within and surrounding the company.

This process can take weeks, maybe months. "Those relationships are built over time. You can't cold call a contact the first time and hit the Holy Grail of information," says Schreiber. "It's very much like detective work." So much so that in 2000 the company asked a retired FBI academy instructor to talk to the analysts about how to develop informants and how to conduct an interview—how to read body language and how to assess whether someone is being straightforward. "It was quite valuable," says Schreiber.

Even though Janus is a growth-oriented money manager, numbers do play a role in their stock-picking process. But it's the research from which they derive all their numbers. They use all of the information they cull from their "informants" and "slice and dice the information to as fine a level as we can," says Schreiber. This often means visiting the various lines of the company business, trying to analyze each one individually. And it often leads to complex earnings models that help the analysts understand what a company is worth and what the operating environment can do to the model. "The ultimate question is, 'Is the idea we had actually a good, investable stock pick?' And many times it's not. But over time, there will be some good stock picks," Schreiber says.

Sometimes the question stirs up a lot of debate—an inevitable by-product of collaboration. But perhaps that's what makes the process work so well.

"There's rarely just one point of view on a stock," says Lammert. A few years ago, for instance, with the emergence of free Internet services, there was a group that questioned whether AOL could maintain its premium pricing. "I was a proponent of that camp," says Lammert, "even though I owned the stock." And there was a time, too, when a faction within Janus believed that digital subscriber lines (DSLs) could represent more effective competition for cable companies in data and video long-term. And there was another that thought that satellite television would take more share. (DSL won in the end.) All told, however, the result is a fairly deep level of research. "From valuation to building the competitive picture, everything receives a fair amount of scrutiny," says Lammert. "Sometimes the dominant camps are wrong."

In any case, it works. Janus was onto Nokia in the early 1990s, long before the stock was traded outside of the European markets. "It was not a stock that was within the vocabulary of anybody in the United States. The biggest share of its revenue was in the television business and they were losing money thanks to their TV exposure," says Lammert. (Nokia stock, despite a recent tumble, has gained 7,131 percent since 1992.) That's just one example of how the research web that Janus weaves is able to turn up good ideas. There have been, of course, the big tech names that generated big returns for the fund company: Dell, Cisco ("One we've owned on the way up and on the way down," Lammert jokes), AOL, Comcast. But there are nontech names, too. In early 1990s, the managers were big into railroad company Wisconsin Central. It climbed 1,113 percent in the first half of the decade.

"Over time, the contact relationships build and our understanding of company strategy and business philosophy builds and we're able to assess changes in a company's fundamentals. And as our ability to detect those changes improves, so does our ability to outperform over time," says Schreiber.

The Last Word

"I think the Janus approach is marked by an intense dedication to research and to working as a team," says Warren Lammert. "Our belief is that to really understand the ecosystems in which companies exist, you have to try to understand the companies on their own terms. And that means talk to not only company managers, but also suppliers, competitors, and customers to get a broad picture of a company and its opportunities. And to do that effectively, you have to develop a way to communicate effectively and you have to build a network. At Janus, ultimately, portfolio decisions are made by the portfolio managers, but they do that based on a research process that is intensive, and it draws together the broader resources of the firm."

APPENDIX

The Right Brokerage Firm for You

Today there are more brokerage firms to choose from than ever before, from classic full-service firms to discounters to even more discounted online brokers. Which is the right one for you? The answer depends on your investing style.

If you're someone who likes to do it yourself (and we'll bet you are, given that you're reading this book), then you should go with a discounter or online firm. You'll save a ton in commissions, and you won't have the bother of a broker calling you with hot tips all the time.

But we won't deny it: There *is* a lot to be said for having some help from a professional, particularly when the market is as choppy as it has been lately. For that reason, many individual investors like the convenience of handing over at least some control of their portfolios to a broker. We call them "delegators."

SmartMoney's favorite brokers, as ranked by our most recent survey of the industry, are Charles Schwab for the do-it-yourselfer and Merrill Lynch for the delegator-type investor. Perhaps that doesn't seem too surprising, given that these *are* the two biggest players in the discount and full-service arenas, respectively. But, in fact, a vast amount of research on our part went into choosing our brokerage-industry winners and losers.

Our team of reporters spent more than six months talking to investors, brokers, and other experts in the business to get their insights. We also collected and analyzed thousands of data points from a 20-page questionnaire we sent to each brokerage firm. The survey gave us details about their products, services, and fees and commissions structures, online and off. Best of all, *SmartMoney* came up with $70,000 to open trading accounts at all 27 online brokers. The mandate: Find the bugs, the blips, and the breakdowns investors should be aware of—and try not to lose a bundle of money in the process. We're happy to report we succeeded nicely at both tasks. (When we finally completed the testing, we had enough data to pick the best brokerage firms, and we had made more than $2,300 in profits, after commissions.)

You'll find all the brokers we ranked in the tables in Figures A.1 and A.2. As you can see, some firms are better at certain things than others. If you want truly cheap trades and little else, for instance, check out Brown & Co. At Brown, trades placed online run as little as $5. Then again, you'll note where Brown falls on our chart—dead last. At the moment, cheap trades are about its only strong feature: The firm's web site offers few research tools, and customer-service help is limited. But forgoing the frills keeps costs low, says CEO Elizabeth Fisher, who explains, "We only take customers with serious experience in trading, and they don't need as much hand-holding."

Interested in opening an account at an online or full-service brokerage? Here's what you need to know.

Online Brokers

During the golden age of online investing—way back in March of 2000—TV ads for brokers made opening an account look as easy as turning on your computer. In reality, there's little instant gratification: Most online brokers require you to mail in an application that you download from their web sites. The forms ask you for basic information; Charles Schwab, for instance, wants your Social Security number, your mother's maiden name, and your driver's license number, along with an estimate of your net worth. Most brokers also ask you to designate a sweep fund, usually a money-market fund, where noninvested cash in your account can earn interest.

Once you finish the paperwork, you mail it in along with a check for your opening balance. Most brokers require a minimum balance in the $1,000 to $2,000 range. Once your check clears, you can get your user ID and a password over the telephone and start poking around online.

Online brokers make basic trades look disarmingly easy. On the web site's trading screen, you type into a preset form whether you'd like to buy or sell, the number of shares you'd like to trade, and the ticker symbol of the stock involved. Most brokers have a direct link from the trading page to a real-time quote on your stock. After you click a "submit order" button, the site presents a summary of the trade for your approval, so you can make sure you didn't mistakenly order 10,000 shares of GE instead of 100. Schwab's and other sites also tell you the amount you'll pay in commission. (Orders at online brokerages sometimes face delays due to significant swings in the price of a market order; so consider opting for a limit order, which lets you set the price at which you'll trade.)

You can keep track of your funds online via the web site's "account balances" or "account positions" page. Schwab and other brokers show the "cost price" of your securities on this page, so you can track your holdings' performance. You can consult a "transaction history" screen that records activity in your account for at least the past 90 days. Most brokers also mail out a monthly paper account statement, although some charge a fee for that service.

Firms generally extend privileges to customers with bigger or more active accounts, which generate more revenue. At Schwab, if you maintain a $100,000 balance or trade 12 times a year (and have account assets of at least $10,000), you qualify for "Signature Services," entitling you to broader research resources, special trading software, and a dedicated customer-service phone line so you don't have to wait on hold behind poorer schmoes. As you might expect, investors with smaller accounts or who seldom trade face extra fees at most brokers: Schwab charges $30 a quarter to accounts with balances under $50,000 that trade fewer than eight times a year.

Full-Service Brokers

Full-service brokers make opening an account a more personal affair. Most of these so-called wirehouse brokers ask you to choose between a traditional account, which charges a commission for each transaction your broker makes for you, and a fee-based account, where you pay a percentage of your assets each year in return for all the services you use. (See Sidebar A.1, "The Flight to Fee-Based Accounts.") The typical fee-based account requires a minimum balance of $50,000; there aren't formal minimums for traditional accounts, but in practice, investors with balances below $100,000 often struggle to get attention from their brokers.

FIRM (2000 RANK)

 STRONG SUITS

1. CHARLES SCHWAB (3)
800-435-4000

Broad investment options and access to financial advice; phone help is polite and speedy.

2. CSFBDIRECT (4)
800-825-5723

Broker-assisted trades cost the same as "solo" transactions ($20); phone reps exceptionally thorough.

3. MURIEL SIEBERT (2)
800-872-0444

Nicely redesigned web site with investing primers and other instructional help for novices.

4. TD WATERHOUSE (1)
800-934-4448

Extensive branch-office network; useful tools for researching and buying bonds, annuities.

5. SCOTTRADE (9)
800-999-9225

Very low commissions (starting at $7) and margin rates; access to unit-investment trusts.

6. MORGAN STANLEY ONLINE (12)
800-688-6896

Programmable e-mail alerts flag changes in portfolio; easy access to market news.

7. FIDELITY (6)
800-343-3548

Well-designed account aggregator; "Powerstreet" gives extra tools to most-active traders.

8. ML DIRECT (10)
877-653-4732

Free access to Merrill Lynch research; web site is reliable and easy to customize.

9. MYDISCOUNTBROKER (8)
888-882-5600

Inexpensive trading ($12); wide array of wireless account-access choices.

10. E*TRADE (7)
800-786-2575

E*Trade Bank, new offerings in financial planning boost choices for customers.

11. AMERITRADE (13)
800-669-3900

Recent acquisitions mean more tools for day traders; low commissions ($8).

12. CITITRADE (NR)
888-663-2484

Trading password enhances web site's security; access to extensive charts, analyst reports.

13. QUICK & REILLY (16)
800-793-8050

Ties to parent company FleetBoston mean access to financial-planning help.

Note: NR=Not ranked in 2000; T=Tie; Quality of Service score includes testing of brokers' web sites by SmartMoney and Gómez Inc.; Commissions and Fees score includes sample margin rates as of 4/30/01; Mutual Funds score reflects availability of mutual funds ranked in the top quartile of their category by research firm Morningstar.

FIGURE A.1   Best Brokers for "Do-It-Yourself" Investors

WEAK POINTS	QUALITY OF SERVICE	COMMISSIONS AND FEES	MUTUAL FUNDS	RESEARCH	PRODUCTS	ACCOUNT AMENITIES
Trading costs ($30) and fees get expensive fast; service calls sometimes become sales pitches.	2	27	12	2	1	1
Lower-asset clients (under $100,000) get left out of goodies like CSFB research. IPO access.	6T	8	16	5T	4	10T
Access to analyst reports is "pay-as-you-go," which can add up.	5	11T	5	11T	8T	5T
Web site slower than average, difficult to read; some commission increases expected.	16T	14T	3	4	2T	5T
Online data on bonds and mutual funds is not always up to date.	11	6	15	10	5	24
Web trades were very slow; gaps between quoted price and execution were sometimes big.	6T	18	18	7T	10	20T
Most expensive fees in survey for nonproprietary mutual funds ($75 to $250 per purchase).	3	26	6	7T	7	3
You'll pay $30 a trade for all those web bells and whistles.	1	25	22T	5T	8T	20T
Lack of access to bonds and money-market funds limits investors' options.	13	4	17	11T	14T	17T
Expect a lot of junk mail; phone reps seemed underfamiliar with web site.	12	19	21	18T	2T	4
New inactivity fees could add up to $60 a year for buy-and-hold investors.	10	5	7T	20T	23T	19
Commissions are steep at $30; no money-market funds online.	4	23	25	1	25T	8
Poor phone service—in April reps promised to call us back with help, and we're still waiting.	19T	13	11	17	11	10T

FIRM (2000 RANK)	STRONG SUITS
14. BIDWELL & CO. (14) 800-547-6337	Exceptional range of mutual funds, and easy online access to them.
15. DREYFUS (22) 800-416-7113	Surprisingly inexpensive for broker-assisted trades ($25) and mutual-fund transactions.
16. AMERICAN EXPRESS (19) 800-297-7378	Strong research tools; easy access to financial advisers and banking services.
17. USAA (213) 800-435-1817	Phone service makes you feel as if your favorite uncle is running your brokerage.
18. WALLSTREET ELECTRONICA (NR) 888-925-5783	Options-trading mechanism is reliable and cheap; clients seeking brokers can contact them via the firm.
19. DATEK (20) 800-823-2835	Ultralow commissions, especially for mutual fund transactions ($10 for a $10,000 buy).
20. JB OXFORD (NR) 800-782-1876	Useful retirement-planning calculator; wireless account access from multiple devices.
21. ACCUTRADE(21) 800-228-3011	Detailed asset-allocation planner; good selection of mutual funds.
22. A.B. WATLEY (18) 888-229-2853	Strong software platform for day traders, e-mail responses were fastest and most thorough in survey.
23. VANGUARD (17) 800-992-8327	"Consolidated View" feature gives detailed overview of client's finances.
24. T. ROWE PRICE (24) 800-225-7720	Reliable web site with easy-to-navigate trading platform and clear commission data.
25. BROWN & CO. (25) 800-822-2021	Dirt-cheap trading on your own ($5 market orders) or with a broker's help ($17).

FIGURE A.1   *(Continued)*

WEAK POINTS	QUALITY OF SERVICE	COMMISSIONS AND FEES	MUTUAL FUNDS	RESEARCH	PRODUCTS	ACCOUNT AMENITIES
Site is slow to load and lacks basic research tools such as stock screens.	16T	7	1T	24T	13	16
Bare-bones operation means no checking, no debit cards, no online money-market funds.	21	3	14	13T	23T	2T
Awkwardly designed web site, particularly the trading page: long phone hold times. (Average time: 5 minutes.)	9	22	27	7T	18	2
Site poorly laid out; would-be clients must become "members" by phone before applying.	14T	21	20	13T	14T	5T
Customer-service staff sounds like it's cheap too; phone reps were beleaguered, bewildered.	14T	24	19	15T	6	14T
Few non-stock investment options available; on phone, long hold times and brusque staff.	19T	2	22T	15T	27	27
Trading web page is slow and cumbersome.	16T	14T	24	18T	22	14T
Only broker surveyed that didn't allow us to activate our account by phone.	22T	16	7T	20T	21	23
Home page is cluttered and crash-prone; difficult to obtain account history online.	24T	9T	1T	26	20	22
Trade confirmation numbers aren't shown online, making orders hard to track; e-mail service is poor.	24T	11T	26	23	19	12T
Research tools are skimpy, especially on stock info.	24T	20	7T	24T	17	17T
Web site short on research tools; difficult to track trades; no e-mail help available.	27	1	13	27	25T	25T

FIRM (2000 RANK)	STRONG SUITS
1. MERRILL LYNCH (1) 877-653-4732	Best stock picks; account statements full of extras, including estimated annual income for each position.
2. MORGAN STANLEY (3) 800-688-6896	Improved web site, with enhanced IPO and real-time account updates; three-year stock picks ranked third.
3. CHARLES SCHWAB (4) 800-225-8570	Two words: the Web. Its workshops and online resources make it easy for investors to educate themselves.
4. A.G. EDWARDS (8) 877-835-7877	Improved online services, including a portfolio tracker and adviser homepages; margin rates ranked third.
5. SALOMON SMITH BARNEY (2) 800-221-3636	Gives clients easy-to-decipher account statements; Citigroup affiliation should bring continued benefits.
6. UBS PAINEWEBBER (6) N/A	Improved research thanks to UBS acquisition; went from eighth to second in one-year stock picks.
7. EDWARD JONES (9) 800-335-6637	All clients work with a personal financial adviser. Excellent research; three-year average beat everyone but Merrill.
8. PRUDENTIAL (7) 800-843-7625	Streamlined stock ratings (now limited to just buy/sell/hold) will help clients act on analyst advice.
9. AMERICAN EXPRESS (5) 800-297-5300	Mortgage refinancing to auto insurance—it's here; lowest margin rates; free bonus trades start with $25,000.

Note: Research score based on performance of stock picks for one-year and three-year periods ended 3/31/01, according to Zacks Investment Research; Commissions and Fees score includes sample margin rates as of 4/30/01; T = Tie. *Reflects performance data of Credit Suisse First Boston, which is one of Schwab's research providers. **Return based on performance of picks by PaineWebber and UBS Warburg. †Return based on performance of the AXP Blue Chip Advantage and AXP Research Opportunities mutual funds.

FIGURE A.2   Best Brokers for the "Delegator" Investor

WEAK POINTS	PRODUCTS AND SERVICES	STOCK RESEARCH	COMMISSIONS AND FEES	ONLINE SERVICES	MUTUAL FUNDS
Hard to take issue with a firm that does lots of things right. One blip: hefty margin rates.	1	1	2T	2	5
Can be pricey investing here, with commissions and margin rates ranking in the bottom half of our survey.	2	4	5	4	3
You'll need $100,000 or active-trader status for perks such as free analyst reports and a personal adviser.	4	5*	2T	1	2
Firm has no online trading after promising a year ago to add it.	5	8	1	8	1
Recommended stock list finished last in our survey; only firm to post losses for past two years.	3	9	6	3	6
Pricey: highest margin rates, and commission schedule ranked eighth.	7	3**	9	5	4
No online trading; 2 percent charge for dividend reinvestment; brokers focus on seven fund families.	9	2	4	9	9
Hit a brick wall in 2000 with recommended stock list; fell from first to seventh overall in research.	6	7	8	7	8
Limited choice of complex products; no access to futures or hedge funds.	8	6†	7	6	7

The Flight to Fee-Based Accounts

The market's turbulence lately has caused investors to flee in two different directions. "While there are people running to brokers for advice," says Gary Schatsky, an independent financial planner in New York, "there are an equal number of people running *from* brokers."

If you want the kind of help that full-service firms are known for but worry that your broker may be churning your account to fatten his or her wallet, consider this alternative: a fee-based account.

These accounts, which are offered by most of the leading brokerages, will exact an annual fee based on your total balance. This way your broker's interests are aligned with yours; the broker makes money by increasing your assets, not by turning them over.

Steven Holtz knows the value of a fee-based account. He says he "feels much better" since switching a couple of years ago from a full-service Merrill Lynch account to the firm's Unlimited Advantage program—and relieving any concerns about commissions. The Livonia, Michigan, attorney says he also values the advice he gets. In 2000, Merrill advisers suggested he sell a good portion of his Microsoft and Intel shares. While initially reluctant, Holtz, 40, now says, "It turned out to be real good advice." Plus, he appreciates the ability to view all his accounts online through Unlimited Advantage.

While fee-based accounts have been around for more than a decade, their popularity has soared in recent years. According to Cerulli Associates, a Boston consulting firm, assets in these accounts are growing 125 percent annually. One reason: They have attracted investors who normally would go the online (read: discounted) trading route. In addition to advice, fee-based accounts offer unlimited online trading. But note: That's not "unlimited" in a day-trading sense of the word. While the firms recognize that a certain level of trading activity is necessary to make this a smart

SIDEBAR A.1

choice for their clients, they'll close off your account if they notice you're routinely darting in and out of positions to make a
quick profit.

The basic rates for these programs don't vary that much.
While Merrill Lynch has no minimum balance, other brokers require at least $25,000, and you can expect to pay an annual fee of
0.25 to 2.5 percent of your assets (the higher the balance, the
lower the percentage). (See Figure A.3.) But keep this in mind: All
the firms we spoke with stressed that their fees were negotiable—
so make sure you strike a deal.

FIRM/PROGRAM	MINIMUM BALANCE	ANNUAL FEE
AMERICAN EXPRESS SPS Advantage	$25,000	0.25% to 2.0% of assets maximum.
MERRILL LYNCH Unlimited Advantage	none	$1,500 minimum; 1.5% of assets maximum.
MORGAN STANLEY Choice	$50,000	$1,000 minimum; 2.25% of assets maximum.
PRUDENTIAL Advisor I	$50,000	$250 minimum; 2.5% of assets maximum; $24.95/trade.
SALOMON SMITH BARNEY AssetOne	$50,000	$750 minimum; 1.5% of assets maximum.
UBS PAINEWEBBER InsightOne	$50,000	$1,250 minimum; 2.5% of assets maximum.

FIGURE A.3   Fee-Based Trading Accounts

Before you've invested a cent, your broker should conduct a lengthy interview to ask you about your financial goals, your needs, and your tolerance for risk. This conversation can cover everything from the assets you already hold to your career plans to your insurance needs. Merrill Lynch calls its initial interview the Financial Foundations report; the report typically produces about 200 pages of data about each client.

Using your answers, your broker will devise an investing strategy and an asset allocation model for your approval. (You should expect to meet at least once a year to tinker with this model.) You should pose these questions to your broker: What is his or her investment philosophy? What kind of research does he or she use to form recommendations, and how have those stocks performed over time? Once you decide you trust a broker with your assets, you'll sign a client relationship agreement which gives him or her the right to trade securities on your behalf.

To cut customer-service costs, full-service brokers like Merrill Lynch encourage their clients to track their accounts online. But they also send out meticulous paper statements: Merrill's are particularly exhaustive, spelling out everything from recent developments in the markets to the year-to-date changes of each item in your portfolio. (See Figure A.4.)

Avoiding Bad Brokers: Look before You Leap

Complaints against brokers have been surging in recent years, according to the Securities and Exchange Commission. So if you're choosing a full-service broker who's going to give you actual investing advice, it's vital that you investigate your broker *before* you invest.

Contact NASD Regulation (at www.nasdr.com or 800-289-9999) to request information on brokers you're considering. The report will list arbitrations and regulatory actions against the firm. Then, advises New York securities lawyer David E. Robbins, ask the broker to explain the research used to make recommendations, clients' performance record, and the broker's investment philosophy. And be sure to state clearly your objectives when opening your brokerage account. A blank form could allow your broker to decide your objectives for you.

If you find anything unusual in your trade confirmations, immediately send a written inquiry to your broker. "The longer it goes without your registering a query," says Robbins, "the more the arbitrators will believe that you authorized it."

JOHN Q. CUSTOMER

3 | 2000 CAPITAL GAIN AND LOSS TRANSACTIONS

Quantity	Security Description	Date of Acquisition or Cover of Short	Date of Liquidation Or Short Sale	Sales Price	Cost Basis	Gain or (Loss)
			SHORT-TERM CAPITAL GAINS			
1000	AMERICAN TEL & TEL	10/15/99	01/18/00	30,799.72	30,000.00	799.72
100	INTL BUSINESS MACH	11/15/99	03/22/00	11,044.82	11,000.00	44.82
1000	US SURGICAL CORP DEL	11/15/99	03/20/00	110,619.10	100,000.00	10,619.10
1000	US SURGICAL CORP	11/15/99	03/22/00	110,619.00	101,870.11 (U)	8,748.89
98000	TIGR SERIES 10%NOV 15 00	12/08/99	08/20/00	50,000.00	50,000.00	0.00
200	AMGEN INC COM PV $0.0001	12/18/99	09/23/00	10,040.60	4,239.08	5,801.52
200	THE SECTOR STRATEGY FUND	11/10/99	11/07/00	20,356.42	20,000.00	356.42
4	CALL IBM JAN 115	11/14/99	11/12/00	1,583.75	413.35	1,170.40
			Subtotal:	345,063.41	317,522.54	27,540.87

(U)-THE COST BASIS FOR THIS TAX LOT HAS BEEN ADJUSTED BY A PORTION OF THE UNLIMITED ADVANTAGE FEE ASSESSED IN THE YEAR 2000. FOR MORE INFORMATION, SEE THE UNLIMITED ADVANTAGE SECTION OF THE TAX REPORTING GUIDE.

Quantity	Security Description	Date of Acquisition or Cover of Short	Date of Liquidation Or Short Sale	Sales Price	Cost Basis	Gain or (Loss)
			SHORT-TERM CAPITAL LOSSES			
2	CALL IBM APR 110	03/15/99	01/10/00 (S)	950.66	1,775.57	(824.91)
6000	MICHIGAN ST HSG DEV AUTH.	04/05/99	04/01/00	5,150.00	6,000.00	(850.00)
25	BELLSOUTH	05/07/99	05/06/00	1,260.73	1,300.00	(39.27)
315	SIEMANS AG FN RT	05/15/99	05/13/00	2,583.03	2,600.00	(17.00)
200	AMER EXPRESS COMPANY	05/20/99	05/18/00	4,819.03	5,000.00	(180.97)
200	UP JOHN CO DEL PV1	03/18/99	12/05/00	7,873.90 (P)	9,236.52	(1,362.62)
100	IBM	05/15/00	12/18/00	11,045.00	11,186.73	(141.73)
1000	AT&T	10/15/00	15/18/00	30,799.00	31,027.86 (U)	(228.86)
			Subtotal:	64,481.32	68,126.68	(3,645.36)
			NET SHORT TERM CAPITAL GAIN (LOSS)			23,895.51

SUMMARY 2000

(P)-INDICATES THAT AN OPTION PREMIUM HAS BEEN INCLUDED IN THE CALCULATION
(S)-SHORT SALE
(U)-THE COST BASIS FOR THIS TAX LOT HAS BEEN ADJUSTED BY A PORTION OF THE UNLIMITED ADVANTAGE FEE ASSESSED IN THE YEAR 2000. FOR MORE INFORMATION, SEE THE UNLIMITED ADVANTAGE SECTION FOR THE TAX REPORTING GUIDE.

Merrill Lynch, Pierce, Fenner & Smith Inc.
Member, Securities Investor Protection Corporation (SIPC).
We urge you to keep the statement with your investment records.

FIGURE A.4 Annual Statement Summary
Source: Merrill Lynch, Pierce, Fenner & Smith, Inc. Reprinted with permission.

Web Site Directory

Our goal is not to bombard you with an exhaustive list of web sites. Rather, these are the sites that *SmartMoney* reporters deem most user-friendly, fast-loading, and most important, informative. No single site will give you everything, so we've organized this directory based on what kind of information you're trying to find.

Actual Earnings per Share

www.moneycentral.msn.com: You can get EPS data at a lot of places, but we like this site's presentation. It shows the information in a table (earnings over the past three years on a quarterly basis as well as year-to-year). But it also includes a colorful bar chart of the data, which allows you to—in a second—take in the company's sequential earnings growth (quarter-to-quarter) as well as the more typical year-to-year. To get this information, we pulled up a stock quote and then clicked (on the left menu) "Financial Results: Highlights." Another bonus: it shows revenue over the past three years (and quarterly) as well. But there is a catch. Graphics appear if you use Internet Explorer, but not Netscape Navigator.

Analysts' Estimates

www.zacks.com: As a database for analysts' estimates (much like First Call), Zacks has a pretty good format for providing estimates on a company-by-company basis. It's easy to get to (by entering a ticker and selecting "Company Estimates" from a menu at the top of the home page). Once there, you'll get estimates for the fiscal year (current and next), the current and coming quarter, and its estimated five-year growth rate. The site lists the information by broker (no names of individuals, just a description of the firm), but it also includes consensus numbers (high, low, and average) for the past 30 days as well as the past 120 days. It's probably more information than you might need, but is still a very thorough accounting of what the Street is thinking about a particular company.

http://finance.yahoo.com: Yahoo!'s Finance site includes a "Research" page on each company that not only gives analysts' estimates for the coming two quarters (as well as for the past two) and the coming two years, but also indicates any analyst adjustments (upward or downward revisions) over the past 90 days. The information is generated by First Call.

Analysts' Reports (Research)

www.multexinvestor.com: Some of the reports you'll have to pay for (around $10 to $25, sometimes more), but this is a great centralized place to find independent research reports. Understand, however, that in some cases you will get abstracts (not the full report).

www.zacks.com: This database is deep. When we searched for Microsoft, we retrieved 298 reports dating back to a year, from reputable firms like CIBC, Robertson Stephens, Bear Stearns, and JP Morgan Hambrecht & Quist, among others. It costs money (prices vary depending on the firm and the kind of report), but most of the time company reports will cost you $10 to $25 each. An industry report might cost as much as $150. Plus, you'll have to register to do it, which includes inputting your credit card information so you can buy the report online.

One last word: Unless you're desperate, we wouldn't spend much time looking around http://finance.yahoo.com for research reports. You won't find top-ranked research firms like Salomon Smith Barney, Merrill Lynch, Morgan Stanley, Lehman Brothers, or Goldman Sachs. Instead there's Adams Harkness & Hill (ranked 44 by the *Wall Street Journal*), Gruntal & Co. (64), Tucker Anthony (33), and Janney Montgomery Scott (42).

Charting

www.bigcharts.com: A free, user-friendly guide to interactive charting. It includes charts, quotes, and reports and allows you to compare the price movement of a stock with other indicators like its price-to-earnings multiple (a truly useful tool) and to show splits and earnings.

www.smartmoney.com or **http://finance.yahoo.com:** Both of these sites' charting services allow you to compare the movement in one stock to another company or an index. Yahoo!'s site loads much faster. Also, be sure to check out *SmartMoney*'s Map of the Market, which shows in colors how the various sectors of the market are doing over four given periods.

Company Snapshot or Profile

www.zacks.com: User-friendly is the key here. The option is at the top of the home page so you can go straight to the profile if you want. Other sites, like Yahoo! Finance, make you pull up a quote first, then click for a profile. Also, the profile page summarizes analysts' recommendations and consensus estimates for the current quarter, the current fiscal year, and the next fiscal year—something you won't get on Yahoo!'s "Profile" page.

http://finance.yahoo.com: You have to pull up a quote first before you can click on "Profile." But once you get there, you'll get a good summary of the kind of business the company does as well as its managers, and its nuts-and-bolts ratios (price-to-book, cash flow, return on equity, etc.).

Five-Year Earnings and Sales Growth

http://finance.yahoo.com: Yahoo!'s Finance site offers a "Research" page for each company that includes consensus estimates from First Call. It also lets you compare a company's quarterly, fiscal-year, and five-year growth with its industry, its sector, and the S&P 500. Unfortunately, this page doesn't have sales growth.

www.moneycentral.msn.com: From the home page, pull up a quote, then click the left menu for the company report. Scroll to the bottom and you'll see a table called "Financials" that provides actual sales and income in the past 12 months, plus five-year average growth in percentage form.

www.hoovers.com: If you pull up a "company capsule" on any stock, you can find the one-year income and sales growth by scrolling down and looking at the box to the right of the page.

Form 10-K or 10-Q

www.freeedgar.com: This user-friendly and fast-loading site is the easiest place to find these SEC filings. But be sure to check the company web site as well.

www.moneycentral.msn.com: Here's a shortcut: If all you want to find out is the company's income or sales figures from its most recent quarterly report, but you don't want to bother with pulling up the entire Form 10-Q, pull up a quote from the home page of MSN Money and then click on "Financial," then "Results," and then "Statements." Up pops a historical (five-year) balance sheet or income statement—you choose.

Price-to-Earnings Ratio

CURRENT OR FORWARD

You'll have to calculate this yourself by finding the average earnings estimate for the current fiscal year or the coming fiscal year. See "Analysts Estimates" at the top of this directory.

TRAILING

Most sites will post the company's trailing P/E when you pull up a quote or chart: www.smartmoney.com; http://finance.yahoo.com; www.multexinvestor.com.

FIVE-YEAR HIGH/LOW

www.smartmoney.com: Get the five-year high/low P/E for a company by pulling up a quote and clicking on the file-tab titled "Key Ratios." This page also shows the current and five-year highs and lows for other ratios like price-to-book, price-to-sales, price-to-cash-flow, as well as return on equity and return on assets.

FIVE-YEAR AVERAGE

This is a toughie. The only place we were able to pull this information from was the stock screener tool on MSN Money (www.moneycentral.msn). You can look up the P/E five-year average, as well as the high and the low through its deluxe stock screener database. The catch is, you'll have to do a screen that will pull up the company—you can't search by ticker. To get the average for Microsoft, for instance, we screened for "application software" companies with greater than "$5 billion in market cap" that trade on the "Nasdaq" exchange.

Price-to-Sales, Price-to-Book, and Other Ratios

www.multexinvestor.com: Compare one company's price-to-book, price-to-cash-flow, and price-to-earnings ratios with its industry, its sector, and the S&P 500. To get there, though, you have to first pull up a "Quote." Then look to the menu on the left (under the heading "Company Information") and you'll find "Ratio Comparison."

http://finance.yahoo.com: Tricky to find, but if you pull up a quote and then click "Profile" and scroll to the table at the bottom of the page, you'll find all the ratios you ever wanted, including profit margin, debt-to-equity, and total cash on books.

www.smartmoney.com: Get the current ratio and five-year high/low for ratios like price-to-book, price-to-sales, and price-to-cash-flow, as well as return on equity and return on assets by pulling up a quote and clicking on the file-tab titled "Key Ratios."

Quotes

DELAYED QUOTES

http://finance.yahoo.com: Speediest quote we know.

www.zacks.com: The thing that sets this site apart is that a chart pops up automatically with the 20-minute-delayed quote (as well as the rest of the customary information: 52-week high/low, daily high/low, market cap, earnings estimates, and average analysts' rating).

REAL-TIME QUOTES

www.smartmoney.com: Where else? (It's free, but you have to register first.)

HISTORICAL QUOTES

http://finance.yahoo.com: Yahoo! Finance goes back to January 1962, and you can opt for daily, weekly, or monthly prices. Be sure to focus on the far right column, which is the split-adjusted price. Ignore the price in bold, unless you're looking for a price that's not adjusted for splits. You can't sort the results on the web page, but you can download the information in a spreadsheet—an invaluable resource if you're trying to study a stock's trading patterns when, say, you're trying to set a target price for the stock. The catch is, this service is tricky to find: To pull up historical prices you have to click "chart" for a stock and scroll halfway down the page to find the "historical prices" option—in small print to the right.

www.siliconinvestor.com: It goes back to January 1968 and you can sort the results (by date, by price, or by volume). Look at the far right column, which is the split-adjusted price and ignore the price in bold—unless you're looking for a price that's not adjusted for splits.

Ratio Comparisons with Competitors

www.smartmoney.com: Pull up a quote and look for the file-tab titled "Competition" to get a look at how a company stacks up next to its peers on a price-to-earnings, price-to-book, sales, or cash flow basis. Or go to "Chart Center" (under Tools) to get the lowdown on a company and its competitors.

www.marketguide.com: Compare one company's price-to-book, price-to-cash-flow, and price-to-earnings ratios with its industry, its sector, and the S&P 500. To get there, though, you first have to pull up a "Quote." Then look to the menu on the left (under the heading "Company Information") and you'll find "Ratio Comparison."

Screening

www.zacks.com and **www.moneycentral.msn.com:** Both sites are good for investors who want to screen without having to set all the parameters. Choose from predefined screens to look for value, growth, or stocks with high dividend yields.

If you plan to move beyond the predefined screens on these web sites, however, there are a couple of things you ought to know: The "custom screening" web site for Zacks Investment Research (www.zacks.com) is slightly clumsy, allowing you to screen for price-to-earnings, price-to-book, or price-to-sales by entering those parameters one at a time. In fact, its custom screening web site only allows you to sift within certain sectors or industries—though you can set a market cap range and you can specify either the New York Stock Exchange or the Nasdaq, for instance. So, for example, you can screen for all basic materials companies that trade on the NYSE with a market cap above $1 billion.

Once you've set those rudimentary parameters, Zacks then spits out a list of companies that you can save and come back to later. You can specify exactly what—and how much or little—information you want to include in the Excel file: all the usual suspects (price, market cap, P/E) as well as earnings estimates and average analysts' recommendations.

To do advanced screens on MSN's Money web site (www.moneycentral.msn.com), you must download a software program, which takes a few seconds (on a cable modem line; two minutes using a 56K modem), but it's well worth the time.

www.quicken.com: There is something for every investor here, beginner or advanced, whether you have a specific request or just want to do a broadbrush screen. It offers three levels of easy-to-navigate screens. The first level offers beginners preset screens just like the ones we described at MSN's Money web site. It has predefined screens, all under the heading "Popular Searches." Then there's "EasyStep" Search, a walk-through screen of the most important variables (industry, then market cap, then P/E, price-to-book, price-to-sales, and so on) a step at a time. And finally a "Full Search" option, which allows you to set 33 different criteria.

www.siliconinvestor.com: If you know exactly what range of P/E you're interested in—say anything above 7 but below 14—then you should check out this site's advanced stock screen tool. It lets you plug in the minimum and maximum metric for nearly every ratio, from P/E to return on equity and more.

Sector Performance

www.smartmoney.com: Go to "Map of the Market" to see how different sectors have been performing. It includes everything from consumer staples and financials to energy and transportation. You can track the performance since the last close, over the past 26 weeks, over 52 weeks, or year-to-date. You can also opt to highlight the top gainers or losers within each sector.

GLOSSARY

accelerated depreciation An accounting method that allows a company to write off an asset's cost at a faster rate than the traditional method. It often results in a larger tax deduction on a company's income statement.

accountant's opinion A signed statement of opinion from an accounting firm regarding a corporation's financial statements. The auditor must follow generally accepted accounting principles. The opinion can be unqualified or qualified. A qualified opinion calls attention to limitations of the audit or unusual items in the statement.

accounts payable Money a company owes to suppliers. By adding accounts payable, short-term debt, and interest on long-term debt together we arrive at a company's current liabilities.

accounts receivable Money owed to a company by its customers. By adding cash, accounts receivable, marketable securities, and inventory we arrive at a company's current assets.

accrual basis Accounting method in which income and expenses are accounted for as they are earned or incurred, although they may not have been received or paid yet. The alternative is cash-basis accounting, in which revenues and expenses are recognized only when cash is received or paid. Accrual-basis accounting is useful for painting a long-term portrait of a company.

affiliate Two companies are affiliated when one owns less than a majority stake of the other, or when both are subsidiaries of a third company. Or, generally, affiliation is any association between two companies that is short of a parent-subsidiary tie.

agency bonds Bonds issued by government-sponsored agencies and federally related institutions. All government agency bonds carry the highest credit ratings—AAA from Standard & Poor's and Aaa from Moody's Investors Service. In quality and liquidity agency issues are considered second only to Treasurys. Normally, agency bonds offer a slightly higher interest rate than comparable Treasury issues. Agency bonds are issued by institutions like the Federal Home Loan Mortgage

Corporation and the Federal National Mortgage Association.

aggressive growth funds   Funds that seek rapid growth of capital and that may invest in emerging-market growth companies without specifying a market capitalization range. They often invest in small or emerging growth companies and are more likely than other funds to invest in initial public offerings or in companies with high price-to-earnings and price-to-book ratios. They may use such investment techniques as heavy sector concentrations, leveraging, and short selling.

alpha   A measure of a fund's risk-adjusted return. Alpha can be used to measure directly the value added or subtracted by a fund's manager. It is calculated by measuring the difference between a fund's actual returns and its expected performance given its level of market risk as measured by beta. An alpha of 1.0 means the fund produced a return 1 percent higher than its beta would predict. An alpha of −1.0 means the fund produced a return 1 percent lower. The accuracy of an alpha rating depends on two factors: (1) the assumption that market risk, as measured by beta, is the only risk measure necessary; (2) the strength of a fund's correlation to a chosen benchmark such as the S&P 500. Correlation is measured by R-squared. An R-squared of less than 50 makes a fund's alpha rating virtually meaningless.

American depositary receipts (ADRs)   Shares of non-U.S. companies that trade in the U.S. stock market. American depositary receipts, or ADRs, offer distinct advantages to the U.S. investor. First, they require no complex currency transactions as they can be purchased in U.S. dollars. Also, most ADR companies are required to report financial details of their operations in accordance with generally accepted accounting principles. That makes their earnings more transparent and less subject to manipulation or fraud.

American Stock Exchange (AMEX)   The third most active market in the United States, behind the New York Stock Exchange (NYSE) and the Nasdaq Stock Market. The exchange was founded in 1842 in New York City. Most stocks traded on it are those of small to midsize companies. Also called both Amex and the curb exchange.

American-style option   An option that may be exercised at any time prior to expiration.

AMEX Market Value Index   A stock index that measures the performance of more than 800 companies representing all major industry groups on the American Stock Exchange.

amortization   The accounting procedure that companies use to write off intangible rights or assets—such as goodwill, patents, or copyrights—over the period of their existence. For fixed assets the term used is depreciation. Both depreciation and amortization expenses are subtracted from a company's operating revenues to calculate net income.

analyst An employee of a brokerage or fund management firm who studies companies and makes buy and sell recommendations on stocks of these companies. Most specialize in a specific industry such as health care, semiconductors, or banks.

annual effective yield The actual annual return on an account after interest is compounded.

annualized return A way to calculate the return on an investment of more than one year. The annualized or average annual return is calculated by adding each year's return on investment and dividing that number by the number of years invested. The return takes into account the reinvestment of dividends (and distributed capital gains for mutual funds) as well as the change in the price of the investment over time. Compare to cumulative return.

annual report An annual report is a record published every year by a publicly held corporation that details its financial condition. The report, which must be distributed to all shareholders, contains a description of the company's operations, its balance sheet, income statement, and other relevant information. The official annual report filed with the SEC is a 10-K form.

annuity A tax-deferred investment product sold by insurers, banks, brokerage firms, and mutual fund companies. Fixed annuities provide a rate of return that is fixed for a year or so but then can move up and down. Variable annuities allow investors to allocate their money among a basket of mutual fund–like subaccounts; the return depends on the performance of the funds selected. Watch out for high sales commissions, expense ratios, and penalties for early withdrawals.

antitrust law Any law that encourages competition by limiting unfair business practices and curbing monopolies' power.

arbitrage The simultaneous buying and selling of a security at two different prices in two different markets. The arbitrageur takes advantage of the price disparity to make money by selling in one market while simultaneously buying in the other. Since the disparity is usually very small, a large volume is required to lock in a significant profit for the arbitrageur. Perfectly efficient markets present no arbitrage opportunities. Fortunately, perfectly efficient markets seldom exist.

ask price The price at which someone is willing to sell a security or an asset. In the stock market, the ask portion of a stock quote is the lowest price a seller is willing to accept at that time. The difference between the ask price and bid price is known as the spread.

asset allocation   An investment technique that diversifies a portfolio among different types of assets such as stocks, bonds, cash equivalents, precious metals, real estate, and collectibles. When it comes to risk and reward, different asset classes behave quite differently. Stocks, for instance, offer the highest return, but they also carry the highest risk of losses. Bonds aren't so lucrative, but they offer a lot more stability than stocks. Money-market returns are puny, but you'll never lose your initial investment. An asset allocation strategy allows you to achieve the optimal blend of risk and reward.

asset-backed securities   Securities backed by loans or accounts receivable. For example, an asset-backed bond is created when a securities firm bundles some type of debt, like car loans, and sells investors the right to receive the payments that consumers make on those loans.

asset-management accounts   All-in-one accounts that allow customers of brokerage firms to buy and sell securities and store cash in one or more money-market mutual funds. Asset-management accounts generally offer check-writing privileges, credit or debit cards, and automatic transfers from one account to another. They often come with an annual fee of up to $100.

asset   Any item of economic value owned by an individual or a corporation, especially that which could be converted to cash. Examples are cash, securities, accounts receivable, inventory, office equipment, a house, a car, and other property.

assets under management   The total market value of a mutual fund. The asset level can change, depending on the flow of money into and out of the fund, as well as the change in market valuation. Asset figures are useful in gauging a fund's size, agility, and popularity. They help determine whether a small-company fund, for example, can remain in its investment-objective category if its asset base reaches an ungainly size.

at-the-money   Refers to an option with a strike price equal to the current price of the instrument, such as a stock, upon which the option was granted.

auction market   Trading securities on a stock exchange where buyers compete with other buyers and sellers compete with other sellers for the best stock price. Trading in individual stocks is managed and kept orderly by a specialist.

auditor's report   An independent accounting firm's opinion on whether a company's financial statements conform to generally accepted accounting principles (GAAP). The auditor's report is included in a company's annual report.

average annual yield   A way to calculate the return on investments of more than one year. It is calculated by adding each year's return on investment and dividing that number by the number of years invested.

averages   In the stock market, averages are indicators that measure price changes in representative stock prices. The most popular indicator is the Dow Jones Industrial Average, which measures the performance of 30 large-capitalization stocks.

back-end load   A sales charge that is imposed when investors redeem shares of a mutual fund. Also known as the contingent deferred sales charge (CDSC), a back-end load generally declines over time. For instance, if you sell the mutual fund shares after one year, you may owe a 5 percent charge, but if you hold them for three years, the charge may decline to 2 percent. Unfortunately, the cumulative 12b-1 fee always compensates any possible loss the fund company might incur by long-term shareholders holding onto their shares until the stated load is 0 percent. Paying the front-end load is often the better deal.

balanced fund   A mutual fund that invests in a mixture of stocks, bonds, and cash. A balanced fund attempts to blend asset classes to produce a conservative growth and income portfolio. It is also known as a hybrid or asset allocation fund.

balance sheet   Financial statement that lists a company's assets and liabilities as of a specified date. The balance sheet presents a company's financial condition by listing what it owns—assets such as cash, inventory, factories, equipment, and accounts receivable—and what it owes—liabilities such as short-term and long-term debt and accounts payable. The difference between assets and liabilities is known as shareholders' equity or book value.

banker's acceptances   A form of financing used in import/export transactions.

bankruptcy   A state of insolvency of an individual or an organization—in other words, an inability to pay debts. The U.S. bankruptcy code is divided into chapters that provide different types of relief from insolvency. Under Chapter 7 bankruptcy, you petition the court to be freed from all your debts following the liquidation of almost all your assets. Certain assets, like your house, are usually exempt from liquidation. Chapter 11 allows you to remain in possession of your assets, but a repayment schedule must be negotiated with creditors.

barrier options   Variations of the standard financial options. They are activated or cease to exist once the price of the underlying security has reached a specified level.

basis point   One-hundredth of one percentage point, or 0.01 percent.

Basis points provide a handy way to state small differences in yield. For example, it's much easier to say one bond yields 10 basis points more than another than it is to say it yields one-tenth of one percentage point more. It is also used for interest rates. An interest rate of 5 percent is 50 basis points greater than an interest rate of 4.5 percent.

bearer stock   Stock certificates that aren't registered in any name. They are negotiable without endorsement by any person.

bear market   Any market in which stock prices are declining for a prolonged period, usually falling by 20 percent or more.

bellwether bond   For the U.S. market, the bellwether bond is the 10-year Treasury note, which recently replaced the 30-year Treasury bond as the benchmark for evaluating the bond market in general.

best three-month return   A fund's highest three-month return measured in rolling three-month periods over the past five years.

beta   A measure of an investment's volatility relative to a chosen benchmark. For stocks or stock funds, the benchmark is usually the S&P 500. For bonds or bond funds, it is Treasury bills. The beta of the benchmark is always 1.00. So a stock fund with a beta of 1.00 has experienced up and down movements of roughly the same magnitude as the S&P 500. Meanwhile, a fund with a beta of 1.25 is expected to do 25 percent better than the S&P in an up market and 25 percent worse in a down market. Generally speaking, the higher the beta, the more risky the investment. But without a high R-squared, a beta statistic can be meaningless. R-squared determines how much an investment's return is correlated to its benchmark.

bid price   The price that someone is willing to pay for a security or an asset. In the stock market, the bid portion of a stock quote is the highest price anyone is willing to pay for a security at that time. The difference between the ask price and bid price is known as the spread.

Big Board   Another name for the New York Stock Exchange (NYSE).

bill of exchange   A signed, written order by one business that instructs another business to pay a third business a specific amount. Also called a draft.

blend fund   Somewhere between growth funds and value funds are blend funds. Applying both strategies, they might, for instance, invest in both high-growth Internet stocks and cheaply priced automotive companies. As such, they are difficult to classify in terms of risk. The S&P 500 index funds invest in every company in the S&P 500 and could therefore qualify as a blend. But other funds are more extreme in using both styles.

block trade   Buying or selling 10,000 shares of stock or $200,000 or more worth of bonds.

blue-chip stocks   Stocks of companies known for their long-established record of earning profits and paying dividends. Blue chips tend to be large, stable, and well known. Most of the top stocks in the S&P 500 are blue chips.

Bollinger bands   A method used by technical analysts, who rely on studying the historical trading patterns of securities to predict their future movements. Bollinger bands are fixed lines above and below a security's average price. As volatility increases, the bands widen.

bond   A debt instrument that pays a set amount of interest on a regular basis. The amount of debt is known as the principal, and the compensation given to lenders for making such funds available is typically in the form of interest payments. There are three major types of bonds: corporate, government, and municipal. A corporate bond with a low credit rating is called a high-yield or junk bond.

bond broker   A bond broker acts as your agent, calling around to different bond dealers to find the best prices for the bonds you want. Brokers may charge a fee for their services or simply make money by increasing the markup (the spread between the purchase and sale price of a bond).

Bond Buyer Municipal Bond Index
An index based on 40 long-term municipal bonds that is often used to track the performance of tax-free municipal bonds. The index is compiled by *The Bond Buyer*, a trade publication that also has several other closely watched municipal bond indexes.

bond dealers   Dealers maintain their own inventory of bonds and make trades with either the general public or brokers. Dealers make money from the difference between the bid price and ask price of a bond. If your broker offers to act as a dealer, that means he can sell you bonds from his own inventory. This is usually a better deal since it removes a layer of commissions that will be added if your broker has to go to another dealer to find you a particular bond.

bond fund   A bond mutual fund specializes in pooling the purchase of bonds into a diversified, managed portfolio. Most bond fund portfolios pay income, which can be reinvested or distributed, on a monthly basis. Bond fund maturities can be as short as one year and as long as 30 years. The disadvantage of a bond fund is that it's not a bond. It has neither a fixed yield nor a contractual obligation to give investors back their principal at some later maturity date—the two key characteristics of individual bonds. However, there are many varieties of bond funds, including government, corporate, and municipal. In the case of corporate bonds, which can be volatile, a diversified fund could be a better option than buying individual issues.

bond rating   An assessment of the likelihood that a bond issuer will pay the interest on its debt on time. Bond ratings are assigned by independent agencies, such as Moody's Investors Service and Standard & Poor's. Ratings range from AAA or Aaa (highest) to D (in default). Bonds rated below BBB are not investment grade and are called high-yield or junk bonds. Since the likelihood of default is greater on such bonds, issues are forced to pay higher interest rates to attract investors.

bond yield   Stated simply, the yield on a bond is the interest you actually earn on your investment. If you buy a new issue, your yield is the same as the interest rate, but if you buy on the secondary market, your yield may be higher or lower. When the yield of a bond goes up, its price has fallen. Conversely, if a bond's yield falls, its market value has risen.

book-to-bill ratio   A measure of sales trends of a company or industry. Book-to-bill is a demand-to-supply ratio of orders on a firm's books to number of orders filled. A number above 1 indicates an expanding market, and a number below 1 is a contracting market. For example, a book-to-bill ratio of 103 means that for every $100 of products shipped,

$103 in new orders was received. This monthly figure is of major interest to investors in the high-technology sector, where sales momentum and inventory control are key to financial health.

book value   The difference between a company's assets and its liabilities, usually expressed in per-share terms. Book value is what would be left over for shareholders if the company were sold and its debt retired. It takes into account all money invested in the company since its founding, as well as retained earnings. It is calculated by subtracting total liabilities from total assets. To calculate price-to-book value divide the result by the number of shares outstanding. Examining the price-to-book ratio (P/B) of an industrial company with a lot of hard assets is a good way of telling whether it's undervalued or overvalued.

bottom fishing   Buying stocks whose prices have bottomed out or fallen to low levels. Value investors favor this investment technique.

bottom line   Accounting term for the net profit or loss.

bourse   A term used for stock exchanges in Europe.

Brady bonds   Securities issued by foreign governments as part of a debt-restructuring program initiated by former U.S. Treasury Secretary Nicholas Brady.

break the buck   When a money-market fund's share price falls below the $1-a-share value it is intended to maintain, the fund is said to "break the buck." Money funds are supposed to be safe investments and easily convertible into cash; thus the stable $1 share price. Cases of breaking the buck have been rare.

broker   A person who gives advice and handles orders to buy or sell stocks, bonds, commodities, and options. Brokers work for full-service and discount brokerage firms. The type of firm you use determines the amount of commissions you pay and advice you receive from your broker.

brokerage firm   When you buy or sell a security, you generally do so through a brokerage firm. Brokerage firms fall into two main camps: full-service brokers and discount brokers. Discount brokers charge far lower commissions than full-service brokers, and a growing number of deep discounters charge especially low commissions. But there is a trade-off. If you use a discount broker, you will get little or no investment advice, so you must be willing to make your own buy and sell decisions. A full-service broker, on the other hand, will help you pick investments and devise a financial plan.

broker call rate   The broker call rate (also known as the broker loan rate) is the interest rate that banks charge brokerages to cover the security positions of the brokerages' customers.

Most brokerages will charge you slightly above this amount when you borrow on margin. Usually the rate is about a percentage point higher than the federal funds rate.

bull market   A bull market is a stretch of time, from several months to years, in which stock prices rise. Excluding a few nasty short-lived corrections, for the 15 years up to June 30, 1999, U.S. stocks experienced a healthy bull market. The S&P 500 soared 1,295 percent during that time. That's an annualized return of 19.2 percent.

business productivity   The U.S. Department of Labor's monthly measurement of output or production per hour of work.

call   The issuer's right to redeem a bond or preferred share before it matures. A bond will usually be called when interest rates fall so significantly that the issuer can save money by floating new bonds at lower rates. The first date when an issuer may call a bond is specified in the bond's prospectus.

callable bond   A bond that the issuer can decide to redeem before its stated maturity date. A call date and a call price are always given. You face a risk with a callable bond that it will be redeemed if its stated coupon is higher than prevailing rates at the time of its call date. If that happens, you won't be able to reinvest your capital in a comparable bond at as high a yield.

call option An agreement that gives an investor the right but not the obligation to buy a stock, bond, commodity, or other instrument at a specified price within a specific time period. Compare with put option.

call risk The risk that an issuer may redeem a security sooner than expected.

capacity utilization The Federal Reserve's estimate of the percentage of factory capacity that is being used. Published monthly, capacity utilization rarely exceeds 90 percent because production costs become too expensive after that point. A high rate of capacity utilization—over 85 percent—suggests inflation is on its way.

capital asset An asset held for more than a year that isn't bought or sold in the normal course of business. Capital assets generally include fixed assets, such as land, buildings, equipment, and furniture. These assets are subject to depreciation.

capital gains Profit realized from the sale of securities, property, or other assets. How much the IRS taxes gain depends on how long the security is held. Gains from stocks held for less than 12 months are considered short-term capital gains, which are taxed at the regular income-tax rate. That can be as high as 39.6 percent. But if a stock is held for more than one year, the gains tax will be a maximum of 20 percent.

capital gains distribution The amount of capital gains a mutual fund distributes to its shareholders per share. Distributions usually occur once or twice per year and can be taxed as long-term or short-term gains, depending on how long the fund manager held the securities in the portfolio. When purchasing a mutual fund, make sure it is not right before a distribution. Otherwise, you'll get slapped with a tax bill for money you didn't make. Also, pay attention to the fund's turnover ratio to see how tax efficient it is.

capital loss Loss suffered from the sale of an asset for less than the price you paid for it. Capital losses can be used to your advantage come tax time. By balancing your capital losses with your capital gains, you can reduce your tax bill. This tactic is called harvesting losses.

cash equivalent The proportion of a fund's assets held in cash or short-term, fixed-income securities. Too much cash in an equity fund's portfolio can be a drag on performance. At the same time, cash can also be used by cautious managers to preserve capital in a down market. It is also used to take advantage of buying opportunities and to meet shareholder redemptions.

cash flow Net earnings before depreciation, amortization, and non-cash charges. Sometimes called cash earnings, cash flow is calculated by adding depreciation to net earnings and subtracting preferred dividends. Many stock analysts think cash flow paints a better picture of a company's true growth potential than net earnings do because company accountants can use crafty write-offs to alter earnings numbers.

cash market   The trading of securities according to their current—or spot—prices. That is in contrast to trading in a security for future delivery.

certificate of deposit (CD)   A certificate issued by a bank or thrift that indicates a specified sum of money has been deposited. The certificate guarantees to repay your principal—the amount you deposited—with interest on a specific maturity date. The amount of interest you receive depends on prevailing interest rates, the length of maturity, and how much you deposited. There are often significant penalties for early withdrawal of your money. CDs are insured by the Federal Deposit Insurance Corporation (FDIC). That makes your investment safe from everything but inflation and a raging bull market.

certified financial planner (CFP) The best-known financial planning designation, given to qualifying planners by the CFP Board of Standards, Denver.

chartered financial consultant (ChFC)   Financial planning designation given to qualifying planners by the American College, Bryn Mawr, Pennsylvania.

Chicago Board of Trade (CBOT)   A commodity-trading market.

Chicago Board Options Exchange (CBOE)   An exchange set up by the Chicago Board of Trade to trade stock options, foreign currency options, and index options of the S&P 500 and other benchmarks.

churning   The practice of trading securities excessively. In taxable investment accounts, churning invariably leads to reduced returns because of the hefty short-term capital gains tax. But even in tax-deferred 401(k)s or IRAs, trading commissions can eat into your return. In fact, brokers that encourage churning to increase their commissions are committing a securities law violation. A fund manager churning the portfolio will also make you feel the tax bite.

circuit breakers   Measures used by some major stock and commodities exchanges to restrict trading temporarily when markets rise or fall too far, too fast. For example, the New York Stock Exchange employs a circuit breaker that will halt trading if the Dow Jones Industrial Average declines by more than 10 percent in one day.

closed-end fund   A type of mutual fund that issues a set number of shares and typically trades on a stock exchange. Unlike more traditional open-end funds, transactions in shares of closed-end funds are based on their market prices as determined by the forces of supply and demand in the marketplace. Interestingly, the market price of a closed-end fund may be above (at a premium) or below (at a discount) the value of its underlying portfolio (net asset value or NAV). Investors in closed-ends will often try to capitalize on large discounts, hoping that eventually they will narrow.

closely held   Refers to a company that has a small group of controlling shareholders. In contrast, a widely held firm has many shareholders. It is difficult or impossible to wage a proxy fight for any closely held firm.

closing price   The last trading price of a stock when the market closes.

collateral   Stock or other property that borrowers are obliged to turn over to lenders if they are unable to repay a loan. Collateral is important for companies that default on their debt. In such cases, hard assets such plant, property, and equipment can be repossessed and liquidated.

collateralized mortgage obligations (CMOs)   Mortgage-backed securities that are carved into an array of bonds of varying maturity, coupon, and risk. The principal payments from the underlying pool of pass-through securities are used to retire the bonds on a priority basis as specified in the prospectus.

commercial paper   Unsecured short-term promissory notes used by companies to obtain cash. The notes are sold through dealers in the open market or directly to investors. The maturity of commercial paper is typically less than 270 days; the most common maturity range is 30 to 50 days or less. Such short maturities make commercial paper a fairly stable, liquid investment. It will often be part of an equity fund's cash position or the cash part of a company's current assets. Money market funds also hold commercial paper.

commodities   Bulk goods such as grains, metals, livestock, oil, cotton, coffee, sugar, and cocoa. They can either be sold on the spot market for immediate delivery or on the commodities exchanges for later delivery. Trade on the exchanges is in the form of futures contracts. Commodities are often viewed as a hedge against inflation because their prices rise with the consumer price index.

common stock   Represents part ownership of a company. Holders of common stock have voting rights but no guarantee of dividend payments. In the event that a corporation is liquidated, the claims of owners of bonds and preferred stock take precedence over those of owners of common stock. For the most part, however, common stock has more potential for appreciation.

composite trading   The total amount of trading across all markets in stocks that are listed on the New York Stock Exchange or American Stock Exchange. This includes transactions on those exchanges, regional exchanges, and the Nasdaq Stock Market.

compounding   Financial advisers love to talk about the magic of compounding. What magic? If your investments make 10 percent a year for five years, you earn not 50 percent but 61.1 percent. Here's the reason: As time goes on, you make money not only on your original investment but also on your accumulated gains from earlier years.

construction spending   The Commerce Department's monthly measure of construction spending. The Commerce Department's report surveys new construction expenditures and is broken down by residential, nonresidential, and public expenditures on new construction. Construction trends are closely related to interest rates and the business cycle. An increase in construction spending is a sign of economic growth and potential inflation.

consumer comfort index   A measure of consumers' feelings about their finances and the economy as a whole. The numbers are calculated through a weekly survey by *Money* magazine and ABC News.

consumer price index (CPI)   A gauge of inflation that measures changes in the prices of consumer goods. The consumer price index is based on a list of specific goods and services purchased in urban areas. These goods include food, transportation, shelter, utilities, clothing, medical care, and entertainment. Index data are released monthly by the Labor Department.

contrarian   An investor who does the opposite of what most investors are doing at any particular time. According to contrarian opinion, if everyone is certain that something is going to happen, it won't. This is because most people who say the market will go up are fully invested so they have no more purchasing power, which means the market is at its peak. When people predict decline they have already sold out, so the market can only go up. Contrarian investing shares many qualities with value investing. The difference is that contrarian stocks aren't just cheap, they are also actively disliked by investors. That can make them risky but potentially lucrative investments.

convertible bond   A bond that investors may exchange for stock at a future date under certain conditions. Convertibles are an intriguing hybrid investment, offering some of the upside potential of stocks but also the downside protection of bonds. On the upside, bonds offer a conversion ratio that dictates how many shares of stock you can receive if you trade in your bonds. Typically, you'll pay a premium for the exchange, but if the underlying stock is on fire, conversion is worthwhile. On the downside, bonds offer a guaranteed dividend yield, even if the underlying stock slides. Because of their complexity, the best way to invest in convertibles is through a convertible bond fund.

corporate bonds   A corporate bond is a debt instrument issued by a private or public corporation. Corporate bonds are rated by Standard & Poor's, Moody's, and other credit rating agencies that assign ratings based on a company's perceived ability to pay its debts over time. Those ratings—expressed as letters (AAA, AA, A, etc.)—help determine the interest rate that a company or government has to pay. A bond with a rating below BBB is considered a high-yield or junk bond. Such bonds pay higher interest rates but have a greater risk of default. Corporate bonds have historically been viewed as safer investments than stocks. The main reason for this is the prior claim corporate bondholders have on a company's earnings and assets.

corporation   A business entity treated as a person in the eyes of the law. A corporation is allowed to own assets, incur liabilities, and sell securities, among other things. It is also able to be sued.

correction   A downward movement in the price of an individual stock, bond, commodity, index, or the stock market as a whole.

cost basis   The original price of an asset, used in determining capital gains. It usually refers to the purchase price of a stock, bond, or other security.

coupon   The stated interest rate on a bond when it is first issued. A $1,000 bond with a coupon of 6 percent will pay you $60 a year until its maturity. Of course, not everyone holds bonds till maturity. The actual dividend yield you get from buying a bond on the secondary market can vary greatly from the coupon rate because the bond can sell above or below its face value.

covered   A derivative investment strategy in which the seller owns the underlying security. For example, an investor constructs a covered call position by buying a security and selling a call option of the same security. A covered call is a market-neutral investment strategy that protects the investor from the downside of owning a stock, while still affording him or her some of the upside.

cram-down   A maneuver in bankruptcy negotiations in which a reorganization plan is forced upon creditors with the least influence.

credit rating   Formal evaluation of a government body's or a company's credit history and ability to repay its debts. An AAA rating is the highest credit rating assigned by Standard & Poor's to a debt obligation. It indicates an extremely strong capacity to pay principal and interest. Bonds rated AA are just a notch below, then single A, then BBB, and so on. (A similar ratings system is available from Moody's Investors Service, with Aaa being the highest rating.) Some ratings show a + or − to further differentiate creditworthiness. Bonds rated BBB and above are considered investment grade, a category to which certain investors, including many pension funds, confine their bond holdings. Bonds rated BB, B, CCC, CC, and C are regarded as speculative. Such bonds are called high-yield or junk bonds. They offer higher interest rates but greater risk of default. A bond rating of D indicates payment default or the filing of a bankruptcy petition.

cumulative return   The total return an investment earned over a specific period. Returns are added year by year instead of averaged as they are with an annualized return. The end result takes into account the reinvestment of dividends (and distributed capital gains for mutual funds) as well as the change in the price of the investment over time.

cumulative voting   A method of voting for corporate directors. Each share has as many votes as there are directors to be elected, and the holder may distribute these votes as he or she wishes.

currency   A country's official unit of monetary exchange. When investing overseas, currency risk can be problematic. Even when foreign economies are doing reasonably well, currency fluctuations can have a negative effect on stock prices. While stocks in the chosen country could be soaring, a decline in the value of the currency's exchange rate to the dollar could eliminate your stock gains.

current account balance   One of the components of a country's balance of payments, the current account balance covers the imports and exports of goods and services. The current account balance helps a country evaluate its competitive strengths and weaknesses and forecast the strength of its currency.

current assets   Assets that can be converted to cash within 12 months. These include cash, marketable securities, accounts receivable, and inventory.

current liabilities   Obligations that must be paid within 12 months. These include accounts payable, short-term debt, and interest owed on long-term debt.

current ratio   A measure of a company's liquidity, or its ability to pay its short-term debts, calculated by dividing current assets by current liabilities. Possession of current assets at least twice current liabilities is considered a healthy condition for most businesses.

current yield You might think the current yield would be the same as the coupon rate on a bond. But, unless you're buying a new issue of a bond trading at face value, it's not. Unlike the coupon rate, which doesn't change, the current yield of a bond fluctuates with a bond's price on the secondary market. To get the current yield, divide the annual payment by the bond's current market price. For example, a bond with a $1,000 face value and a coupon of 6 percent purchased at $900 has a current yield of 6.7 percent (60/900). When the current yield of a bond rises, its market price declines. Conversely, when the current yield declines, the price of the bond rises.

CUSIP number An identification number for securities. CUSIP is an acronym for Committee on Uniform Securities Identification Procedures.

cyclical stocks Stocks that tend to rise quickly during an upturn in the economy and fall quickly during a downturn. Examples are housing, steel, automobiles, and paper. These economically sensitive stocks are the bread and butter of value investors who pick them up during economic troughs and wait for the recovery.

day order An investor's order to buy or sell stock that will be canceled by the end of the day if not filled.

debenture A common kind of corporate bond, often issued by a firm during restructuring. Debentures are backed only by the credit quality or essentially the good name of the issuer. Since there is no collateral, these bonds may carry a higher risk, and therefore a higher rate of return, when compared to an asset-backed bond. However, debentures of solid companies may be very highly rated.

debt Securities such as bonds, notes, mortgages, and other forms of paper that indicate the intent to repay an amount owed. A company that takes on too much debt can wind up in dire financial straits.

debt-to-equity ratio A measure of financial leverage, the debt-to-equity ratio is calculated by dividing long-term debt by shareholders' equity. (Shareholders' equity is the same as book value.) The higher the ratio, the greater the chance a company won't be able to pay its debts in the future.

debt-to-total-capital ratio This ratio indicates how much financial leverage a company has. It is calculated by dividing total debt by total invested capital. Total invested capital is a tally of all the outside investments a company's management has used to finance its business—everything from equity (the amount of stock sold) to long-term debt. The major difference between the debt-to-equity ratio and this ratio is that debt-to-capital includes long-term debt as part of the denominator. The higher the ratio, the greater the chance a company will not be able to pay its debts in the future.

default   Failure to pay principal or interest on a debt security. Owners of a bond that is in default can usually make claims against the assets of the issuer to recover their loss. A bond that is in default is rated D by Standard & Poor's. A default generally does not mean that the investor loses his or her entire investment. Sometimes the default will be the result of a temporary cash crunch and won't result in a bankruptcy filing. In other cases, a company will enter bankruptcy and either liquidate or reorganize its capital structure and business operations. In either case, the bond investor will generally recover some percentage of the bond's face value.

defensive securities   Stocks with investment returns that tend not to decline as much as the market in general in times when stock prices are falling. These include companies with earnings that tend to grow despite the business cycle, such as food and drug firms, or companies that pay relatively high dividends, like utilities.

defined-benefit plan   A defined-benefit plan is a traditional pension plan usually paid for by your employer. Upon retirement, you receive a fixed monthly check based on your age, salary, and length of service. Unlike a 401(k) or other defined contribution plan, it does not

necessarily require you to contribute any portion of your salary to receive a retirement benefit.

defined-contribution plan   A pension plan in which the level of contributions is fixed at a certain level, while benefits vary depending on the return from the investments. In some cases, such as 401(k), 403(b), and 457 plans, employees make voluntary contributions into a tax-deferred account, which may or may not be matched by an employer. Defined-contribution plans, unlike defined-benefit plans, give the employee choices of where to invest the account, usually among stock, bond, and money-market mutual funds.

deflation   A decline in the general price level of goods and services that results in increased purchasing power of money. The opposite of inflation. Deflation is not always good for an economy, because companies have no pricing power.

delta   A measure of the relationship between an option price and its underlying futures contract or stock price.

demand-pull inflation   A general increase in prices that occurs when demand exceeds supply.

depreciation   A noncash charge that represents a reduction in the value of assets due to wear, age, or obsolescence. Hard assets such as factories and machinery depreciate in value over time and must eventually be replaced. Accountants write off these depreciation costs over the estimated useful life of the asset. Because of the reductive effects of depreciation on earnings, some financial analysts prefer to look at cash flow, which separates depreciation costs from net income.

depression   A severe downturn in an economy that is marked by falling prices, reduced purchasing power, and high unemployment. The Great Depression began in 1929 and continued through most of the 1930s. But even depressions haven't stopped the upward trend of stock prices and earnings.

derivative   A derivative is a security whose value is "derived" from the performance or movement of another financial security, index, or other investment. For example, derivatives may be futures, options, or mortgage-backed securities. Derivatives may be used to short sell a security or to hedge against downside risk.

derivative suit   A shareholders' suit made on behalf of the company or mutual fund and its shareholders. If damages are awarded, they are paid to the company or mutual fund. Originally, derivative suits were a way for shareholders to challenge the actions of a self-interested or entrenched board that allowed mismanagement of a company.

devaluation   Lowering of the value of a country's currency relative to the currencies of other nations. When a nation devalues its currency, the goods it imports become more expensive, while its exports become less expensive abroad and thus more competitive.

dip   A slight decline in securities prices followed by a rise. Analysts often advise investors to buy on the dips, meaning buy when a price is momentarily weak.

discount   When the market price of a closed-end fund is less than its underlying net asset value (NAV), it is said to be trading at a discount. That discount allows you to buy a dollar's worth of securities for less than a dollar. So if a closed-end fund trading at a 10 percent discount owns a portfolio of stocks collectively worth $10 a share, you can buy that portfolio for $9 a share. Unlike open-end funds, closed-ends trade like stocks on an exchange, so a closed-end fund's price is determined by investor demand for its shares. A lack of demand can cause the fund's market price to be less than its underlying portfolio value—the source of the discount.

discount bond   A bond that sells at a current market price that is less than its face value. Bonds sell at a discount when the coupon on the bond is lower than prevailing rates. For example, you might have to pay only $812 for a bond with a 6.5 percent coupon if new issues yielding 8 percent are available for $1,000.

discount brokers   Brokers who charge lower commissions than full-service brokers. Investors often give up the benefits of stock-picking advice, updates on news affecting their investments, and research services normally provided by full-service brokers. Increasingly, however, the line between discount and full-service brokers has begun to blur.

discount rate   The interest rate the Federal Reserve charges its member banks for loans. This rate influences the rates these financial institutions then charge to their customers. The Fed uses this rate as one method of influencing monetary policy. The rate is also very important to the bond and stock markets as it provides a clue to interest rate trends and future Federal Reserve policy.

disinflation   A slowdown in the rate of price increases. Disinflation occurs during a recession, when sales drop and retailers are unable to pass higher prices along to consumers.

diversification   When you diversify, you spread your money among a slew of different securities, thereby avoiding the risk that your portfolio will be badly bloodied because a single security or a particular market sector turns sour.

dividend   A portion of a company's net income paid to stockholders as a return on their investment. A stock's dividend yield is determined by dividing a company's annual

dividend by its current share price. So a stock selling for $20 a share with an annual dividend of $1 a share yields the investor 5 percent. Dividends are declared or suspended at the discretion of the company's board of directors. A prime benefit of dividends is that once paid, they are money in the bank and provide your only return when stocks are weak. One disadvantage is that dividends are taxed as ordinary income, which, if you're in a high tax bracket, can ramp up your tax bill.

dividend yield   A company's annual dividend expressed as a percentage of its current stock price. As a stock's price declines, its dividend yield goes up. So a stock selling for $20 a share with an annual dividend of $1 a share yields an investor 5 percent. But if the same stock falls to $10 a share, its $1 annual dividend yields 10 percent. Value investors often see high dividend yields as a sign that a stock is cheaply priced. A high yield also acts as a cushion in a declining market, which is attractive to risk-averse investors. The downside is that dividends are taxed as ordinary income. The greater the yield, the more taxes you will have to pay.

dollar-cost averaging   A strategy to invest fixed amounts of money in securities at regular intervals, regardless of the markets' movements. Dollar-cost averaging is another form of diversification—only instead of spreading your money over a bunch of different stocks or bonds, it diversifies your investments over time. As a result, when the price is lower more shares of the security are purchased than when prices are higher. Investing $300 into the same stock every month will get you a lot more shares when the stock is depressed than when it's flying high. This strategy causes your overall cost of investment to go down.

Dow Jones averages   There are four Dow Jones averages that track price changes in various sectors. The Dow Jones Industrial Average tracks the price changes of the stock of 30 industrial companies. The Dow Jones Transportation Average monitors the price changes of the stocks of 20 airlines, railroads, and trucking companies. The Dow Jones Utility Average measures the performance of the stock of 15 gas, electric, and power companies. The Dow Jones 65 Composite Average monitors the stock of all 65 companies that make up the other three averages. One consistent criticism of the averages is that they're price-weighted, not market capitalization–weighted like the S&P 500. Since each Dow index calculates the average price of its participants, higher-priced stocks have a greater influence on index movements than lower-priced stocks. But a stock's price is less significant to the broader market than its market capitalization.

Dow Jones Equity Market Index
An index that measures price changes

in more than 100 U.S. industry groups. The stocks in the index represent about 80 percent of U.S. market capitalization and trade on the New York Stock Exchange, the American Stock Exchange, and the Nasdaq Stock Market. The equity market index is market capitalization–weighted, which means that a stock's influence on the index is proportionate to its size in the market.

Dow Jones Global Indexes   Some 2,700 companies' stocks in 29 countries worldwide are tracked by Dow Jones Global Indexes. These indexes subdivide the companies by geographic region and industry group. Collectively, the indexes represent more than 80 percent of the equity capital on stock markets around the world. All of them are weighted by market capitalization, which is the product of price times shares outstanding. Thus, each country carries a weight proportionate to the value of its equities relative to all those in the world. The U.S. market is the world's biggest, and the U.S. component of the global indexes has the most stocks—more than 700.

Dow Jones Industrial Average
Often referred to as the Dow or DJIA, the Dow Jones Industrial Average is the best known and most widely reported indicator of the stock market's performance. The Dow tracks the price changes of 30 large blue-chip stocks. Their combined

market value is equal to roughly 20 percent of the market value of all stocks listed on the New York Stock Exchange (NYSE). That said, the Dow is frequently criticized for lacking the breadth of the S&P 500, which accounts for more than 80 percent of NYSE's market value. It is also a price-weighted index, weighting higher-priced stocks more than lower-priced ones. The S&P 500 is market capitalization–weighted index, weighting the total market value of each stock's shares. Some financial analysts believe a market cap–weighted index paints a more accurate picture of the stock market.

Dow Jones World Stock Index   An index that measures the performance of more than 2,000 companies worldwide that represent more than 80 percent of the equity capital on 25 stock markets. It is a composite of the Dow Jones Global Indexes.

downtick   A sale of a listed security that occurs at a lower price than the previous transaction.

draft   A signed, written order by one party that instructs another party to pay a third party a specific amount. It also may be called a bill of exchange.

drag on returns (drag grade)   The negative impact of three factors—sales charges, annual expenses, and portfolio turnover—on mutual fund returns. High-turnover funds can lead to large capital gains distributions and tax inefficiency. If you aren't careful, management expenses and capital gains taxes can shave hundreds—if not thousands—of dollars from your returns over the years.

durable goods orders   The durable goods orders data measure the number of new orders for goods intended to last at least three years placed with domestic manufacturers for immediate and future delivery. The financial markets view this report as an excellent indicator of manufacturing sector trends. It is provided by the Census Bureau and U.S. Department of Commerce near the end of each month for the prior month's orders. The report is divided into broad categories, including defense, nondefense, capital, and noncapital goods.

duration   A way to measure part of the risk in a bond or bond fund. Duration tells you how long it will take to recoup your principal. It's a complicated calculation, so you'll have to get the number from your fund company or bond dealer, but it makes for a handy way to judge interest rate risk. If a bond or a bond fund has a duration of seven years, a 1 percent drop in interest rates will raise its value by 7 percent, while a 1 percent rise in interest rates will lower its price by 7 percent. The greater the duration of a bond, the greater its percentage volatility. In general, duration rises with maturity and falls with the frequency of coupon payments.

Dutch auction   A procedure for buying and selling securities named for a system used for flower auctions in Holland. A seller seeks bids within a specified price range, usually for a large block of stock or bonds. After evaluating the range of bid prices received, the seller accepts the lowest price that will allow it to dispose of the entire block. U.S. Treasury bills are sold under this system.

earnings   The amount of profit a company realizes after all costs, expenses, and taxes have been paid. It is calculated by subtracting business, depreciation, interest, and tax costs from revenues. Earnings are the supreme measure of value as far as the market is concerned. The market rewards both fast earnings growth and stable earnings growth. Earnings are also called profit or net income.

earnings growth   The percentage change in a company's quarterly or annual earnings per share versus the same period from the previous year. For example, a company that earned $1 a share in the second quarter of 1998, then earned $1.25 in the second quarter of 1999 would have experienced a 25 percent growth in earnings. To gauge how successful a company is at growing its earnings, you should compare its earnings growth to other companies in its industry.

earnings per share (EPS)   The portion of the company's earnings allocated to each share outstanding. EPS is a company's net income divided by its number of outstanding shares. If a company earning $2 million in one year had 2 million shares of stock outstanding, its EPS would be $1 per share. In calculating EPS, the company often uses a weighted average of shares outstanding over the reporting term. EPS is the denominator in the price-to-earnings ratio.

earnings yield   A company's per-share earnings expressed as a percentage of its stock price. This provides a yardstick for comparing stocks with bonds, as well as with other stocks.

EBIT   Earnings before interest and taxes. EBIT is calculated by subtracting costs of sales and operating expenses from revenues. The figures are often used to gauge the financial performance of companies with high levels of debt and interest expenses.

EBITDA   Earnings before interest, taxes, depreciation, and amortization. Also known as operating cash flow, EBITDA is calculated by subtracting costs of sales and operating expenses from revenues. Depreciation and amortization expenses aren't included in the costs. EBITDA is a useful measure of cash flow for companies that have low earnings because of large restructuring, capital buildout, or acquisition costs.

economic indicators   Key statistics used to analyze business conditions and make forecasts. Among them are the unemployment rate, inflation rate, factory utilization rate, and balance of trade.

emerging markets   The financial markets of developing countries such as Mexico, Malaysia, Chile, Thailand, and the Philippines. Emerging-markets securities are the most volatile in the world. They have tremendous growth potential, but also pose significant risks—political upheaval, corruption, and currency collapse, to name just a few.

employee stock ownership plan (ESOP)   A program encouraging employees to buy stock in their company and thereby have a greater stake in its financial performance.

equity   Ownership interest possessed by shareholders in a corporation—stocks as opposed to bonds. It is the part of a company's net worth that belongs to shareholders.

equity income funds   Funds that seek current income by investing a minimum of 65 percent of their assets in dividend-paying securities. Equity income funds are most akin to value funds in their investment philosophy because stocks with high dividend yields tend to be the cheapest stocks. Since dividends are the primary criterion by which these funds select stocks, they often lose out on capital appreciation. This means that as the market rallies, these funds will often lag. Conversely, when the market

declines, the income generated by the stocks held in equity income funds provides a buffer against losses.

ERISA   Acronym for the Employee Retirement Income Security Act, a law governing most private pension and benefit plans.

escalator clause   A clause in a contract providing for increases in costs such as labor expenses and materials.

European Monetary System   An exchange-rate system adopted by European Union members in an effort to move toward a unified European currency, which was rolled out in early 2002.

European-style option   An option that may be exercised only on its expiration date.

exchange   A centralized place for trading securities and commodities, usually involving an auction process. Examples include the New York Stock Exchange (NYSE) and the American Stock Exchange (AMEX).

exchange-traded fund (ETF)   A basket of stocks that can be traded like a single stock. Unlike traditional mutual funds, which are priced once per day after the market closes, an ETF can be bought or sold at the market price any time the exchanges are open. Investors can choose from many different ETFs, including Spiders, which tracks the Standard & Poor's 500, Diamonds, which tracks the 30 stocks in the Dow Jones Industrial Average, and Qubes, which tracks the Nasdaq 100.

ex-dividend   A period of time immediately before a dividend is paid, during which new investors in the stock are not entitled to receive the dividend. A stock's price is revised lower to reflect the dividend value on the first day of this period. On that day, a stock is said to "go ex-dividend." Usually indicated in newspapers with an x next to the stock's or mutual fund's name.

expense ratio   The percentage of mutual fund assets deducted each year for expenses, which include management fees, operating costs, administrative fees, 12b-1 fees, and all other costs incurred by the fund. Recently, the average expense ratio for domestic equity funds was 1.4 percent. For fixed-income funds it was 1.1 percent. International funds have higher expense ratios, averaging around 1.8 percent. There is no reason to buy funds with expense ratios higher than that. Sometimes the fund's management may elect to waive part of the expenses charged to shareholders in order to boost returns. But this is usually a temporary waiver, so be careful—such funds often raise their expenses once the waiver period ends.

expiration date   The date after which an option may no longer be exercised.

extension risk   For mortgage-backed securities, the risk that rising interest rates may slow down mortgage prepayment. Because investors' money is tied up in the securities, they may miss the opportunity to earn a higher rate of interest on a different investment.

extraordinary items   A nonrecurring event that must be explained to stockholders in an annual or quarterly report. Examples include expenses related to acquisitions or plant shutdowns, results of legal proceedings, or unanticipated tax benefits. Earnings are usually reported before and after taking into account the effects of extraordinary items. Pay close attention to these items because they can make earnings look better or worse than they actually are.

face value   Just like it sounds: the value a bond has printed on its face, usually $1,000. Also known as par value, it represents the amount of principal owed at maturity. The bond's actual market value may be higher or lower. When a bond's market price fluctuates, it has an impact on its yield. If the price drops below the bond's face value, its yield goes up. If the price rises above face value, the yield goes down.

factors   Companies that buy accounts receivable, which are debts for merchandise or services bought on credit. Factors assume the job of collecting the money due.

federal budget deficit   The amount of money the federal government owes because it spent more than it received in revenue for the past year. To cover the shortfall, the government usually borrows from the public by floating long- and short-term bonds. Federal deficits, which started to rise in the 1970s, exploded to hundreds of billions of dollars per year in the 1980s and 1990s. Some economists think massive federal deficits can lead to high interest rates and inflation, since they compete with private borrowing from consumers and businesses, but such was not the case during the 1980s and 1990s. The cumulative unpaid debt of all past deficits is called the federal debt or national debt.

federal debt   The total amount the federal government owes because of past deficits. The federal debt is made up of such debt obligations as Treasury bills, Treasury notes, and Treasury bonds. Congress imposes a ceiling on federal debt, which has been increased on occasion when accumulated deficits neared the ceiling. In the mid-1990s the federal debt was more than $5 trillion. The interest due on the federal debt is one of the major expenses of the federal government. The federal debt, which is the total debt accumulated by the government over many years, should not be confused with the federal budget deficit, which is the excess of spending over income by the federal government in one fiscal year.

federal funds   Funds deposited by commercial banks at Federal Reserve district banks. Designed to enable banks temporarily short of their reserve requirement to borrow reserves from banks having excess reserves.

federal funds rate   The interest rate that banks charge each other for the use of federal funds. This rate is used for overnight loans to banks that need more cash to meet bank reserve requirements. It changes daily and is the most sensitive indicator of general interest rate trends. The rate is not set directly by the Federal Reserve, but fluctuates in response to changes in supply and demand for funds. It is reported daily in the business section of most newspapers.

Federal Open Market Committee (FOMC)   The policy-making arm of the Federal Reserve Board. It sets monetary policy to meet the Fed's objectives of regulating the money supply and credit. The FOMC's chief tool is the purchase and sale of government securities, which increase or decrease the money supply, respectively. It also sets key interest rates, such as the discount rate. The FOMC has 12 members. Seven are the members of the Federal Reserve Board, appointed by the president of the United States. The other five are presidents of the 12 regional Federal Reserve Banks.

Federal Reserve   The central bank of the United States that sets monetary policy. The Federal Reserve oversees money supply, interest rates, and credit with the goal of keeping the U.S. economy and currency stable. Governed by a seven-member board, the system includes 12 regional Federal Reserve Banks, 25 branches, and all national and state banks that are part of the system. Also called the Fed.

Financial Accounting Standards Board (FASB)   An independent board responsible for establishing and interpreting generally accepted accounting principles (or GAAP). U.S. companies that adhere to GAAP are said to be more transparent and easier to analyze financially than companies in many foreign countries. In fact, the differences in accounting standards make it difficult to compare the earnings of companies in different countries.

financial planner   A type of financial adviser, ideally with broad knowledge of all areas of personal finance. But no particular training or credentials are required, and many incompetents and even some outright crooks call themselves planners. Fee-only planners are paid solely by their clients—that is, they do not receive sales commissions or compensation from other sources. Fee-plus-commission planners charge fees for advice and other services, and also receive commissions on the sale of investment and insurance products. When choosing a financial planner, see that the individual has a certified

financial planner (CFP) designation. It is the best-known financial planning designation, requiring that the adviser be certified by the CFP Board of Standards.

fiscal year (FY)   The 12-month period that a corporation or government uses for bookkeeping purposes. A company's fiscal year is often, but not necessarily, the same as the calendar year. A seasonal business will frequently select a fiscal rather than a calendar year so that its year-end figures will show it in its most liquid condition, which also means having less inventory to verify physically. The fiscal year of the U.S. government ends September 30.

fixed assets   Tangible property used in the operations of a business but not expected to be consumed or converted into cash in the ordinary course of events. Plant, machinery and equipment, furniture and fixtures, and leasehold improvements comprise the fixed assets of most companies. Companies with a lot of fixed assets can be accurately valued with the price-to-book ratio.

fixed-income security   A security that pays a fixed rate of return. This usually refers to government, corporate, or municipal bonds, which pay a fixed rate of interest until the bonds mature, and to preferred stock that pays a fixed dividend. Since fixed-income investments guarantee you an annual payout, they are inherently less risky than stocks, which do not.

float   The number of outstanding shares in a corporation available for trading by the public. A small float means the stock will be more volatile, since a large order to buy or sell shares can influence the stock's price dramatically. A large float will mean a stock is less volatile. Since small-capitalization stocks tend to have less shares outstanding than larger companies, their float is smaller and they tend to be more volatile. The same is true for closely held companies.

floating an issue   Offering stocks or bonds to the public for the first time. It can be an initial public offering or an offering of issues by companies that are already public.

401(k) plan   An employer-sponsored retirement-savings plan funded by employees with contributions that are deducted from pretax pay. Employers frequently add matching contributions up to a set limit. Employees are responsible for managing the money themselves, allocating the funds among a selection of stock, bond, and cash investment funds. Investment gains aren't taxed until the money is withdrawn.

403(b) plan   A retirement-savings plan for employees of colleges, hospitals, school districts, and nonprofit organizations. The plan, which is similar to the 401(k) plan offered to many corporate employees, is funded by employees with contributions that are deducted from pretax pay.

Employees manage the money themselves, selecting from fixed and variable annuities, and mutual funds. Investment gains aren't taxed until the money is withdrawn.

FT-SE 100   Abbreviation for the *Financial Times*–Stock Exchange 100-Share Index, an index of 100 large companies, on a capitalization basis, on the London Stock Exchange. The FT-SE 250 is an index of the largest 250 companies after the top 100.

full-service brokers   Brokers who execute buy and sell orders, research investments, help investors develop and meet investment goals, and give advice to investors. They charge commissions for their work. During a bull market, when stocks are going up consistently, good ideas are a dime a dozen. But when the markets turn choppy, solid advice can save you. Some full-service firms offer a range of good mutual funds, estate-planning services, and tax advice. A broker will set up a financial profile for you—based on your assets, income, and goals—and advise you appropriately. All of this, of course, will cost you a lot more than using a bare-bones discount broker.

fundamental analysis   Fundamental analysis asserts that a stock's price is determined by the future course of its earnings and dividends. The fundamental analyst tries to find what the intrinsic value of a stock's underlying business is by looking at its financial statements and its competitive position within its industry. If this intrinsic value is greater than the market price of the stock, the stock is said to be undervalued. In other words, the company has greater earning potential than its stock price would indicate. Fundamental analysis is the antithesis of technical analysis, which focuses on stock-price movements instead of underlying earnings potential.

fund company   Fund companies are business entities that manage, sell, and market mutual funds to the public. They typically offer a wide variety of funds, investing in both the equity and fixed-income markets. Companies also perform administrative tasks, such as fund accounting and customer service, although these responsibilities are sometimes contracted out. Some of the larger fund companies are Fidelity, Vanguard, Franklin-Templeton, and T. Rowe Price. In many cases, investors may move their assets from one fund to another within a fund company at little or no cost. Also called fund family.

futures contract   An agreement to buy or sell a set amount of a commodity or security in a designated future month at a price agreed upon today by the buyer and seller. A futures contract differs from an option because an option is the right but not the obligation to buy or sell, whereas a futures contract is the promise to actually make a transaction. A future is part of a class of securities called derivatives, so named because such securities derive their value from the worth of an underlying investment.

futures option   An option on a futures contract.

generally accepted accounting principles (GAAP)   Guidelines that explain what should be done in specific accounting situations as determined by the Financial Accounting Standards Board. U.S. companies that adhere to GAAP are said to be more transparent and easier to analyze financially than companies in many foreign countries. In fact, the differences in accounting standards make it difficult to compare the earnings of companies in different countries.

general-obligation bond   A government bond that is approved by either the voters or their legislature. The government's promise to repay the principal and pay the interest is constitutionally guaranteed, based on its ability to tax the population. Also called a full-faith-and-credit bond.

global funds   A fund that invests in stocks located throughout the world while maintaining a percentage of assets (normally 25 percent to 50 percent) in the United States. Global funds tend to be the safest foreign-stock investments, but that's because they typically lean on better-known U.S. stocks.

goodwill   In accounting, goodwill is any advantage, such as a well-regarded brand name or symbol, that enables a business to earn better profits than its competitors. During an acquisition, goodwill value in excess of the acquired company's liquidation value is treated as an intangible asset. Because this intangible asset has no independent market or liquidation value (unlike, say, a factory, which can be sold for cash), accepted accounting principles require that goodwill be written off by the acquiring company over a period of time—up to 40 years. The process of writing off goodwill is called amortization. Both depreciation and amortization expenses are subtracted from a company's operating revenues to calculate net income.

government-sponsored enterprise
A government-sponsored agency such as the Federal National Mortgage Association (Fannie Mae), the Federal Home Loan Mortgage Corporation (Freddie Mac), the Student Loan Marketing Corporation (Sallie Mae), and the Tennessee Valley Authority (TVA). Bonds issued by these organizations are called agency bonds. Agency bonds are almost as safe and liquid as Treasurys but have slightly higher yields.

Great Depression   The worldwide economic hard times that began after the stock market collapse on October 28, 1929, and continued through most of the 1930s. Even the Great Depression didn't stop the long-term upward trend of stock prices and earnings. If in 1929 you'd invested $100 in the S&P 500, you'd be sitting on $83,000 in 1999 (assuming you reinvested all the dividends).

gross domestic product (GDP)   The total value of goods and services produced by a nation. The GDP is made up of consumer and government purchases, private domestic investments, and net exports of goods and services. In the United States it is calculated by the Commerce Department every quarter, and it is the main measure of economic output. Because GDP measures national output, and strong output is indicative of a healthy economy, bond prices react negatively to strong GDP data. A strong economy ignites inflationary fears, which is a negative for bond prices. Equities, on the other hand, tend to perform well when GDP is rising since earnings-growth prospects are better during economic expansions.

gross margin   A company's profitability after the costs of production have been paid. Gross margin is calculated by dividing gross income (revenue after production costs are subtracted) by revenue and then multiplying by 100. The result is expressed as a percentage. Gross margin shows you how profitable the basic business of a company is before administrative costs, taxes, and depreciation have been taken out.

Operating margins may paint a truer picture of a company's profitability.

gross spread   The difference between the price that investors are charged for a security and the amount of proceeds that are paid to the issuer. In the securities-underwriting business, those proceeds are the total amount of fees that a company pays to an underwriting group in connection with a public offering of its stock or bonds. This includes the selling concession paid to members of the underwriting group and the underwriting and management fees that are paid to the securities firms in charge of the offering.

growth and income fund   A mutual fund that seeks long-term growth of capital as its primary objective. Current income is a secondary objective. Growth and income funds typically buy shares of large companies that have good prospects for future earnings growth and solid dividend payment histories. They are generally more value-oriented than growth-oriented in style, since value stocks produce more dividend income than growth stocks. From a risk perspective, growth and income funds tend to move in tandem with the broad market averages, such as the S&P 500. The upside is that growth and income funds tend to be less volatile than the overall market. The downside is that such funds aren't generally the leaders on a total-return basis.

growth fund   As its name implies, this type of fund tends to look for the fastest-growing companies on the market. Growth managers are willing to take more risk and pay a premium for their stocks in an effort to build a portfolio of companies with above-average earnings momentum or price appreciation. Growth stock funds usually have higher return volatility than most funds. This means that if the market declines, a growth fund's return will tend to decline more than the overall market. On the upside, if the market rallies, growth funds typically outperform most market measures such as the S&P 500. A growth fund invests in stocks of all market capitalization ranges—small, medium, and large.

growth investing   An investment style that looks for companies with above-average current and projected-earnings growth. Growth investors believe in buying stocks with superior earnings growth no matter what the price. Thus, growth stocks tend to have very high earnings-growth rates but very low dividend yields. These firms all trade at high valuation levels, meaning they usually have high price-to-book (P/B), price-to-earnings (P/E), and price-to-sales (P/S) ratios. Because of their high prices and low yields, growth stocks tend to have less downside protection and more volatility than cheaper companies. They are particularly sensitive to rising interest rates, which can put a damper on their rapid earnings growth. Contrast with value investing.

guaranteed investment contract (GIC)   An investment offered by an insurance company that promises preservation of principal and a fixed rate of return. Many defined-contribution plans, such as 401(k) and 403(b) plans, offer GICs as retirement options to employees. Although the insurance company takes all market, credit, and interest rate risks on the investment portfolio, it can profit if its returns exceed the guaranteed amount. Only the insurance company backs the guarantee, not any government agency; so if the insurer fails, it is possible there could be a default on the contract. But overall, GICs offer a stable way to achieve a fixed rate of return.

hard asset   Also known as a tangible asset, a hard asset is one whose value depends on particular physical properties. These include reproducible assets such as buildings or machinery and nonreproducible assets such as land, a mine, or a work of art. Assets that have no physical presence, such as goodwill or a copyright, are called intangible assets. An industrial company with a lot of hard assets (factories, machinery, etc.) is best valued by its price-to-book ratio. But companies that have a lot of intangible intellectual assets (such as software makers or pharmaceutical companies) should be valued by other means.

hedge fund   A private investment partnership, owned by wealthy individuals and institutions, which is allowed to use aggressive strategies that are unavailable to mutual funds, including short selling, leverage, program trading, swaps, arbitrage, and derivatives. Since these funds are restricted by law to less than 100 investors, the minimum hedge-fund investment is typically $1 million.

hedging   A strategy designed to reduce investment risk using call options, put options, short selling, or futures contracts. A hedge can help lock in existing profits. Examples include a position in a futures market to offset the position held in a cash market, holding a security and selling that security short, and a call option against a shorted stock. A perfect hedge eliminates the possibility for a future gain or loss. An imperfect hedge insures against a portion of the loss.

high-yield bond   These are the lowest-quality bonds (other than those in default). Bonds with credit ratings below BBB from Standard & Poor's or Baa from Moody's Investors Service are considered speculative because they have a greater chance of default than investment-grade bonds. High-yield or junk bonds are usually issued by smaller companies without long track records or by companies with questionable credit ratings. To compensate for the additional risk, issuers offer higher yields than investment-grade bonds. In recent years, however, junk-bond yields have declined as their popularity has increased and default rates have slowed.

holding company   A company whose principal assets are the securities it owns in companies that actually provide goods or services. A holding company enables one corporation and its directors to control several companies by holding large stakes in the companies.

hot issue   A stock that attracts attention because its share price has risen substantially, and in many cases is expected to rise further.

housing completions   The Commerce Department's monthly survey of the number of completed single- and multifamily homes. The level of housing completions can be seen as an indicator of economic growth, although housing starts is usually considered more relevant.

housing starts   The Commerce Department's monthly survey of the number of housing permits issued by local government authorities.

illiquid   Not readily convertible into cash. Illiquid investments include antique cars, paintings, and stamp collections. An illiquid security is one without an active secondary market, making it difficult for an owner of the security to sell it. Small-capitalization stocks tend to be more illiquid than

large-cap stocks because they have fewer shares outstanding and lower trading volumes. That can make them more volatile to own.

incentive stock options   A compensation plan that gives executives the right to purchase stock at a specified price during a specific period of time. The options are free of tax when they are granted and when they are exercised.

income bond fund   A mutual fund that seeks a high level of steady income by investing in a mix of corporate and government bonds.

income equity fund   A mutual fund that seeks a high level of steady income by investing in stocks of companies with consistent records of paying dividends.

income fund   A mutual fund that seeks a high level of current income by investing in income-producing securities, including both stocks and bonds.

index   A composite of stocks, bonds, or other securities selected to represent a specific market, industry, or asset class. Examples include: the S&P 500, which represents large U.S. stocks; the Russell 2000, which represents smaller U.S. stocks; the Morgan Stanley EAFE Index, a foreign stock index that represents Europe, Australasia, and the Far East; and the Lehman Brothers Aggregate Bond Index, which represents the total U.S. bond market. Investors use these composites to measure the overall health of specific markets and as benchmarks of comparison. For example, if you own a large-cap mutual fund, you can compare its total return to the S&P 500 to see whether it is performing well.

index arbitrage   Buying or selling baskets of stocks while at the same time executing offsetting trades in stock-index futures. For example, if stocks are temporarily cheaper than futures, an arbitrageur will buy stocks and sell futures to capture a profit on the difference, or spread, between the two prices. By taking advantage of momentary disparities between markets, arbitrageurs perform the economic function of making those markets trade more efficiently.

index fund   A mutual fund that seeks to produce the same return that investors would get if they owned all the securities in a particular index. The most common variety is an S&P 500 index fund, which tries to mirror the return of the Standard & Poor's 500-stock index. Index funds have the lowest expense ratios in the fund universe and are also very tax-efficient because of their low turnover ratios. They are good funds for novice investors.

indexing   A passive investment strategy that tracks the total return of a securities index, such as the S&P 500. Robotic indexing offers some unique advantages over active portfolio man-

agement. Discipline and style consistency are first and foremost. If you buy an S&P 500 index fund, it will never invest in anything but the S&P 500. That kind of consistency is necessary if you want the asset allocation in your portfolio to be precise. An active fund manager could be guilty of style drift, investing in parts of the market that don't suit your asset-allocation scheme. Other advantages of indexing are low expenses and tax-efficiency.

index option   An agreement that gives an investor the right, but not the obligation, to buy or sell the basket of stocks represented by a stock-market index at a specific price on or before a specific date. Index options allow investors to trade in a particular market or industry group without having to buy all the stocks individually.

individual retirement account (IRA) A tax-deferred retirement plan that can help build a nest egg. Individuals whose income is less than a certain amount or who aren't active participants in an employer's retirement plan—such as a 401(k) or 403(b)—generally can deduct some or all of their annual IRA contributions when figuring their income tax. Others can make nondeductible IRA contributions. A single person can contribute up to $3,000 (deductible) and a married couple up to $6,000 annually. The contributions grow tax-deferred until withdrawn. (In contrast, a Roth IRA's nondeductible contributions are tax-free upon withdrawal.) Withdrawals before age $59^{1}/_{2}$ are subject to a 10 percent penalty charge.

industrial production   Monthly report by the Federal Reserve that measures output at factories, utilities and mines. The industrial production index rises during economic expansions and falls during recessions. Analysts often use the index as a proxy for gross domestic product (GDP). Financial markets pay a great deal of attention to this report. Bond prices react negatively when industrial production increases because inflation pressures eat away at their yield returns.

inflation   The rate at which the general level of prices for goods and services is rising. Inflation has an uncanny ability to erode the value of securities that don't grow fast enough. That's why investing only in a money market fund can be more risky than it appears on the surface. If inflation is rising at 3 percent a year and your money market is growing at 5 percent or 6 percent, you won't have much money left over for your retirement. Measures of inflation include the consumer price index (CPI) and the producer price index (PPI).

inflation-indexed bonds   These Treasurys are designed to keep pace with inflation. The principal is adjusted to match changes in the con-sumer price index (CPI), while the interest rate remains fixed. In this way, inflation cannot erode the value of your principal. New in 1997, they are officially known as Treasury Inflation Protection Securities, or TIPS.

initial public offering (IPO)   The first time a company issues stock to the public. This process often is called "going public." Securities offered in an IPO are often, but not always, those of young, small companies seeking outside equity capital and a public market for their stock. Investors purchasing stock in IPOs generally must be prepared to accept very large risks for the possibility of large gains.

insider   A person, such as an executive or director, who has information about a company before the information is available to the public. An insider also is someone who owns more than 10 percent of the voting shares of a company. All insider trades must be disclosed to the Securities and Exchange Commission. However, it is illegal for insiders to trade on corporate information that hasn't been released to the public yet. Many professional investors watch insider activity closely for clues to a company's future.

insider trading   In one respect, it refers to the legal trading of securities by corporate officers based on information available to the public. In another respect, it refers to the illegal trading of securities by any investor based on information not available to the public. Many professional investors watch insider activity closely for clues to a company's future.

intangible assets   Assets that have no physical substance, such as patents, goodwill, copyrights, and trademarks. Because an intangible asset has no independent market or liquidation value (unlike, say, a factory, which can be sold for cash), it is subject to a lot of accounting manipulation. Generally accepted accounting principles require intangibles to be written off over a period of time—up to 40 years. The process of writing off an intangible asset is called amortization. Both depreciation and amortization expenses are subtracted from a company's operating revenues to calculate net income.

interest rate   The rate of interest charged for the use of money, usually expressed as an annual percentage rate. The rate is derived by dividing the amount of interest by the amount of principal borrowed. For example, if a bank charged $50 a year to borrow $1,000, the interest rate would be 5 percent. Interest rates are quoted on bills, notes, bonds, credit cards, and many kinds of consumer and business loans. Rates in general tend to rise with inflation and in response to the Federal Reserve raising key short-term rates. A rise in interest rates has a negative effect on the stock market because investors can get more com-

petitive returns from buying newly issued bonds instead of stocks. It also hurts the secondary market for bonds because rates look less attractive compared to newer issues.

interest rate risk   This is the danger that prevailing interest rates will rise significantly higher than the rates paid on bonds you are holding. This drives down the price of your bonds, so if you sell you'll lose money. This is a serious risk for anyone investing in long-term bonds, including Treasurys, because the longer the maturity, the higher the interest rate risk.

interest rate swap   A derivative in which one party agrees to pay a fixed interest rate in return for receiving a floating interest rate from another party.

intermediate-term bonds   Treasury notes that mature in 2 to 10 years, or corporate bonds that mature in 5 to 15 years.

internal rate of return   An accounting term for the rate of return on an asset. It is the discount rate on an investment that equates the present value of its cash outflows to the present value of its cash inflows.

international funds   Funds that primarily invest in stocks located outside the United States. While having international exposure adds diversification to your portfolio, there are some risk factors to note: currency risk, political risk, and economic risk. In particular, currency risk can cause investment returns to vary considerably. Also, because of the high cost of investing abroad, most international funds have higher expense ratios than their domestic peers.

International Monetary Fund (IMF)
An organization that makes loans and provides other services intended to stabilize world currencies and promote orderly and balanced trade. Member nations may obtain foreign currency when needed, making it possible to make adjustments in their balance of payments without currency depreciation.

in-the-money   A term used to describe an option that is worth something if exercised immediately. In the case of a call option, it means the current price is higher than the strike price. In the case of a put option, it means the current price is below the strike price.

intrinsic value   The underlying value of a business separate from its market value or stock price. In fundamental analysis, the analyst will take into account both the quantitative and qualitative aspects of a company's performance. The quantitative aspect is the use of financial ratios such as earnings, revenue, and so on, while the qualitative perspective involves consideration of the company's management strength. Based on such analysis, the fundamental analyst will make a forecast of future earnings and prospects for the company to arrive at

an intrinsic value of its shares. The intrinsic value of a share can be at odds with its stock market price, indicating that the company is either overvalued or undervalued by the market.

inventory   The monetary value of a company's raw materials, work in progress, supplies used in operations, and finished goods. Excess inventory on a company's balance sheet could indicate a slowdown in sales and a lack of pricing power.

inventory turnover   For a company, the ratio of annual sales to inventory; or equivalently, the fraction of a year that an average item remains in inventory. Low turnover is a sign of inefficiency, since inventory usually has a rate of return of zero. For example, if a company had $20 million in sales last year but $60 million in inventory, then inventory turnover would be 0.33, an unusually low number ($20/$60). It would take three years to sell all the inventory.

investment bank   A securities firm, financial company, or brokerage house that helps companies take new issues to market. An investment bank purchases new securities from the issuer, then distributes them to dealers and investors, profiting on the spread between the purchase price and the offering price. Additionally, an investment bank handles the sales of large blocks of previously issued securities and private placements. Most investment banks also maintain brokerage operations and other financial services.

investment grade   An assessment of a bond by a credit rating firm that indicates whether investors are expected to receive principal and interest payments in full and on time. A grade of BBB or higher from Standard & Poor's or Baa or higher from Moody's Investors Service is considered investment grade. Lower grades (BB, Ba, B, etc.) are considered speculative. Investment-grade bonds have less risk of default but lower yields than speculative bonds. Speculative bonds are also called high-yield or junk bonds.

junior security   A security that has lower priority in claims on assets and income than other securities.

junk bond   These are the lowest-quality bonds. Bonds with credit ratings below BBB from Standard & Poor's or Baa from Moody's Investors Service are considered junk because they have a greater chance of default than investment-grade bonds. Junk bonds are usually issued by smaller companies without long track records or by companies with questionable credit ratings. To compensate for the additional risk, issuers offer higher yields than investment-grade bonds. In recent years, however, junk-bond yields have declined as their popularity has increased and default rates

have slowed. Also called high-yield bonds.

knock-in option   An option activated only when the price of the option's underlying instrument or market reaches a certain level above or below an agreed-upon range.

knock-out option   An option that becomes worthless when the price of the option's underlying instrument or market reaches a previously agreed-upon point.

ladder   A portfolio strategy where investors stagger the maturities of their bond holdings in order to provide regular income as the bonds come due and smooth out the effects of interest rate fluctuations. For those with enough assets allocated to bonds, we recommend putting equal amounts of money into Treasurys due to mature in one-, three-, five-, seven-, and nine-year periods. That gives your portfolio an average maturity of five years. As the principal comes due every two years, you can reinvest that amount in bonds due to mature in 10 years. That way, you keep your portfolio's average maturity at five years or so.

lagging economic indicators Economic indicators that lag behind the overall pace of economic activity. The Commerce Department publishes the Index of Lagging Indicators monthly along with the Index of Leading Indicators and Index of Coincident Indicators. The six components of the lagging indicators are the unemployment rate, business spending, unit-labor costs, bank loans outstanding, bank interest rates, and book value of manufacturing and trade inventories.

large-capitalization stock   A share of a large publicly traded corporation, typically with a total market capitalization of greater than $5 billion (also called large-cap stocks, large caps, and blue chips). These companies play an especially significant role in driving the economy. The two most watched indexes—the Dow Jones Industrial Average and the S&P 500—are both composed of large-cap stocks. The Dow tracks 30 of the biggest stocks on the New York Stock Exchange. The S&P tracks 500 companies with an average market value of $7.85 billion. Because of their sheer size, large caps tend to grow more slowly than small-capitalization stocks, but they also tend to be much more stable.

leading economic indicators   A composite of 11 economic measurements developed to help forecast likely changes in the economy as a whole. It is compiled by the Conference Board. The components are: average work week, unemployment claims, orders for consumer goods, deliveries, plant and equipment orders, building permits, durable-order backlog, materials prices, stock prices, M2 money supply, and consumer expectations.

leverage   The degree to which an investor or business is utilizing borrowed money. For companies, leverage is measured by the debt-to-equity ratio, which is calculated by dividing long-term debt by shareholders' equity. The more long-term debt there is, the greater the financial leverage and the greater the risk of the company falling on its face. For investors, leverage means buying on margin or using derivatives such as options to enhance return on value without increasing investment. Leveraged investing can be extremely risky because you can lose not only your money but the money you borrowed as well.

leveraged buyout   The purchase of a company by a small group of investors financed largely by debt, often in the form of junk bonds. Most often the target company's assets serve as security for the loans taken out by the acquiring firm, which repays the loans out of cash flow of the acquired company. The buyout firm maintains control by converting the acquired business from a public company to a private one.

liabilities   The claims against a corporation or other entity. They include accounts payable, wages and salaries, dividends, taxes, and obligations such as bonds, debentures, and bank loans.

limit order   An order to buy or sell a stock at a specific price or better. The broker will execute the trade only within the price restriction. This type of trade provides more investment control than a market order, which will buy or sell the security at any price.

liquidation   The process of converting stock or other assets into cash. When a company is liquidated, the cash obtained is first used to pay debts and obligations to holders of bonds and preferred stock. Whatever cash remains is distributed on a per-share basis to the holders of common stock.

liquidity   The ease with which financial assets can be converted to cash without creating a substantial change in price or value. Liquidity is influenced by the amount of float in the security, investor interest, and size of the investment being converted to cash. A blue-chip stock like Microsoft is liquid because it is actively traded so its share price won't be dramatically affected by a few buy or sell orders. Money-market funds and checking accounts provide instant liquidity because you can write a check on the assets.

load   A sales charge for buying or selling a mutual fund. For initial, or front-end, loads, this figure is expressed as a percentage of the initial investment and is incurred upon purchase of fund shares. For back-end loads, the amount charged is based on the lesser of the initial or final value of the shares sold.

load factor   A measurement of business and efficiency for airlines. It is the percentage of available seats that are occupied.

load fund   A mutual fund that charges a sales commission, as opposed to a no-load fund, which doesn't levy a fee when you buy or sell. To compensate brokers, load funds usually charge either a front-end sales commission when you buy the fund or a back-end sales commission when you sell. In addition, many broker-sold funds charge an annual 12b-1 fee, which is also used to compensate brokers. The 12b-1 fee is included in the fund's expense ratio. The supposed advantage of a load fund is that the broker/salesperson will provide you with financial advice, telling you when it is appropriate to sell the fund or buy more shares.

loan-participation fund   A fund that invests in loans that are made by banks to companies with low credit ratings. The loans are not investment grade, but they are secured by assets, which means they are the first to be paid off in case of a bankruptcy. (And that makes them higher quality than junk bonds.) Because of the nature of their portfolios, the funds are able to offer higher yields than investment-grade and government-bond funds. Also, since the rates on these loans are reset every 30, 60, or 90 days to reflect changes in current interest rates, these funds have little interest-rate risk. That makes them fairly stable investment vehicles. Also called floating-rate funds.

long   The opposite of short selling, establishing a long position means to own a security with the expectation that it will appreciate. One would say, "I'm long bank stocks but short semiconductor companies."

long bond   Slang for a 30-year Treasury bond, which the government stopped issuing in 2001.

long-term bonds   Treasury bonds with maturities of more than 10 years; corporate bonds with maturities more than 15 years. Long-term bonds pay higher yields but have greater inflation and credit risk.

long-term debt   Debt that must be paid in a year or more. A company's long-term debt could be in the form of bank debt, mortgage bonds, debenture bonds, or other obligations. Analysts examine long-term debt to see how much leverage a company has.

long-term equity anticipation securities (LEAPS)   Options that won't expire for a period from nine months up to three years.

Major Market Index   This stock index encompasses 20 blue-chip stocks, including 17 that are also in the Dow Jones Industrial Average. Options and futures are based on this index.

margin   To buy on margin means to borrow money from a broker to buy securities. The margin is the amount you must deposit with the broker in order to borrow. The minimum is 50 percent of the purchase, or short sale price, in cash. So if you want to buy $10,000 in stock on margin, you have to put up at least $5,000 to make the purchase. Buying on margin poses the threat of not only losing your own money but the money you borrowed as well.

margin account   A brokerage account allowing customers to buy securities with money borrowed from the brokerage.

margin call   A demand from a broker for additional cash or securities to bring a margin account back within minimum maintenance limits. The National Association of Securities Dealers (NASD) requires that a margin be maintained equal to 25 percent of the market value of securities in established margin accounts. Brokerage firm requirements are typically a more conservative 30 percent. If an investor fails to meet the minimum, securities in the account may be liquidated.

market capitalization   The total market value of a company or stock. Market capitalization is calculated by multiplying the number of outstanding shares by their current market price. Investors generally divide the U.S. market into three basic market caps: large-cap, mid-cap, and small-cap. Large-cap stocks typically have market capitalizations upwards of $5 billion. Because they are more liquid, large caps tend to be less volatile than small caps, which have capitalizations less than $1 billion.

market maker   In the over-the-counter market, a trader responsible for maintaining an orderly market in an individual stock by standing ready to buy or sell shares. The market maker's job is to maintain a firm bid and ask price for the assigned security. If a broker wants to buy a stock but there are no offers to sell it, the market maker fills the order by selling shares from his or her own account. And vice versa—if a broker wants to sell but no one wants to buy, the market maker buys the shares. On a stock exchange like AMEX or NYSE, a market maker is known as a specialist.

market order   Market orders execute buy or sell orders for securities at whatever price is available when the order reaches the exchange floor. Unlike a limit order, a market order gives you no control over the price at which you buy the security. But it does guarantee you will get the security if it's available.

market timing   Shifting money in and out of investment markets in an effort to take advantage of rising prices and avoid being stung by downturns. For example, investors in mutual funds will shift from an equity fund to a money-market fund if the stock market outlook turns ugly.

Unfortunately, few, if any, investors manage to be consistently successful in timing markets.

match trading   Stock transactions made outside of an auction or negotiation process. Buy and sell orders for the same security, at the same price, are paired and executed, often by computer.

maturity date   When a bond expires and the principal must be paid back in full. The later the bond's maturity date, the greater the risk of it defaulting or being negatively impacted by a rise in inflation or interest rates.

merger   The formation of one company from two or more previously existing companies through pooling of common stock, cash payment, or a combination of both. Mergers where common stock is exchanged for common stock are nontaxable and are called tax-free mergers.

microcap fund   Fund that invests primarily in equity securities issued by companies with very small market capitalizations; they typically have median market caps of approximately $250 million or less. With stocks this small, the volatility is always extremely high, but the growth potential is exceptional.

mid-capitalization stock   Shares of medium-sized publicly traded corporations, typically with a total market capitalization between $1 billion and $5 billion (also called mid-cap stocks or mid-caps). Mid-caps are established companies that haven't quite become household names yet. They make excellent diversifiers, having both the growth characteristics of small-cap stocks and the stability of larger companies. One of the most watched mid-cap indexes is the S&P MidCap 400, which has an average market capitalization of $2.30 billion.

monetary policy   The regulation of the money supply and interest rates by a central bank, such as the U.S. Federal Reserve, in order to control inflation and stabilize currency. If the economy is heating up, the Fed can withdraw money from the banking system, raise the reserve requirement, or increase the discount rate to make it cool down. If growth is slowing, the Fed can reverse the process—increase the money supply, lower the reserve requirement, and decrease the discount rate.

money-market account   A federally insured account available at many banks, credit unions, and savings and loan associations. Money-market accounts are liquid—because you can usually write three checks against the account per month—and are very stable—because they invest only in short-term debt instruments with maturities of less than a year. Accounts are also insured by the Federal Deposit Insurance Corporation (FDIC), unlike money-market funds. But since the interest rates on money-market accounts are so low, if you're not careful, the value of your investment can be eroded by inflation.

money-market fund   A type of mutual fund that invests in stable, short-term securities. Money-market funds are easily convertible into cash and usually maintain an unchanged value of $1 a share, but aren't insured by the federal government. There are various types of money-market funds based on the type of securities they buy, but the most important distinction is whether your dividends are taxable or tax-free.

money supply   Total stock of money in the economy, consisting primarily of currency in circulation and deposits in savings and checking accounts. Too much money in relation to the output of goods tends to push interest rates down and push inflation up; too little money tends to push rates up and prices down, causing unemployment and idle plant capacity. The Federal Reserve manages the money supply by raising and lowering the reserves banks are required to hold and the discount rate at which they can borrow money from the Fed. The Fed also trades government securities (called repurchase agreements) to take money out of the system or put it in. There are various measures of money supply, including M1, M2, M3, and L; these are referred to as monetary aggregates.

mortgage-backed securities   Debt issues backed by a pool of mortgage loans. Investors receive payments from the interest and principal payments made on the underlying mortgages. These bonds are extremely interest-rate sensitive because homeowners have a tendency to prepay and refinance their mortgages when interest rates decline.

MSCI EAFE index   The MSCI EAFE index is a widely accepted benchmark of foreign stocks. EAFE refers to Europe, Australasia, and the Far East. The index, which is compiled by Morgan Stanley Capital International, is an aggregate of 21 individual country indexes that collectively represent many of the major markets of the world. Most international mutual funds measure their performance against this index. It is market capitalization–weighted.

municipal bond   Bond issued by local government authorities, including states, cities, and their agencies.

municipal bond fund   Mutual fund that invests in municipal bonds. There are two main types of municipal bond fund: national tax-free funds and state tax-free funds. National tax-free funds invest in municipalities across the United States and are exempt from federal income taxes. State tax-free funds invest in a specific state and are exempt from federal and state taxes if you live in the state of issue. National funds offer more diversification and less risk but also less tax benefits.

mutual fund   An investment company that pools the money of many individual investors to purchase stocks, bonds, or other financial instruments. Professional management and diversification are the two primary benefits of mutual fund investing. A management fee is charged for these services, typically 1 percent or 2 percent a year. Funds also levy other fees and charge a sales commission (or load) if purchased from a financial adviser. Funds are either open-end or closed-end. An open-end fund issues new shares when investors put in money and redeems shares when investors withdraw money. The price of a share is determined by dividing the total net assets of the fund by the number of shares outstanding. Closed-end funds issue a fixed number of shares in an initial public offering, trading thereafter in the open market. Open-end funds are the most common type of mutual fund.

Nasdaq   An electronic stock market run by the National Association of Securities Dealers. Brokers get price quotes through a computer network and trade via telephone or computer network. The index that covers all the stocks that trade on this market is called the Nasdaq Composite index. Since there is no centralized exchange, Nasdaq is sometimes referred to as an over-the-counter market or a negotiated marketplace. Many of the stocks traded through Nasdaq are in the technology sector.

Nasdaq Composite index   An index that covers the price movements of all stocks traded on the Nasdaq Stock Market.

Nasdaq National Market   A subdivision of the Nasdaq Stock Market that contains the largest and most actively traded stocks on Nasdaq. Companies must meet more stringent standards to be included in this section than they do to be included in the other major subdivision, the Nasdaq Small-Cap Market.

National Association of Securities Dealers (NASD)   A self-regulating securities industry organization responsible for the operation and regulation of the Nasdaq Stock Market and other over-the-counter markets. NASD members include almost all investment banking houses and firms dealing in the over-the-counter market. The organization sets guidelines for ethics and standardized industry practices, and has a disciplinary structure for looking into allegations of rules violations.

net assets   The total assets (net of liabilities) held in a fund. Pay close attention to this statistic when investing in small-cap or aggressive equity funds. Because of the illiquidity and volatility of the companies they buy, such funds need to be able to move quickly in and out of positions. Having too much in assets—more than $1 billion—can be a real detriment to their performance.

net asset value (NAV)   Net asset value, also known as price per share, is the value of a fund's assets divided by the number of its outstanding shares. The NAV is calculated daily at the close of the markets. Open-end funds always trade at NAV, but closed-end funds often trade at a premium or discount to their asset values.

net income   Also known as the bottom line, this is the profit a company realizes after all costs, expenses, and taxes have been paid. It is calculated by subtracting business, depreciation, interest, and tax costs from revenues. Investors often pay too much attention to net income, the calculation of which can be easily manipulated by accountants. A better measure of corporate growth, some analysts say, is cash flow. Net income is also called earnings or net profit.

net margin   A company's profitability after all costs, expenses, and taxes have been paid. The net margin is calculated by dividing net earnings by revenue and then multiplying by 100. The result is expressed as a percentage. Net margin is used to measure operating efficiency at a company. It is the one profit margin investors watch most closely because it takes into account all expenses of running the company. But operating margins may paint a truer picture of a company's profitability.

net worth   The amount by which total assets exceed total liabilities. Also known as shareholders' equity or book value, net worth is what would be left over for shareholders if the company were sold and its debt retired. It takes into account all money invested in the company since its founding, as well as retained earnings. Examining the price-to-book (P/B) ratio of an industrial company with a lot of hard assets is a good way of telling if it's undervalued or overvalued.

New York Stock Exchange (NYSE)   The oldest and largest stock exchange in the United States, the New York Stock Exchange is located on Wall Street in New York City. The total market value of the roughly 2,300 companies whose shares are listed on the NYSE is about $5 trillion. It was founded in 1792. Also called the Big Board.

Nikkei   A price-weighted index of 225 large-capitalization stocks on the Tokyo Stock Exchange. This is the Japanese equivalent of the Dow Jones Industrial Average. In fact, it was called the Nikkei Dow Jones Stock Average until 1985. Like the Dow, it is composed of representative blue chips and is price-weighted, not market capitalization–weighted.

no-load mutual fund   A mutual fund that sells its shares without a sales charge or commission. Investors buy shares of no-load funds directly from the fund companies rather than from a broker. Buying a no-load fund is a good way to cut costs. The listing of the price of a no-load fund in the newspaper is accompanied with the designation NL.

note   A bond with a maturity greater than one year and less than 10 years.

NYSE Composite index   An index that covers the price movements of all stocks listed on the New York Stock Exchange (NYSE). It is a market capitalization–weighted index.

odd lot   Purchase or sale of securities in any amount less than 100 shares. An investor buying or selling an odd lot often pays a higher commission rate than someone making a round lot trade. This odd-lot differential varies between brokers.

open-end mutual fund   A type of fund that issues as many shares as investors demand. This contrasts with a closed-end fund, which has a fixed number of shares that trade over-the-counter or on a stock exchange. The share price of an open-end fund is determined by dividing the total net assets of the fund by the number of shares outstanding. This figure is called the fund's net asset value (NAV). The net asset value of an open-end fund is calculated at the end of each trading day. Most mutual funds are open-end funds.

open interest   A measure of liquidity in futures and options. Open interest is the total number of futures contracts or options that have been opened with either a purchase or a sale and not yet closed by an offsetting opposite purchase or sale.

operating income   A measure of a company's earning power from ongoing operations, equal to earnings before deduction of interest payments and income taxes. Operating income is calculated by subtracting costs of sales and operating expenses from revenues. It is often used to gauge the financial performance of companies with high levels of debt and interest expenses. Also called operating profit or EBIT (earnings before interest and taxes).

operating margin   A company's profitability after all operating costs have been paid. Operating margin is calculated by dividing cash flow by revenue and then multiplying by 100. The result is expressed as a percentage. Operating margin shows you how profitable a company is before interest expenses on debt and depreciation costs have been deducted. Since accountants often manipulate depreciation and amortization costs on income statements, many analysts feel operating profit paints a truer picture of a company's profitability.

option   An agreement that gives an investor the right, but not the obligation, to buy or sell a stock, bond, or commodity at a specified price within

a specific time period. A call option is an option to buy the security; a put option is an option to sell. If the option is not exercised before the expiration date, all monies paid for the option are forfeited. Options are traded on several exchanges, including the Chicago Board Options Exchange, the American Stock Exchange, the Philadelphia Stock Exchange, the Pacific Stock Exchange, and the New York Stock Exchange.

out-of-the-money   A term used to describe an option worth nothing if exercised immediately. In the case of a call option, it means the strike price is higher than the current price of the underlying security. In the case of a put option, it means the strike price is lower than the current price of the underlying security.

over-the-counter (OTC) derivative A financial contract, whose value is designed to track the return on stocks, bonds, currencies, or some other benchmark, that is traded over-the-counter or off organized exchanges.

over-the-counter market   A market in which securities transactions are conducted by dealers through a telephone and computer network connecting dealers in stocks and bonds. Also called OTC trading.

over-the-counter securities Securities that aren't listed and traded on an organized exchange, but rather via a telephone and computerized network linking OTC security dealers. The National Association of Securities Dealers (NASD) oversees over-the-counter transactions and regulations. Nasdaq is the best-known market for trading OTC securities.

par   A bond that is trading at par is selling for the same amount as its face value (par value).

par value   The nominal dollar amount assigned to a bond by its issuer. Par value represents the amount of principal you are owed at a bond's maturity. The bond's actual market value may be higher or lower. Any fluctuation in a bond's market price has an impact on its yield. If the price drops below the bond's par value, its yield goes up. If the price rises above par value, the yield goes down. Also called face value.

pass-through security   A security that comprises a pool of debt instruments. The income from the debt is passed through an intermediary—usually a government agency or investment bank—to the investors.

payment date   The date that a stock's dividend or a bond's interest payment is scheduled to be paid.

payout ratio   The percentage of a company's earnings paid to shareholders as dividends. It is calculated by dividing the quarterly dividend by the quarterly earnings per share and multiplying by 100. Typically, growth companies retain earnings to spur fur-

ther growth, while old-line companies, banks, and utilities tend to have higher payout ratios.

penny stocks   Many penny stocks do indeed have a share price of less than $1, but this informal designation now often includes stocks that are priced at $5 and below. While many legitimate companies have share prices that low, the term "penny stocks" usually refers to speculative companies with little or no real business that are heavily promoted by unscrupulous, hard-selling brokerage firms.

percent in top five holdings   Proportion of total assets in a mutual fund's largest five positions. Funds that have too much money invested in their top five holdings may not be properly diversified.

personal financial specialist   Financial planning designation given to qualifying accountants by the American Institute of Certified Public Accountants, based in New York.

pink sheets   The printed quotations of the bid and ask prices of over-the-counter stocks, published by National Quotation Bureau.

poison pill   A takeover defense tactic designed to make a hostile takeover prohibitively expensive. For instance, a firm may issue a new series of preferred stock that gives shareholders the right to redeem shares at a premium price after a takeover. Or a poison pill can allow all existing shareholders of the target company except the acquirers to buy additional shares at a bargain price. Such measures raise the cost of acquisition and cause dilution, hopefully deterring a takeover bid.

portfolio A collection of securities held by an investor. Portfolios tend to consist of a variety of securities in order to minimize investment risk.

portfolio insurance A method of hedging, or protecting, the value of a stock portfolio by selling stock-index futures contracts when the stock market declines. The practice was a major contributor to the October 1987 stock market crash.

portfolio manager The manager of a mutual fund or an investment trust.

precious metals Commodities such as gold, silver, and platinum that are used as investment instruments. Investors can buy physical metal in bullion or jewelry or can purchase precious metals futures and options contracts or mining stocks. A precious metals investment is often considered a hedge against inflation.

preferred stock A stock that pays dividends at a specified rate and that has preference over common stock in the payment of dividends and the liquidation of assets. Preferred stock enjoys prior claim to company assets over common stock in the case of a bankruptcy. But the stock does not usually carry voting rights.

premium When a closed-end fund's market price is higher than its underlying net asset value (NAV), it is said to be trading at a premium. So if a fund trading at a 10 percent premium owns a portfolio of stocks collectively worth $10 a share, the market price for the fund is actually $11 a share. Unlike open-end funds, closed-ends trade like stocks on an exchange, so a fund's price is determined by investor demand for its shares. An excess of demand can cause the fund's market price to be more than its underlying portfolio value—the source of the premium.

premium bond A premium bond sells at a current market price that is more than its face value. Bonds sell at a premium when the coupon on the bond is higher than prevailing rates. For example, you might have to pay $1,090 for a bond with a 6 percent coupon if new issues yielding 5.5 percent are available for $1,000.

price-to-book (P/B) ratio A company's stock price divided by its per-share book value. Examining the P/B of an industrial company with a lot of hard assets is a good way of telling if it's undervalued or overvalued.

price-to-cash-flow (P/C) ratio A ratio that shows how much investors are paying for a company's cash flow. There are various calculations because there are various definitions of cash flow. But the one used most often divides a company's price per share by its earnings before interest expense, taxes, depreciation, and amortization (EBITDA) per share. Many stock analysts think cash flow paints a better picture of a company's true growth potential than net earnings do because company accountants can use crafty write-offs to alter earnings numbers. Cash flow is harder to manipulate.

price-to-earnings-growth (PEG) ratio The PEG ratio is calculated by dividing a stock's forward P/E by its projected three-to-five-year annual earnings-per-share growth rate. It is used to find companies that are trading at a discount to their projected growth. A PEG ratio of less than one is considered a sign that a stock is a good value. Generally speaking, the higher the PEG, the pricier the stock.

price-to-earnings (P/E) ratio A ratio to evaluate a stock's worth. It is calculated by dividing the stock's price by an earnings-per-share figure. If calculated with the past year's earnings, it is called the trailing P/E. If calculated with an analyst's forecast for next year's earnings, it is called a forward P/E. The biggest weakness with either type of P/E is that companies sometimes manage their earnings with accounting wizardry to make them look better than they really are. That's why some analysts prefer to focus on the price-to-cash-flow measure instead.

price-to-sales (P/S) ratio The ratio of a stock's latest closing price divided by revenue per share. (Sales are the same thing as revenues.) Revenue per share is determined by dividing revenue for the past 12 months by the number of shares outstanding. This ratio is particularly useful for companies that have little or no earnings.

principal The face value or par value of a bond. It represents the amount of money you are owed when a bond reaches its maturity. So if you buy a 10-year Treasury note with a 5 percent coupon rate and a $1,000 face value, $1,000 is the principal owed to you in 10 years.

private placement The sale of stocks or other investments directly to an investor. The securities in a private placement don't have to be registered with the Securities and Exchange Commission.

producer price index (PPI) An index that measures inflation in wholesale goods. The producer price index tracks the prices of food, metals, lumber, oil, and gas, as well as many other commodities, but does not measure the price of services. It is reported monthly by the Bureau of Labor Statistics. Economists look at trends in the PPI as an accurate precursor to changes in the consumer price index (CPI) because upward or downward pressure on wholesale prices is usually passed through to the consumer over time. Bond prices are perhaps the most responsive to PPI data. This is because inflation undercuts the value of the future interest and principal payments that bonds yield. With the consumer price index coming only days after this release, the stock market's reaction is usually delayed until the CPI either confirms or refutes what the PPI trend is indicating.

profit   The earnings a company realizes after all costs, expenses, and taxes have been paid. It is calculated by subtracting business, depreciation, interest, and tax costs from revenues. Profit is the supreme measure of value as far as the market is concerned. Profit is also called earnings or net income.

profit margin   A measure of a company's profitability, cost structure, and efficiency, calculated by dividing earnings or cash flow by revenue. There are four basic types of profit margin: gross, operating, pretax, and net. Net margin is the one investors pay the most attention to. It shows a company's profitability after all costs, expenses, and taxes have been paid. The net margin is calculated by dividing earnings by revenue and then multiplying by 100. Margins are particularly helpful since they can be used both to compare profitability among many companies and to look for financial trouble at a single outfit.

profit-taking   Selling securities after a recent, often rapid price increase.

This is often the action of short-term traders cashing in on gains from the rise. Profit-taking pushes down prices, but only temporarily; the term implies an upward market trend.

pro forma results   A projection of a financial statement that shows how the actual statement would look under certain conditions. For example, pro forma results are used to show the earnings that newly merged companies would have achieved had they been combined throughout the entire period.

program trading   Stock trades involving the purchase or sale of a basket including 15 or more stocks with a total market value of $1 million or more. Most program trades are executed on the New York Stock Exchange, using computerized trading systems. Index arbitrage is the most prominently reported type of program trading.

prospectus   A formal, written offer to sell securities that sets forth the plan for a proposed or existing business. The prospectus must be filed with the Securities and Exchange Commission and given to prospective buyers. A prospectus includes information on a company's finances, risks, products, services, and management. Prospectuses are also used by mutual funds to describe the fund objectives, risks, fees, and other essential information.

proxy   A proxy is the authorization or power of attorney, signed by a stockholder assigning the right to vote the stockholder's shares to another party. A company's management mails proxy statements to registered stockholders prior to the annual shareholder meetings. The statement contains a brief explanation of proposed management-sponsored voting items, along with the opportunity to vote for or against each individual issue or transfer the right to vote to company management or another party.

proxy fight   A contest for control of a company in which one or more companies, groups, or individuals seek proxies from a company's shareholders to back a takeover attempt. The acquirer tries to persuade the shareholders of the target company that the present management of the firm should be ousted in favor of a slate of directors favorable to the acquirer. If the shareholders, through their proxy votes, agree, the acquiring company can gain control without paying a premium price for the firm.

proxy statement   Information that the Securities and Exchange Commission requires must be provided to shareholders before they vote by proxy on company matters. The statement contains proposed members of the board of directors, inside directors' salaries, and any resolutions of minority stockholders or management.

public company   A company that sells shares of its stock to the public. Public companies are regulated by the Securities and Exchange Commission. Also called a publicly held company.

put/call volume ratio   The volume of trading in puts (options to sell) divided by the total calls (options to buy) for a security or an index.

put option   An agreement that gives an investor the right, but not the obligation, to sell a stock, bond, commodity, or other instrument at a specified price within a specific time period.

qualitative analysis   Qualitative analysis is security analysis that uses subjective judgment in evaluating securities based on nonfinancial information such as management expertise, cyclicality of industry, strength of research and development, and labor relations. Compare with quantitative analysis.

quant   Slang reference to an analyst who uses quantitative analysis techniques.

quantitative analysis   A research technique that deals with measurable values as distinguished from such qualitative factors as the character of management or labor relations. Quantitative analysis uses financial information derived from company balance sheets and income statements to make investment decisions. Examples of quantitative analysis include a review of company financial ratios, the cost of capital, asset valuation, and sales and earnings trends. Although quantitative and qualitative analysis are distinct, they must be used together to arrive at sound financial judgments.

quote   A quote, or quotation, is the highest bid price and lowest ask price currently available for a security in a given market. The difference between the bid and ask is called the price spread.

real estate investment trust (REIT) A publicly traded company that manages a portfolio of real estate to earn profits for shareholders. Patterned after mutual funds, REITs hold a diverse portfolio of real estate such as apartment buildings, offices, industrial warehouses, shopping centers, hotels, and nursing homes. Shareholders receive income in the form of dividends from the rents received on the property. To avoid taxation at the corporate level, 75 percent or more of a REIT's income must come from real property and 95 percent of its net earnings must be distributed to shareholders annually. Because REITs must distribute most of their earnings, REITs pay high yields of 5 percent to 10 percent or more.

reallowance   In the securities underwriting business, the fee that the underwriting group pays to a securities firm that isn't a member of the group to sell the shares or bonds that are being offered.

recession   A downturn in economic activity, broadly defined by many economists as at least two consecutive quarters of decline in a nation's gross domestic product (GDP).

record date   The date on which a shareholder must own a company's stock to be entitled to receive a dividend. For example, a company's board of directors might declare a dividend on October 1, payable on November 1 to stockholders of record on October 15. Investors who buy after October 15 wouldn't be entitled to the dividend. After the record date, the stock is said to be ex-dividend.

recovery   In a business cycle, the period after a downturn or recession when economic activity picks up and the gross domestic product (GDP) increases.

redemption fee   A fee charged when money is withdrawn from a mutual fund. Unlike a back-end load, this fee doesn't go back into the pockets of the fund company, but rather into the fund itself, and doesn't represent a net cost to shareholders. Also, redemption fees typically operate only in short, specific time frames, commonly 30, 180, or 365 days. Charges aren't imposed after the stated time has passed. These fees are typically imposed to discourage market timers, whose quick movements into and out of funds can be disruptive. The typical redemption fee is 1 percent or 2 percent of withdrawn assets.

regional exchange   Securities exchange located outside of New York City, including the Boston, Philadelphia, Chicago, Cincinnati, and Pacific stock exchanges. Stocks listed on the New York Stock Exchange or the American Stock Exchange also may trade on regional exchanges. These exchanges usually list only securities traded within their regions.

reserve requirement   The Federal Reserve's limit on the level of financial assets banks must keep on reserve and not lend out or reinvest. These reserves help determine how much money the banks can lend.

retail sales   A monthly survey by the Commerce Department that measures the sales of durable and nondurable goods sold to consumers. (A durable good is a product that is expected to last more than three years.) The changes in retail sales are seen as the most timely indicator of broad consumer spending patterns. Bondholders favor a decline in retail sales because such weakness signals a slowing economy. A strong economy brings fears of inflation, which hurts bond prices.

return on assets (ROA)   The rate of investment return a company earns on its assets. An indicator of profitability, ROA is determined by dividing net income from the past 12 months by total assets and then multiplying by 100. Within a specific

industry, ROA can be used to compare how efficient a company is relative to its competitors. Unlike return on equity, ROA ignores a company's liabilities.

return on equity (ROE)   The rate of investment return a company earns on shareholders' equity. An indicator of profitability, ROE is determined by dividing net income from the past 12 months by net worth (or book value). This statistic shows how effectively a company is using its investors' money. Within a specific industry, it can be used to compare how efficient a company is relative to its competitors. Contrast with return on assets.

return on investment (ROI)   A measure of how much the company earns on the money the company itself has invested. It is calculated by dividing the company's net income by its net assets.

revenue   Revenue is the earnings of a company before any costs or expenses are deducted. It includes all net sales of the company plus any other revenue associated with the main operations of the business (or those labeled as operating revenues). It does not include dividends, interest income, or nonoperating income. Also called net sales.

revenue bond   A municipal bond issued to finance public works such as bridges, tunnels, or sewer systems and supported directly by the revenues of the project. For instance, if a municipal revenue bond is issued to build a bridge, the tolls collected from motorists using the bridge are committed for paying off the bond. Holders of these bonds have no claims on the issuer's other resources.

rights offering   Offering of additional shares, usually at a discount, to existing shareholders who have rights to those shares. The shares can be actively traded.

risk   Risk is the financial uncertainty that the actual return on an investment will be different from the expected return. Factors of risk that can affect an investment include inflation or deflation, currency exchange rates, liquidity, default by borrower, and interest rate fluctuation.

Roth IRA   A type of individual retirement account established in the Taxpayer Relief Act of 1997 that allows taxpayers, subject to certain income limits, to save for retirement while allowing the savings to grow tax-free. Taxes are paid on contributions, but withdrawals, subject to certain rules, aren't taxed at all. A single person can contribute up to $3,000 and a married couple up to $6,000 annually to this type of IRA.

R-squared   A measure of a fund's correlation to the market calculated by comparing monthly returns over the past three years to those of a benchmark. The benchmark for equity funds is the S&P 500. For fixed-income funds, it is the Treasury bill. The R-squared number ranges from zero to 100. A score of 100 means a perfect correlation with the benchmark. A score of 85 means an 85 percent correlation. Generally, a higher R-squared will indicate a more useful beta figure. For instance, if a fund is earning a return near its most closely related index (indicated by an R-squared near 100), yet has a beta below one, it is probably offering higher risk-adjusted returns than the benchmark. If the R-squared is lower, then the beta is less relevant to the fund's performance.

Russell 2000 Index   A market capitalization–weighted index that is the best-known benchmark of small-cap stocks. It measures the 2,000 smallest companies in the U.S. market. These stocks represent only about 8 percent of the total market's capitalization (as represented by the broader Russell 3000 index). As of the latest reconstitution, the average market capitalization of the Russell 2000 was approximately $526.4 million. The largest company in the index had an approximate market capitalization of $1.3 million. There are a number of index funds that track the Russell 2000.

sales   Money a company receives from the goods and services it sells. In some cases, the amount includes receipts from rents and royalties. Also called revenue.

sales charge   Also referred to as a load. This is the fee investors must pay to buy shares in a mutual fund. There are front-end loads that are charged upon the initial investment and back-end loads (deferred sales charges) that are assessed upon withdrawal.

sales growth percentage   The annualized growth rate of sales or revenue expressed as a percentage. Sales growth can be useful for measuring the growth rate of young companies with no earnings. It is also harder for accountants to manipulate sales figures than earnings.

savings bond   Similar to zero-coupon bonds, savings bonds are sold at a discount to their face value, which is fully paid at maturity. They are exempt from state and local taxes and you can defer paying federal taxes until maturity. They can be purchased for as little as $50 or up to $10,000. The cost and the maturity depend on the series (E, EE, and HH) and the interest rate being paid. They can be bought or redeemed (after six months) at your local bank, the Federal Reserve, or the Bureau of Public Debt. Call 800-872-6637 or go to the United States Savings Bonds web site (www.savingsbond.gov) to get more information and current rates.

secondary market   The market where previously issued securities are traded. Most trading is done in the secondary market. The New York Stock Exchange, American Stock Exchange, Nasdaq, bond markets, and so forth are secondary markets.

secondary offering   The sale of already issued stock, typically a large block of stock that is owned by an institution. As with a primary offering (or IPO), secondary distributions are usually handled by an investment banker who purchases the shares from the seller at an agreed-upon price, then resells them at a higher public offering price, making a profit from the spread.

sector fund   Mutual fund that invests in a single-industry sector, such as biotechnology, gold, or regional banks. Sector funds tend to generate erratic performance, and they often dominate both the top and bottom of the annual mutual fund performance charts.

secular   Long term as opposed to seasonal or cyclical.

Securities and Exchange Commission (SEC)   The federal agency that enforces securities laws and sets standards for disclosure about publicly traded securities, including mutual funds. It was created in 1934 and consists of five commissioners appointed by the U.S. president and confirmed by the Senate to staggered five-year terms. To ensure its independence, no more than three members of the commission may be of the same political party.

Securities Investor Protection Corporation (SIPC)   The nonprofit corporation that insures the securities and cash in the customer accounts of brokerage firms up to $500,000 in the event a firm fails. All brokers and dealers registered with the Securities and Exchange Commission are required to be members.

security   Generally, a stock or a bond. Specifically, a piece of paper that indicates the holder owns a share or shares of a company (stock) or has loaned money to a company or government organization (bond).

sell-off   A period of intensified selling in a market that pushes stock or bond prices sharply lower.

senior security   A security with claims on income and assets that rank higher than certain other securities. Debt, including notes, bonds, and debentures, is senior to stock. In the event of bankruptcy, senior securities have first claim on corporate assets.

share   A unit of ownership in an equity or mutual fund. This ownership is represented by a certificate that names the shareowner and the company or fund. The number of shares a company is authorized to issue is detailed in its corporate charter. Open-end mutual funds can issue unlimited shares.

shareholders' equity   The amount by which total assets exceed total liabilities. Also known as net worth or book value, shareholders' equity is what would be left over for shareholders if the company were

sold and its debt retired. It takes into account all money invested in the company since its founding, as well as retained earnings. Examining the price-to-book (P/B) ratio of an industrial company with a lot of hard assets is a good way of telling if it's undervalued or overvalued.

shell merger   A method for a company to go public when it is unable to do so by an initial public offering. The company wishing to go public merges with a shell company—a publicly traded company that has no significant operations. The merger is done under state merger and acquisition laws, requiring fewer, less extensive filings with the Securities and Exchange Commission than a conventional initial public offering. Also called a back-door merger.

short covering   Trades that reverse, or close out, short-sale positions. For instance, when a stock rises sharply in price, investors who shorted the stock, expecting it to fall, are often forced to purchase the shares they borrowed from their brokers. That can push the price of the stock up even higher.

short interest   Total number of shares of a given stock that have been sold short and not yet repurchased. Usually, investors sell short to profit from price declines. As a result, the short interest is often an indicator of the amount of pessimism in the market about a particular security. On the flip side, short interest represents dormant demand for a stock that may come to life if short sellers must cover their positions due to a marked rise in the stock's price. So a large short interest can ultimately push the stock higher. There are also other reasons to short that are not related to pessimism. For example, hedging strategies for mergers and acquisitions as well as derivative positions may involve short sales.

short interest ratio   The ratio of shares of a security that investors have sold short divided by average daily volume of the security, measured over 30 days or 90 days. The short interest ratio tells you how many days—given the stock's average trading volume—it would take short sellers to cover their positions (i.e., buy stock) if good news sent the price higher and ruined their negative bets.

short selling   A trading strategy that anticipates a drop in a share's price. Stock or another financial instrument is borrowed from a broker and then sold, creating a short position. That position is reversed, or covered, when the stock is repurchased to repay the loan. If the stock price falls, the short seller will profit by replacing the borrowed shares at a lower cost.

short squeeze   Situation that occurs when the price of a security rises sharply, causing many short sellers to buy the security to cover their positions and limit losses. That buy-

ing leads to even higher prices, increasing the losses of short sellers who haven't covered their positions.

short-term bonds   Treasury bills that mature in 90 days to one year, or corporate bonds that mature in one to five years. Because of their short maturities, these bonds are particularly safe from default and interest-rate risk, but they also pay lower yields.

short-term gain or loss   For tax purposes, the profit or loss from selling capital assets or securities held 12 months or less. Short-term gains are taxed at your regular income-tax rate, which can be as high as 39.6 percent. It pays not to trade. At the moment, the maximum federal tax rate on long-term capital gains is only 20 percent.

sidecar   A so-called circuit breaker that restricts some trading on the New York Stock Exchange and the Chicago Mercantile Exchange when the price of a Standard & Poor's 500 index futures contract falls by 12 points. Such a decline is equal to roughly 90 points on the Dow Jones Industrial Average.

small-capitalization stocks   Shares of relatively small publicly traded corporations, typically with a total market capitalization of less than $1 billion. (Also called small-cap stocks or small caps.) Small-cap stocks tend to grow faster than larger-capitalization companies, but they also tend to be more volatile. Because they have fewer shares outstanding, their price movements are necessarily more erratic. When good news hits the tape, investors clamoring to get in will drive the price up quickly. When bad news hits, the opposite is true. The Russell 2000 is the most widely known small-cap index.

specialist   A stock exchange member who is designated to maintain a fair and orderly market in a specific stock. The specialist's job is to prevent imbalances in supply and demand for the assigned security. If a broker wants to buy a stock but there are no offers to sell it, the specialist fills the order by selling shares from his or her own account. And vice versa—if a broker wants to sell but no one wants to buy, the specialist buys the shares. A specialist is also known as a market maker.

spin-off   A form of corporate divestiture that results in a subsidiary or division becoming an independent company. In a traditional spin-off, shares of the new company are distributed to the parent corporation's shareholders. Spin-offs can also be accomplished through a leveraged buyout by the subsidiary's or division's management.

spot market   A market for buying or selling commodities or foreign exchange for immediate delivery and for cash payment. Trades that take place in futures contracts expiring in the current month are also called spot market trades.

spot price   The price of a commodity or currency available for immediate sale and delivery.

spread   In stocks, the difference between the bid price and the ask price. In bonds, the difference between the yields on securities of the same credit rating but different maturities or the difference between the yields on securities of the same maturity but different ratings. The term also represents the difference between the public offering price of a new issue and the proceeds the issuer receives.

stagflation   A combination of high inflation and slow economic growth. A term coined in the 1970s, stagflation described the previously unprecedented combination of high unemployment (stagnation) with rising prices (inflation). The principal factor was the fourfold increase in oil prices imposed by OPEC in 1973, which raised prices throughout the economy while slowing economic growth. Traditional fiscal and monetary policies aimed at reducing unemployment only exacerbated the inflationary effects.

Standard & Poor's 500 stock index (S&P 500)   The Standard & Poor's 500 index—or S&P 500—is an index of 500 stocks chosen for their market size, liquidity, and industry group representation. Experts use the S&P

500 as a benchmark for the overall market performance. It is a broader, more comprehensive index than the Dow Jones Industrial Average, and represents the largest U.S. companies in 11 diversified sectors of the market. It is also a capitalization-weighted benchmark, with each stock's weight in the index proportionate to its market value. So price fluctuations in big companies in the index count proportionately more than little ones. In contrast, the Dow is a price-weighted index; it weights price movements for all of its stocks equally, regardless of company size.

standard deviation   A measure of a fund's volatility derived by looking at its range of historical returns. The higher the standard deviation, the greater the potential for volatility. Say a fund has an average annual return of 12 percent and a standard deviation of 20. By adding and subtracting 20 from 12, you can figure what the fund's high and low returns have been in two-thirds of the time periods over the past three years. In this case, the high would have been 32 percent (12 + 20). By multiplying the standard deviation by 2 and doing the same calculations, you can figure the fund's high and low returns for 95 percent of its history.

stock   An investment that represents part ownership of a company's assets and earnings. There are two different types of stock: common and preferred. Common stocks provide voting rights but no guarantee of dividend payments. Preferred stocks provide no voting rights but have a set, guaranteed dividend payment. Preferred stock also enjoys prior claim to company assets over common stock in the case of a bankruptcy. Contrast with bond.

stock fund   A mutual fund that invests in stocks. Stock funds have different investment strategies—growth, blend, and value—and invest in companies of different market capitalizations—small-cap, mid-cap, and large-cap. There are also index funds that track specific stock benchmarks such as the S&P 500 and sector funds that invest in specific industries such as technology and health care. One of the key advantages of owning a stock fund is diversification and active portfolio management.

stock index future   A contract to buy or sell the cash value of a stock index by a specified date. Investors can speculate on general market performance, short selling an index with a futures contract, or they can buy a contract to hedge a long position against a decline in value. Among the most popular indexes traded are the New York Stock Exchange Composite index on the New York Futures Exchange (NYFE) and the S&P 500 index on the Chicago Mercantile Exchange (CME).

stock index option   A call or put option based on a stock market index.

Index options allow investors to trade in a particular market or industry group without having to buy all the stocks individually. For instance, someone who thought technology stocks were going to fall could buy a put on a technology index instead of short selling a dozen tech companies.

stock option   An option in which the underlying security is the common stock of a corporation, giving the holder the right to buy or sell its stock at a specified price by a specific date. Also, it is a method of employee compensation that gives workers the right to buy the company's stock during a specified period of time at a stipulated exercise price. In recent years, offering top executives stock options as compensation has become increasingly popular.

stock split   A change in a company's number of shares outstanding that doesn't change a company's total market value or each shareholder's percentage stake in the company. Additional shares are issued to existing shareholders at a rate expressed as a ratio. A 2-for-1 stock split, for instance, doubles the number of shares outstanding. So an investor holding 100 shares of a $60 stock would have 200 shares of a $30 stock following a 2-for-1 split, but the stockholder's percentage of equity in the company remains the same. Typically, management will split a stock to make the shares more affordable to a greater number of investors.

stop order   An order to buy or sell a security when a definite price is reached, either above (on a buy) or below (on a sell) the price that prevailed when the order was given. This type of trade provides more investment control than a market order, which will buy or sell the security at any price. A stop order to buy, always at a higher price than the current market price, is usually designed to protect a profit or limit a loss on a short sale. A stop order to sell, always at a lower price than the current market price, is usually designed to protect a profit or limit a loss on a security already purchased at a higher price.

strike price   A specified price at which an investor can buy or sell an option's underlying security. For example, a call option may allow the buyer to purchase 100 shares of a company in the next three months at a strike price of $50 a share. If the stock is currently trading at $75 a share and that's as high as you think it will go, you can exercise the call option at $50 and earn $25 a share less commissions. Also called exercise price.

STRIPS   A bond, usually issued by the U.S. Treasury, whose two components, interest and repayment of principal, are separated and sold individually as zero-coupon bonds. STRIPS generally have a slightly higher return than regular Treasury bonds, but they don't pay regular interest payments. Instead the buyer receives the return by the gradual appreciation of the security, which is redeemed at face value on a specified maturity date. STRIPS is an acronym for separate trading of registered interest and principal of securities.

stub stock   Publicly traded shares with drastically reduced stock-market values. Typically, this happens when the company takes on debt for leveraged buyouts or pays a large one-time dividend.

subordinated debenture   A debt security that will be paid off after the issuer first pays off debt to senior creditors in the event of the dissolution of the company.

subsidiary   A company of which more than 50 percent of its voting shares are owned by another corporation, called the parent company. Compare with affiliate.

technical analysis   The study of all factors related to the supply and demand of stocks. Unlike fundamental analysis, technical analysis doesn't look at underlying earnings potential of a company when evaluating a stock. Rather, the technical analyst uses charts and computer programs to study the stock's trading volume and price movements in hopes of identifying a trend. Technical analysts don't care about a business's intrinsic value, only the movements of its stock. Most technical analysis is used for short-term investing.

tender offer   A formal offer by a company to buy a certain amount of its own securities or another company's securities at a stated price within a specified time limit. The offer price is usually at a premium above the current market price. When the offer is for another company's shares, it usually involves a takeover attempt. The Securities and Exchange Commission requires any corporate suitor that acquires more than 5 percent of a company to disclose its position.

10-year Treasury note   Debt obligation of the U.S. Treasury that has a maturity of 10 years. The 10-year Treasury note replaced the 30-year Treasury bond as the benchmark bond in determining interest rate trends. As a group, Treasurys are regarded as the safest bond investments, because they are backed by the full faith and credit of the U.S. government.

30-year Treasury bond   Debt obligation of the U.S. Treasury that has a maturity of 30 years but since 2001 is no longer being issued. Before being replaced as a bellwether by the 10-year Treasury note, the 30-year Treasury bond was considered the benchmark bond in determining interest rate trends. (Also known as the long bond.) As a group, Treasurys are regarded as the safest bond investments, because they are backed by the full faith and credit of the U.S. government. Treasury bonds pay interest semiannually and can be purchased in minimum denominations of $1,000 or multiples thereof.

ticker symbol   Letters that identify a security for trading purposes. Trades are reported on the consolidated tape and on quote machines by the company's symbol. For example, MSFT is Microsoft's ticker. Also called a stock symbol.

total assets   A company's total current assets plus total noncurrent assets. Noncurrent assets include property, plant and equipment, and other noncurrent receivables and investments. Total assets can be found on a company's balance sheet. It is a crucial figure for calculating return on assets (ROA), an efficiency ratio. Also, total assets minus total liabilities equals book value.

total invested capital   Total invested capital is a tally of all the outside investments a company's management has used to finance its business—everything from equity (the amount of stock sold) to long-term debt. It is calculated by taking the sum of common and preferred stock equity, long-term debt, deferred income taxes, investment credits, and minority interest. Total invested capital is the denominator of the debt-to-total-capital ratio, a ratio that measures how leveraged a company is.

total liabilities   A company's total current liabilities plus long-term debt and deferred income taxes. Total

assets can be found on a company's balance sheet. Total assets minus total liabilities equals book value or net worth.

total return   The full amount an investment earns over a specific period of time. When dealing with mutual funds or securities, total return takes into consideration three factors: changes in the NAV or price, the accumulation/reinvestment of dividends, and the compounding factor over time. The return is presented as a percentage and is usually associated with a specific time period such as six months, one year, or five years. Total return can be cumulative for the specific period or annualized. If it is cumulative, it describes how much your investment grew in total for the entire period. If it is annualized, it describes the average annual return over the period of years described.

trader   An individual who buys and sells securities for his or her own account as a dealer or principal, not as an intermediary (broker). A secondary meaning is a short-term investor who buys or sells frequently in anticipation of a quick profit.

Treasury bills (T-bills)   Debt obligations of the U.S. Treasury that have maturities of one year or less. Maturities for T-bills are usually 91 days, 182 days, or 52 weeks. Unlike Treasury bonds and notes, which pay interest semiannually, Treasury bills are issued at a discount from their face value. Interest income from Treasury bills is the difference between the purchase price and the Treasury bill's face value. Bills are issued in denominations of $10,000 with increments of $5,000 for amounts above $10,000.

Treasury bonds (T-bonds) Debt obligations of the U.S. Treasury that have maturities of 10 to 30 years. Treasury bonds pay interest semiannually and can be purchased in minimum denominations of $1,000 or multiples thereof. Until recently, the 30-year Treasury bond was considered the benchmark bond in determining trends in interest rates. (It was replaced by the 10-year Treasury note and is no longer issued.) As a group, Treasurys are regarded as the safest bond investments, because they are backed by the full faith and credit of the U.S. government.

Treasury notes (T-notes) Debt obligations of the U.S. Treasury that have maturities of 2 to 10 years. Treasury notes pay interest semiannually and can be purchased in minimum denominations of $1,000 or multiples thereof. Treasury note yields typically are lower than those of Treasury bonds, which have longer maturities, but notes typically are about half as volatile as long bonds. The 10-year note now is considered the benchmark for determining interest rates.

Treasurys Debt securities issued by the U.S. Department of the Treasury. Because principal and interest are backed by the U.S. government, Treasurys are viewed as having no credit risk. They are issued as bills, which have maturities of a year or less; notes, which have maturities of 2 to 10 years; and bonds, which have maturities of 10 to 30 years. Because Treasury issues have low liquidity risk and are considered to have no credit risk, required yields are typically lower than those of all other debt issues at any given maturity. Many other bonds, including corporate, municipal, and mortgage-backed bonds, are evaluated on a spread basis to Treasurys.

triple witching hour Slang for the quarterly expiration of stock index futures, stock index options, and options on individual stocks. Trading associated with the expirations inflates stock market volume and can cause volatility in prices. Occurs on the Friday preceding the third Saturday of March, June, September, and December.

turnover ratio A measure of a fund's trading history that is expressed as a percentage. A fund with a 100 percent turnover generally changes the composition of its entire portfolio each year. A low turnover figure (20 percent to 30 percent) would indicate a buy-and-hold strategy. High turnover (more than 100 percent) would indicate an investment strategy involving considerable buying and selling of securities. Funds with higher turnover incur greater brokerage fees for effecting the trades. They also tend to distribute more capital gains than low-turnover funds, because high-turnover funds are constantly realizing the gains. A change in a fund's general turnover pattern can indicate changing market conditions, a new management style, or a change in the fund's investment objective.

12b-1 fees   These are fees the fund charges for marketing and distribution expenses. They are included in the expense ratio, but often are talked about separately. These fees are charged in addition to a front- or back-end load, and you'll find that many no-load funds charge them, too. If a 12b-1 fee puts a fund's expense ratio above the average for that class of fund, think twice before buying.

underwriter   An investment banker who purchases shares of a company that is going public, then resells them to investors for a higher price. When an underwriter brings shares of a new company to market it is called an initial public offering (IPO). Investment banks can also underwrite secondary offerings of existing public companies.

unemployment rate   The percentage of people in the workforce who aren't working and are looking for jobs. The numbers are compiled monthly by the U.S. Labor Department and are adjusted for seasonal variations. The unemployment report is one of the most closely watched of all government reports, because it gives the clearest indication of the direction of the economy. A rising unemployment rate will be seen by analysts and the Federal Reserve as a sign of a weakening economy, which might call for an easing of monetary policy by the Fed. On the other hand, a decline in the unemployment rate shows that the economy is growing, which may spark fears of higher inflation. The Fed might raise interest rates as a result. When interest rates rise, the stock and bond markets tend to take a dive.

value funds   These funds like to invest in companies that the market has overlooked. Companies favored by value funds may have an undistinguished track record because they are cyclical companies in industries such as steel or auto manufacturing, which are tied to the ups and downs of the business cycle. Value funds try to buy such stocks when they are near the bottom of a down cycle. The big risk is that the undiscovered gems they try to spot sometimes remain undiscovered. Still, because these fund managers tend to buy stocks and hold them until they turn around, expenses and turnover are low. That makes them suitable for conservative, tax-averse investors.

value investing   Value investors are the stock market's bargain hunters. They often lean toward beaten-down companies whose shares appear cheap when compared to current earnings or corporate assets. Value investors typically buy stocks with high dividend yields, or ones that trade at a low price-to-earnings (P/E) ratio or low price-to-book (P/B) ratio. The value investment style often is contrasted with the growth style. The two styles tend to take turns being popular on Wall Street. One year growth stocks will be all the rage; the next year value stocks may dominate.

volatility   The characteristic of a security or market to fall or rise sharply in price in a short-term period. A measure of the relative volatility of a security or mutual fund to the overall market is beta. A stock may be volatile because the outlook for the company is particularly uncertain, because there are only a few shares outstanding (i.e., it's illiquid) or for various other reasons. While beta can apply to both stocks and funds, standard deviation is more widely used to measure the volatility of mutual funds. Standard deviation examines a fund's range of historical returns, thus determining a portfolio's potential to swing between high and low returns.

volume   Number of shares traded in a company or an entire market during a given period. Days with unusually high volume typically correspond with the announcement of company news, either positive or negative. In the absence of news, high volume can indicate institutional (or professional) buying and selling. Technical analysis places a great emphasis on the amount of volume that occurs in the trading of a security. A sharp rise in volume is believed to signify future sharp rises or falls in price because it reflects increased investor interest in a security or a market.

warrant   A security entitling the holder to buy a proportionate amount of stock at some specified future date at a specified price, usually one higher than the current market price. Warrants are issued by corporations and often used as a sweetener bundled with bonds or preferred stock to enhance their marketability. They are like call options, but with much longer time spans that can stretch into years. In addition, warrants are offered by corporations, whereas exchange-traded options are not.

Wilshire 5000   A market capitalization–weighted index of approximately 7,000 U.S.-based equities traded on the New York Stock Exchange, American Stock Exchange, and Nasdaq. The Wilshire 5000 is the best measure of the entire U.S. stock market. Contrast with S&P 500 and Dow Jones Industrial Average.

window dressing   Trading activity near the end of a quarter or fiscal year that is designed to dress up a portfolio to be presented to clients or shareholders. For example, mutual fund managers may sell losing positions in their portfolios right before their semiannual reports are released so they can display only positions that have gained in value.

working capital   The excess of current assets over current liabilities. This statistic shows a company's level of solvency. A company with a lot of working capital has cash to reinvest and make its business grow.

wrap account   An investment plan that wraps together money management and brokerage services. Wrap plans are popular for their simplicity. For one all-inclusive annual fee, an investment firm provides the services of a professional money manager, who creates a portfolio of stocks and bonds or mutual funds and takes care of all the trading.

writer   In the options market, the seller of put and call options.

yield   The annual rate of return on an investment, as paid in dividends or interest. It is expressed as a percentage, generally obtained by dividing the current market price for a stock or bond into the annual dividend or interest payment. As the price of a stock or bond declines, its yield rises. So a stock selling for $20 a share with an annual dividend of $1 a share yields an investor 5 percent. But if the same stock falls to $10 a share, its $1 annual dividend yields 10 percent.

yield curve   This is a graph showing the yields for different bond maturities. It can be used not only to show where the best values in bonds are, but also as an economic indicator. A normal yield curve is upward sloping, with short-term rates lower than long-term rates. An inverted yield curve is downward sloping, with short-term rates higher than long-term rates. A steep upward-sloping yield curve indicates the bond market anticipates an economic expansion. An inverted yield curve anticipates an economic decline.

yield spread   The difference between the yields of various securities. Yield spreads are often used to compare bonds of different maturities or credit ratings. Bonds with lower credit ratings and longer maturities tend to have higher yields than those with good ratings and short maturities. In evaluating a lower-quality bond, you must decide whether the yield spread to better-rated issues is worth the extra risk of default.

yield to call   The yield on a bond assuming the bond is redeemed by the issuer at the first call date. A bond's call provision is detailed in its prospectus. Yield to call differs from yield to maturity in that yield to call uses a bond's call date as the final maturity date (most often, the first call date). The price at which an issuer can call a bond is the call price. The call price generally includes a call premium that is greater than the bond's face value. Conservative investors calculate both a bond's yield to call and yield to maturity, selecting the lower of the two as a measure of potential return.

yield to maturity   Yield to maturity is similar to current yield on a bond, but it also takes into account any gain or loss of principal at maturity. For example, if a $1,000 par bond was bought at a discount of $900, at maturity there would be a $100 gain. Likewise, if a $1,000 par bond is purchased for $1,090, there will be a $90 loss in principal at maturity. Yield to maturity is a precise measure that allows you to compare bonds with different maturities that sell for more or less than par. The trouble is, it is a complex calculation that isn't printed in the newspaper, so you'll have to get it from your broker or bond dealer.

zero-coupon bond (zeros)   Zero-coupon bonds (the Treasury's version of zeros are known as STRIPS) don't pay out interest annually. Rather, they are purchased at a deep discount to their face value. At maturity, all compound interest is paid, and the bondholder collects the face value of the bond. However, since interest is technically earned and compounded semiannually, holders of zeros are obliged to pay taxes each year on the interest as it accrues. Many investors like to time the maturity of their zero-coupon bonds to coincide with certain anticipated expenses, such as college tuition.

INDEX